1984

SHELLEY AND THE SUBLIME

SHELLEY AND THE SUBLIME

An Interpretation of the Major Poems

ANGELA LEIGHTON

Lecturer in English, University of Hull

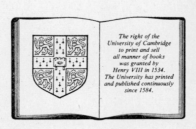

The right of the
University of Cambridge
to print and sell
all manner of books
was granted by
Henry VIII in 1534.
The University has printed
and published continuously
since 1584.

CAMBRIDGE UNIVERSITY PRESS

Cambridge

London   New York   New Rochelle
Melbourne   Sydney

Published by the Press Syndicate of the University of Cambridge
The Pitt Building, Trumpington Street, Cambridge CB2 1RP
32 East 57th Street, New York, NY 10022, USA
296 Beaconsfield Parade, Middle Park, Melbourne 3206, Australia

First published 1984

Printed in Great Britain by
New Western Printing Ltd, Bristol

Library of Congress catalogue card number: 83–7818

British Library cataloguing in publication data
Leighton, Angela
Shelley and the sublime.
1. Shelley, Percy Bysshe – Criticism and interpretation
I. Title
821'.7   PR5438
ISBN 0 521 25089 7 hard covers
ISBN 0 521 27202 5 paperback

WP

CONTENTS

v

PREFACE

In this book I trace the development in Shelley's work of an inspirational theory of poetry and examine the ways in which the language of some of the major poems reflects the tensions and paradoxes of such a theory. Shelley's aesthetic of inspiration, which finds its fullest expression in 'A Defence of Poetry', draws on the profuse and tangled tradition of the sublime in the eighteenth century. As an aesthetic of the vast in nature, and of an equivalent largeness of soul in the spectator, the eighteenth-century sublime may be seen to offer a challenge to the principle of representative perception which is the basis of English empiricism. It protects from the evidence of mere sense perception the ideas of original genius, imagination and inspiration, and thus protects an element of the mystical and inexplicable in the work of art.

Shelley's own indebtedness to the eighteenth century is wide and eclectic. It is not my purpose to give a detailed study of influence, but I would argue that he moves progressively from reliance on empirical arguments, which support his radicalism and atheism, to an interest in the sublime, as a theory and language of creativity which is congenial to his own imaginative temperament. But although there is a shift of emphasis in Shelley's thinking, the two perspectives remain in conflict throughout his life. On the one hand, he consistently denies the religious basis and reference of an aesthetic of the infinite, and he does so with arguments drawn from the principle of sense perception in empiricism. On the other hand, he finds in such an aesthetic a stronghold for that Power of inspiration or vision which directs the writing of poems, and which is central to his own theory of creativity. The tension between his religious scepticism and poetic need is a tension which Shelley never fully resolves, and which underlies and orders the language of many of his poems.

I aim to give a formalist interpretation of a number of the major poems, showing how Shelley's use of certain rhetorical devices reveals an anxiety about composition which is central to his own sceptical aesthetic of declining inspiration. It is particularly in those poems which present a landscape of sight-defeating heights and depths that this anxiety becomes evident. It has been customary to dismiss the language of the Shelleyan sublime with accusations of weak thinking or rhetorical escapism. But I would answer that such language expresses a dilemma of gain and loss in writing which is far from sentimental or escapist. Shelley's aesthetic of creativity is strangely modern in its scepticism and imaginative relativism. According to this aesthetic, all writing is a loss of that original inspiration which prompts composition. As a result, poetry continually acknowledges both the inadequacy and the sufficiency of its own rhetoric. This aesthetic is not separate from the philosophical and political subject matter of Shelley's poetry, but is intricately connected to it. Philosophy and politics are presented as problems of poetic utterance. For Shelley, the task of change and renovation is conducted in the language of inspired composition, which is the prerogative and aspiration of the radical poet.

ACKNOWLEDGEMENTS

My thanks, first of all, to James Booth, who has read this book in many stages of its writing, and whose comments and criticisms have been unfailingly apposite, perceptive and often chastening. My thanks, too, to Marilyn Butler, who has made innumerable helpful suggestions, particularly on passages dealing with the eighteenth century, and to Roy Park for his invaluable directions on the philosophical argument of the early parts. Marion Shaw has generously read a number of chapters and given me much useful advice. I am also grateful to Timothy Webb for reading and commenting on some earlier drafts of chapters, and to Paul Hamilton who, formally and informally, has made both general and detailed criticisms of the whole. Lastly, my thanks to Harriet Marland, who has been a wonderfully patient general reader, and to Margaret Bowen who has typed it all.

My main debt of thanks, however, must be to all those Shelley scholars whose work has been a stimulus to many of my own ideas and interpretations. In particular, I am aware of having been influenced by the work of Harold Bloom, Timothy Webb and Judith Chernaik. But I am grateful, too, for the more indirect influence of scholars and enthusiasts at successive Shelley conferences, and for the sustaining interest of my students, for whom this book is written.

Two earlier and different versions of chapter 6 have been printed in the *Keats–Shelley Memorial Bulletin* (Autumn, 1980), and in *Shelley Revalued* (Leicester University Press, 1983), to whose editors, Timothy Webb and Kelvin Everest respectively, I am grateful for permission to reprint.

ix

ABBREVIATIONS

P.W.   *Shelley: Poetical Works*, ed. Thomas Hutchinson, corr. G. M. Matthews, London, Oxford University Press, 1970.

Letters *The Letters of Percy Bysshe Shelley*, 2 vols., ed. Frederick L. Jones, Oxford, Clarendon Press, 1964.

References by volume and page number only are from *The Complete Works of Percy Bysshe Shelley*, 10 vols., ed. Roger Ingpen and Walter E. Peck, London, Ernest Benn, New York, Charles Scribner's Sons, 1926–30.

THE SUBLIME IN THE EIGHTEENTH CENTURY

It is possible to detect the influence of two main traditions of eighteenth-century thought on Shelley's work. The first of these is the influence of empirical philosophy. Shelley finds in the writings of Locke and Hume a description of the mind's relation to the outside world to accord with his own radical atheism. The philosophy of Locke in particular furnishes the young poet with an argument to refute both Deism and orthodox Christianity. Locke, in *An Essay Concerning Human Understanding*, attacks the Cartesian principle that there are innate ideas in the mind, and instead derives all knowledge from the perception of the senses. Shelley then uses this empirical theory of representative perception to put in question the existence of a benign God. However, if empirical philosophy provides the youthful poet with a method of countering religious orthodoxy and of undermining the institutionalised dogmas of Christianity, it fails to provide him with a sympathetic account of poetic creativity. As a result, Shelley turns gradually to another tradition of thought in the eighteenth century: the tradition of the sublime. It is in a sublime aesthetic, which develops alongside empirical philosophy but is in many ways antagonistic to it, that Shelley finds a language to protect inspiration as the original and mysterious Power of poetry.

One of the main features of empirical philosophy is its emphasis on the passivity of the mind as it receives sense perceptions of the external world. Knowledge is derived from the way in which external objects act upon the senses, and impinge upon the mind as ideas. Locke writes: 'Whatsoever the Mind perceives in it self, or is the immediate object of Perception, Thought, or Understanding, that I call *Idea*.'[1] The ideas of the mind mediate between the

external world and our recognition of it. However, in this mediation the mind itself remains inactive. As C. R. Morris writes, 'the
nature of the ideas arriving in our minds through the senses is
entirely determined by the nature of the objects, and not at all
by the nature of the mind'.[2] This epistemology therefore seeks to
return all forms of mental experience to the influence of simple
ideas, which the mind receives passively. Locke distinguishes two
kinds of ideas: ideas of sensation and of reflection, the first deriving
from external objects and the second deriving from the internal
operations of the mind. But in both cases the ideas are not shaped
or created by the mind; they are the objects of its perception or
contemplation. It is interesting that when Locke makes his large
claim that all knowledge derives from ideas, his argument is
hardest pressed to include the sublime. He writes that all 'sublime
Thoughts, which towre above the Clouds, and reach as high as
Heaven it self, take their Rise and Footing here: In all that great
Extent wherein the mind wanders, in those remote Speculations, it
may seem to be elevated with, it stirs not one jot beyond those
Ideas, which *Sense* or *Reflection*, have offered for its Contemplation.'[3] It is these 'sublime Thoughts' which might be thought to
out-distance the grounding effort of empiricism.

If the characteristic of Locke's argument is to present ideas as
objects of the mind's perception or contemplation, it is also a
characteristic of his method to fall back upon a metaphor of sight.
In fact, he uses the word '*Perception*' to refer widely to what man
does 'when he sees, hears, feels, *etc.* or thinks'.[4] Similarly Hume
divides the mind's perceptions into '*Ideas*' and '*Impressions*', and
the latter are defined as 'all our more lively perceptions, when we
hear, or see, or feel, or love, or hate, or desire, or will'.[5] But
although these definitions include all the senses, a bias towards
sight predominates. Locke states that the 'Perception of the Mind'
is 'most aptly explained by Words relating to the Sight',[6] but his
use of a visual vocabulary is not just a verbal convenience. The
status of the mind's ideas becomes very nearly that of mental
images. Their truth is assessed according to their clarity, distinctness and completeness, and in opposition to any weakness or

2

obscurity. It is a metaphor of the eye which governs Locke's arguments on behalf of empirical truth. To perceive ideas is to look with the mind's eye.

This bias towards sight is also evident in the works of Hume. When, at the beginning of *An Enquiry Concerning Human Understanding*, he attacks a metaphysics founded upon superstitions and religious prejudices instead of on a proper science, he distinguishes between obscure and clear knowledge. 'Obscurity, indeed, is painful to the mind as well as to the eye,' he writes, 'but to bring light from obscurity, by whatever labour, must needs be delightful and rejoicing.'[7] Hume's division of knowledge into ideas and impressions is an affirmation of what is clear, vivid and perspicuous against what is obscure, confused or distant. Once again, it is the imagination's ability to go beyond the boundaries and limits of reality which seems to pose the greatest challenge to Hume's argument, and it does so because it might seem to escape the control of the eye. The realm of the imagination is in 'the most distant regions of the universe; or [goes] even beyond the universe, into the unbounded chaos, where nature is supposed to lie in total confusion'.[8] This Miltonic landscape reflects a capacity of thought which might challenge Hume's sceptical empiricism, by being irreducible to visibility and sense perception. Like Locke, Hume is concerned to bring even the province of the sublime within the gravitational pull of empiricism. He writes that 'when we analyze our thoughts or ideas, however compounded or sublime, we always find that they resolve themselves into such simple ideas as were copied from a precedent feeling or sentiment'. This resolution into simple ideas also applies to that other large imagining of the human mind: the 'idea of God'.[9] Hume's swift and cunning move from the fictionalising imagination, which ventures into the unbounded regions of the sublime, to the 'idea of God', reveals an association of the two which is inherent in much eighteenth-century thinking and which will prove awkward for Shelley; for the atheist, radical and empiricist who would also be a poet.

Both Locke and Hume present an epistemology based on the

3

authenticity of sense perception. This authenticity is determined mainly by the criterion of clarity or vividness; by a language which falls back, willingly or unwillingly, on a metaphor of sight. The mind's ideas or impressions are the source of true knowledge to the extent that they are clear, distinct, simple. However, this emphasis on the accuracy and clarity of perception in empirical philosophy results in another problematic assumption. If truth is to be found in perceiving ideas vividly and distinctly, it is not to be found in the language by which ideas are communicated. Michel Foucault, in *The Order of Things*, claims that this fall in the status of language is the result of a general post-Cartesian emphasis on truth as 'evident and distinct perception', which it is 'the task of words to translate'.[10] In English empirical philosophy the translating function of words is deeply distrusted. As language is reduced to being the mere necessary conveyor of the mind's ideas, its rhetorical and figurative susceptibilities become all the more menacing.

Locke devotes much of Book III of his *Essay* to cautioning against a careless use of language, by which he means a language unaccompanied by clear ideas. He writes that the 'use then of Words, is to be sensible Marks of *Ideas*; and the *Ideas* they stand for, are their proper and immediate Signification'.[11] Again the main threat to this empirical proposition comes from the realm of aesthetics. What Locke denounces as antagonistic to the cause of truth is a non-literal language, which has for its object, not clear perception, but emotional effect. He comprehensively asserts that 'all the Art of Rhetorick, besides Order and Clearness, all the artificial and figurative application of Words Eloquence hath invented, are for nothing else but to insinuate wrong *Ideas*, move the Passions, and thereby mislead the Judgment; and so indeed are perfect cheat'.[12] Rhetorical language, according to Locke, cheats us of the different order and logic of ideas. True knowledge resides in this separate and autonomous system of mental discourse.

It is Berkeley who challenges the extremism of Locke's position. In *A Treatise Concerning the Principles of Human Knowledge*, he claims that 'the communicating of ideas...is not the chief and only end of language', because language also has as its aim the arousal

4

of 'passion'.[13] He reinstates the very example of literary and rhetorical language which Locke is at pains to banish. However, although Berkeley makes some space for a language which communicates the force of passion rather than clear ideas, when he wishes to distinguish the philosophical cause of truth, he too would dispense with 'names' and take only 'ideas' which are 'bare and naked' into 'view'.[14] The source of true knowledge is still located in a purely mental order, of which language is too often a falsification. Hume, in his *Enquiries*, has very little to say about the working of language, except occasionally to remark on its irrelevance to philosophy. 'A moral, philosophical discourse needs not enter into all these caprices of language,'[15] he claims. He refuses 'to engage in disputes of words' because these encroach upon 'the province of grammarians',[16] and the philosopher's commitment must be to mental and moral systems that lie beyond the wily and capricious tendencies of words.

In general, the tradition of empirical philosophy, with its emphasis on theories of representative perception, seeks to expel language as far as it can from the domain of knowledge. Above all, it seeks to expel any rhetorical or aesthetic language, which obscures the mind's ideas by moving the passions. If empiricism starts by attacking the verbal intricacies of medieval Scholasticism, it ends by banning all forms of verbal ornamentation or subtlety. In order to communicate the clear and distinct perceptions of the mind, language must be as nearly nominal and literal as it can. Ideally, the empiricist's language will be perfectly transparent to the ideas it would convey, and this transparency is equivalent to a linguistic literalism. Such an ideal is mainly threatened, therefore, by figurative and metaphorical devices, which are commonly regarded, in the eighteenth century, as manifestations of the passions. Unlike literal language, these devices obtrude themselves upon the mind's eye and cloud its vision of the ideas. The measure of truth is to be found in the rule of sight once again, as empirical philosophy broadly distinguishes between a literal language which is transparent and true, and a metaphorical language which is opaque, and cheats. Locke, however, is uneasily aware that the distinction is loose, and that the obscuring effect of rhetorical and metaphorical language might extend to all forms of verbal representation. He writes that words by their very nature 'interpose themselves so much between our Understandings, and the Truth, which it would contemplate and apprehend, that like the *Medium* through which visible Objects pass, their Obscurity and Disorder does not seldom cast a mist before our Eyes, and impose upon our Understandings'.[17] It is the very fact that words tend to interpose and mediate between the mind and the visible truth that makes them suspect. They interfere with the act of seeing.

Broadly, then, it might be said that the predominant criterion of truth in empirical philosophy, which is the criterion of sight, is subtly endangered by two factors: by the large and chaotic vistas of the sublime and by the opaque and passion-moving devices of rhetoric. By presenting these two as most distant from, or antipathetic to, the pursuit of true knowledge, empirical philosophy points to a dilemma which will haunt the imaginative poet who claims to be an empiricist in religious belief. Locke and Hume advocate a distinction between verifiable knowledge and superstitious imagining, between clear ideas and rhetorical obscurantism, which will be present in Shelley's own thought and work as a long unresolved choice.

Although this empirical emphasis on clear sight results in a deep suspicion of rhetorical language, Locke's general precepts become highly influential on studies of rhetoric and aesthetic in the eighteenth century. His basic premise, that to perceive an idea clearly and distinctly is to avoid error and confusion, is transferred to the study of aesthetics, and comes to describe the effect of rhetorical images on the imagination. Joseph Addison, at the beginning of the eighteenth century, is one of the first to attempt to link empirical philosophy with aesthetics, and he does so by stressing the model of the eye. In his Papers on the 'Pleasures of the Imagination' of 1712, he unequivocally asserts the supremacy of sight, which is 'the most perfect and most delightful of all our Senses', and which 'furnishes the Imagination with its Ideas'.[18] He elides the Lockean principle of accuracy with the very different principle of delightfulness, and he similarly transfers the Lockean ideas from the philosophical mind to the literary imagination. Addison uses the words idea and image interchangeably, and although the latter is not yet associated with the devices of metaphor and simile for which Coleridge is mainly responsible,[19] it is already associated with the poetic imagination which represents things in words. Although Addison defers to Locke's privileging of sight as the source of true knowledge, he in fact turns Locke's argument on its head when he writes that words have 'so great a Force in them, that a Description often gives us more lively Ideas than the Sight of Things themselves'.[20] Words, and particularly descriptive words, are no longer condemned for obscuring ideas, but are praised instead for being more forcefully visualisable than things. Verbal eloquence begins to compete with clear ideas for the attention of the mind's eye.

This eliding of ideas and images, of mental discourse and rhetorical discourse, is evident in innumerable works of rhetoric and aesthetic in the eighteenth century. Hugh Blair, Lord Monboddo, Lord Kames, William Drummond, for instance, all describe metaphorical or poetic language in terms of its visual effect. Blair advises that poetic description 'should be as marked and particular as possible, in order to imprint on the mind a distinct and complete image'.[21] The purpose of metaphor, according to Lord Monboddo, is to express 'the thing in a more lively and forcible manner',[22] and according to Blair it is 'to make intellectual ideas, in some sort, visible to the eye'.[23] Lord Kames emphasises the dramatic element in this visibility of language when he writes that the 'force of language consists in raising complete images; which have the effect to transport the reader as by magic into the very place of the important action, and to convert him as it were into a spectator, beholding every thing that passes'.[24] William Drummond, in his *Academical Questions* (1805) which Shelley so admired, writes that 'it is always a beauty in the figures of rhetoric, when they represent what may be conceived as placed before the eyes, and what is agreeable to truth and probability'.[25] All these writers describe rhetorical figures as seen. But the emphasis has shifted somewhat, from Locke's insistence on clarity and distinctness, to an insistence on forcefulness and delightfulness. For Drummond, figures of rhetoric are visually beautiful as well as truthful.

Although Locke remains one of the main influences on eighteenth-century theories of rhetoric and aesthetics, his actual principles are somewhat ungratefully distorted. Rhetorical language, the figurative language of the passions, which Locke dismisses as the source of error and mystification, now takes pride of place. The visual clarity of the Lockean ideas gives way to the visual force and beauty of rhetorical images. Locke's plea for a pared and literal language which would not hinder the passage of mental ideas gives way to a celebration of figures of speech which work strongly and visually upon the imagination. The importance of the model of sight remains. But seeing is no longer the condition of philosophical truth; it is the measure of aesthetic effect.

Because empiricism is the dominant eighteenth-century philosophy, at least until the Scottish Common-Sense philosophers, Thomas Reid and Dugald Stewart, begin to challenge its theory of ideas in the later decades of the century, it is difficult for any other discipline to ignore its influence. Yet it seems that Lockean empiricism can be aligned with the cause of aesthetics only by a curious transmogrification of its principles. It is a comment on the nature of empiricism, that it makes no easy liaison with aesthetic theory. Its epistemology is based on the new scientific method drawn from the study of the natural sciences in the seventeenth century, and from the start it is in opposition to the metaphysical and theological formulations of Scholasticism. Locke and Hume repeatedly inveigh against metaphysical subtleties which are the product of verbal ingenuity and have no reference to true ideas. Their distrust of language, therefore, is mainly directed against Scholasticism, and is only incidentally directed against aesthetic language. Nonetheless, the effect of their reaction is to condemn all ingenious or figurative verbalising as tending towards the dissemination of dangerous fictions and grosser superstitions. The attempt of eighteenth-century theories of rhetoric to align themselves with a Lockean empiricism only reveals more acutely how tricky such an alignment must be. One of the whispered assumptions of empiricism, which Peacock will echo in 'The Four Ages of Poetry' to Shelley's dismay, is that imaginative writing is itself a lingering superstition from the dark ages of man's development. This association of aesthetics with religious belief is not, however, just an incidental corollary of empiricism. It finds support in another strong tradition of seventeenth- and eighteenth-century thinking, to which Shelley will be drawn in spite of himself.

The first English translation of the treatise *On the Sublime* attributed to Longinus appeared in 1652, but it was not until the 1730s that the work achieved widespread popularity. Boileau's famous and seminal translation became available in English in 1736, while the most important English translation of the original by William Smith was published in 1739. The enormous popularity of the work throughout the century seems, however, less due to the instrinsic value of the treatise itself than to a resurgent need on the part of the age which rediscovered it. The age finds in Longinus an aesthetic vocabulary to meet its own requirements. This is a vocabulary not so much of rhetorical style as of literary sensibility. Longinus in fact contains both. The five sources of the sublime which he lists are grandeur of thought, strong passion, skilful figures of speech, graceful expression and careful organisation of sentences. However, of the two main definitions of the sublime in Longinus' work: that it is 'a certain Eminence or Perfection of Language',[26] and that 'the Sublime is an Image reflected from the inward Greatness of the Soul',[27] the eighteenth century shows a marked preference for the second. The Longinian sublime gives to the age, not a series of rules about poetic style, but a language for celebrating the act of creativity. It is 'the inward Greatness of the Soul' which will become the main preoccupation of eighteenth- and nineteenth-century aesthetics.

Boileau, in the Preface to his translation of Longinus, first uses a psychological terminology which will be repeated unashamedly in innumerable accounts of the sublime. He argues that the main characteristic of the Longinian sublime is not to be found in stylistic conventions, but in something extraneous to language. It is described as 'cet extraordinaire et ce merveilleux qui frappe dans le discours, et qui fait qu'un ouvrage enlève, ravit, transporte'.[28] To raise, ravish and transport are the signs of some force in language which is strange and marvellous, and which therefore defies reduction to any linguistic process. The sublime, according to Boileau, is neither style nor theme; it is psychological effect. Furthermore, it is an effect which draws heavily on the language of religious mysticism. The sublime is a mysterious and violent force, irreducible to anything in the work, which strikes and uplifts the involuntary reader without warning. Such a description seeks to preserve an element of the unknown and unwritten in aesthetic works: something extraordinary and marvellous.

Although Longinus' treatise is an outstanding landmark in the development of the sublime in England, the tradition does not originate here. In an essay entitled 'Space, Deity, and the "Natural Sublime"', Ernest Tuveson argues that the general concept of sublimity, or grandeur, first emerges in the seventeenth century, in religious writings which attempt to account for the nature of God in a philosophical terminology acceptable to the new scientific age: a terminology of infinite space and time.[29] Although the word 'sublime' does not come into general use before the English translations of Boileau, the sensibility which it expresses is already evident in the works of the Cambridge Platonists, for instance, and in the writings of Thomas Burnet. Burnet's *The Sacred Theory of the Earth* was finally published in English in 1690 and foreshadows many later descriptions of the workings of the sublime. Natural grandeur, for Burnet, becomes an image of divine presence. It is the vast in nature which points to and approximates the incomprehensible vastness of God. As a result, Burnet explicitly equates two kinds of mental state: the mind susceptible to natural grandeur is also the mind able to achieve religious ecstasy. Burnet had crossed the Alps in 1671, and the landscape which he describes in the *Sacred Theory* is familiar in retrospect, as one of the favourite locations of the sublime. It is precisely the emptiness and barrenness of this landscape which, paradoxically, makes it seem filled with a divine presence.

Such a presence is not realised, however, by any kind of intellection, but by an emotional response which registers the presence of the divine in a defeat of the senses. Burnet writes that, in contemplating the vast perspectives of nature, we 'do naturally, upon such occasions, think of God and his greatness: and whatsoever hath but the shadow and appearance of INFINITE, as all things have that are too big for our comprehension, they fill and over-bear the mind with their Excess, and cast it into a pleasing kind of stupor and admiration'.[30] The nature of the Deity is synonymous with a vastness which defeats comprehension, and provokes instead a state of pleasurable awe. There is what will become a characteristic grammatical transference of activity, from the human spectator to the objects contemplated. These 'fill and over-bear the mind with their Excess'. Out of the emptiness of the landscape comes a sense of plenitude almost too large to bear. Before the vast images of the divine the human mind experiences a loss of power and autonomy, and suffers passively a violent 'Excess' of the desired object.

Burnet's *Sacred Theory* is a work dear to the Romantic imagination. Wordsworth and Coleridge both admired it, and the latter considered translating it into blank verse.[31] Although there is no evidence of Shelley having read it at first hand, he had certainly read Buffon's 'La Théorie de la Terre' which refers to Burnet. While the theological context of Burnet's writing is explicit, there is already in progress what Angus Fletcher describes as a 'conversion of awe from the religious to the aesthetic sphere'.[32] A mystical experience of the Deity is the necessary accompaniment to an admiration of the natural landscape. Grandeur, vastness or infinitude are qualities of the natural landscape which compel the mind to think them a manifestation of the divine. This equivalence between natural and supernatural grandeur is repeated throughout the eighteenth century, and very quickly becomes a commonplace of the sublime.

This means however, as Hume cunningly implies, that the sublime rarely loosens its allegiance to theology. As an aesthetic of the limitless, the terrible, the grandiose, the sublime continues to point beyond the visible distances of nature to the invisible presence or power which they manifest. Thus Addison, who read Burnet in his youth, writes that we 'delight in the Apprehension of what is Great or Unlimited' because of a natural, divinely originating desire to contemplate God.[33] Longinus gives his support to this already flourishing association when he writes that 'the Sublime makes near Approaches to the Height of God'.[34] Thomas Reid also, writing in the 1780s, still recalls Burnet, when he claims that of 'all objects of contemplation, the Supreme Being is the most grand. His eternity, his immensity, his irresistible power...fill the utmost capacity of the soul, and reach far beyond its comprehension.'[35] The sublime is dependent on, and in its turn protects, the idea of the divine. It is because the infinite spaces of the natural world are capable of holding an infinite presence that they are worthy of our creative admiration. Such heights and depths are possible approaches by which human creativity seeks out the Creator. 'All versions of the sublime', writes Thomas Weiskel in his book *The Romantic Sublime*, 'require a credible god-term.'[36] Although the god may have changed, the Romantic poets tread the same landscapes as Burnet, and find there, too, a divinely patented signpost.

If an aesthetic of the sublime originates with seventeenth-century theological speculation, and retains thereafter this element of mystical confrontation with a hidden power within the landscape, it also develops into an influential and at times sophisticated theory of creativity. In his book, *The Sublime*, Samuel Monk argues that, after the mid-eighteenth century, the 'tendency to regard the sublime as a quality residing in objects' is superseded by an interest in 'the subject'.[37] There is a dismally large quantity of writing which seeks to classify the external landscape according to aesthetic formulae in the eighteenth century. Thus the picturesque would be exemplified by variety, the beautiful by smoothness and the sublime by magnitude. It is also a favourite habit to list the kinds of objects that fall into the different categories. Addison confidently enumerates 'Mountains, high Rocks and Precipices, or a wide Expanse of Waters'[38] as characteristic of the sublime. Edmund Burke, who in *A Philosophical Enquiry into the Origin of our*

Ideas of the Sublime and Beautiful (1757) advocates a theory of the sublime based on the emotion of terror, claims therefore that a 'cloudy sky' is more sublime than a 'blue', and 'night' more than 'day'.[39] Even Dugald Stewart as late as 1810 feels obliged to remind us, in his essay 'On the Sublime', of the 'sublime effect of rocks and of cataracts; of huge ridges of mountains; of vast and gloomy forests; of immense and impetuous rivers; of the boundless ocean'.[40] These classifications, if stultifying, do generally hold good even for the Romantics. Coleridge is reported by Dorothy Wordsworth to have been highly indignant at a fellow traveller who referred to the Falls of the Clyde as majestic and also sublime and beautiful.[41] Wordsworth wrote an unfinished essay on 'The Sublime and the Beautiful', where he claims that 'it is of infinite importance ... that the forms of Nature should be accurately contemplated',[42] and he goes on to distinguish carefully between the two main aesthetic categories. Shelley, too, is fairly scrupulous in referring, for instance, to the lower and lusher slopes of the Alps as beautiful and to the higher, more desolate peaks as sublime. The eighteenth-century classifications thus persist well into the nineteenth century. However, it is when studies of the sublime centre on the human subject rather than on the natural object, that there develops a new and even complex theory of creativity as a psychological activity.

Although, as Monk points out, there is a shift in emphasis from object to subject in the development of the sublime, nature is still the touchstone of artistic authenticity. As a result, this aesthetic joins the lists of the long debate of nature versus art, and adds its own voice in favour of the first. It is the natural world, especially that which gives a promise of the supernatural, which is properly the locus of the sublime. The rude and irregular formation of natural scenery is more sublime than the most masterful artistic rendering of it. As a result, that art is sublime which most nearly approximates the condition of nature. It is this sense of priorities which lies behind Addison's statement that there is 'something more bold and masterly in the rough careless Strokes of Nature, than in the nice Touches and Embellishments of Art'.[43] The submerged image upon which this distinction turns is that of the

13

painter at his easel. The first kind of artist is impetuous and original and works to no rules, while the second merely adds a little colouring or finish. Addison is making out a case for original genius as opposed to imitative genius, a case that will be championed by theorists of the sublime throughout the century. However, there is a further implication to his opposition of nature and art. This is that true artistry, a 'more bold and masterly' ability, belongs to nature itself. The opposition collapses, as art deserts its own meaning and becomes nature instead. Nor does Addison intend by nature, human nature. The strongest kind of art is that of the natural world, particularly the rough and careless landscapes of the sublime, so that nature here in fact refers to the creation. As a result, the opposition broadens to imply the difference between God's natural creation and man's imitative creativity. The first original genius is God.

It is William Duff, in *An Essay on Original Genius* published in 1767, who advances this association between the natural creation and a natural creativity. His defence of the artist born, not taught, leads to just such a distinction as Addison's. He writes that the sublime is the proper sphere of original genius, adding that such a genius is 'much more delighted with surveying the rude magnificence of nature, than the elegant decorations of art', for 'the former throws the soul into a divine transport of admiration and amazement, which occupies and fills the mind'.[44] He too opposes the vast and rude appearance of nature to the little, ornamental elegancies of art. Here nature is quite specifically the external world, which induces in the receptive genius a state of 'divine transport'. Duff uses the familiar language of religious ecstasy and emotional violence. However, he too relies on a distinction which is in danger of forfeiting creativity to the Creator. The role of the artist, it seems, is merely to survey and admire. His genius is affirmed by a passivity and subservience to the already finished work of nature. Human art and originality are preceded by the original artistry of the Creator. The paradox that emerges from Duff's argument, and which will haunt subsequent writers of the sublime, is that nature is only gained at the cost of becoming art, and that originality is only gained at the cost of coming second.

Duff's problematic championing of original genius is centred on another keynote of the sublime: the concept of enthusiasm. Locke and Hume both use the word pejoratively, to signify religious fanaticism, or a form of revelation unchecked by reason and common sense. However, although Duff claims to use the word in a newly non-pejorative sense, he is in fact preceded by John Dennis, who, in *The Grounds of Criticism in Poetry* (1704), writes that poetry excites either vulgar passion or enthusiastic passion, and that the latter 'is moved by the Idea's in Contemplation or the Meditation of Things, that belong not to common Life'.[45] He then makes a comparison between two ideas of the sun, which startlingly foreshadows Blake's later distinction between the visible and the visionary sun. Dennis writes that 'the Sun mention'd in ordinary Conversation, gives the Idea of a round flat shining Body, of about Two Foot Diameter. But the Sun occurring to us in Meditation, gives the Idea of a vast and glorious Body, and the top of all the visible Creation, and the brightest material Image of the Divinity.'[46] Dennis is in fact comparing, as Blake consciously or unconsciously recognised, the sun seen literally and the sun imagined metaphorically. It is this second idea of the sun, seen innerly and meditatively, and therefore with what Dennis terms enthusiasm, which will become Blake's ideal of poetic vision when he writes, at the end of the *Vision of the Last Judgement*, that he sees the sun, not as 'a round Disk of fire somewhat like a Guinea', but as 'an Innumerable company of the Heavenly host crying "Holy Holy Holy is the Lord God Almighty" '.[47]

The notion of enthusiasm, therefore, not only brings to the aesthetic of the sublime a specifically religious term, but also an internalisation of sight which radically disturbs its empirical value. For Duff, enthusiasm still retains its etymological meaning of divine possession, but it is possession by a different god: 'that ENTHUSIASM of Imagination, which as it were hurries the mind out of itself'.[48] In this its new literary ascendancy, enthusiasm comes to stand for a kind of imaginative energy which distorts and troubles the calm outward seeing of the eye. Art is authenticated, not so

15

much by its representational accuracy, as by the psychological energy which directs it. Duff writes that enthusiasm is the mark of the artist who expresses 'the natural dictates of the heart, not fictitious or copied, but original'.[49] The heart is the original speaker, and enthusiasm is the emotional speed with which 'the natural dictates of the heart' can be externalised in language.

This definition of enthusiasm as energy and force is emphasised by Robert Lowth, in his *Lectures on the Sacred Poetry of the Hebrews* (1787) which Shelley read and admired. Lowth writes that enthusiasm is found in 'a style and expression directly prompted by nature itself, and exhibiting the true and express image of a mind violently agitated'.[50] To be true and express, the work must issue directly from the violently agitated mind. Between the expression and the inner prompting of nature there must be no disruptive pause or calm. It is enthusiasm which ensures a swift transcription of what nature prompts into what the poet writes. The work is authenticated, therefore, by reference to a kind of psychological good faith which compels expression and forbids delay. Artistic value is now described in terms of power, force or speed; by the emotional urgency or even violence by which the heart is translated into words.

Thus the eighteenth-century sublime tends to centre on the figure of the poet, rather than on the workings of poetry. Furthermore, it presents the poet in the role of traveller or spectator or even painter. He is concerned, not with pen and words, but with landscapes or pictures; not with language, but with external forms. The poet is essentially one who sees the world, and it is the quality of that seeing which is the touchstone of artistic value. But although the sublime fixes on the acts of contemplating, surveying, seeing, as the original artistic endeavours of the mind, it also emphasises the emotional intensity that accompanies them. As a result of this accompanying enthusiasm, sight comes to be something which is almost its own opposite. The empirical model, which affords an accurate copy of the external world, is challenged by an alternative seeing, which has the intensity, at times, of blindness.

Just as Addison elides the Lockean ideas with images, and the principle of accuracy with the principle of delight, so he also exposes the limitations of the empirical eye as a register of poetic effect. He writes that 'in the Survey of any Object we have only so much of it painted on the Imagination, as comes in at the Eye; but in its Description, the Poet gives us as free a View of it as he pleases'.[51] There is a difference between the first 'Survey' and the second 'View'. The first is a visual copy, in a loosely Lockean sense, while the second is a kind of seeing which is free from the constraints of accuracy. Furthermore, this imaginative view, which is communicated through description, is in a sense autonomous; the poet can see as freely as he chooses.

This freedom of sight, the imaginative mobility of the poet's eye, is also, of course, a freedom to range over landscapes which are potentially infinite. The free view of imaginative description coincides with its sublime objects: the space and indeterminacy of wild landscapes. Addison transfers this freedom to the object when he writes that 'a spacious Horison is an Image of Liberty, where the Eye has Room to range abroad'.[52] The 'Horison' here is not so much a line which the eye can fix, as a space which permits the eye's ranging. This pushing out of visual boundaries is another way in which the aesthetic of the sublime disturbs and alters the sense of sight. Burke's sublime of terror, which commends all forms of obscurity, is based on the notion that 'to see an object distinctly, and to perceive its bounds, is one and the same idea'.[53] For Burke, distinctness and clarity are limitations upon the eye, which seeks the sublime in what lies on the other side of the world's outlines. Finally, it is Kant, in his *Critique of Judgement* (1790), who brings together the diverse strands of the eighteenth-century sublime in a philosophical system. He contends that the sublime belongs properly to the mind and not to natural objects, claiming that it 'is to be found in a formless object, so far as in it or by occasion of it *boundlessness* is represented'.[54] Once again, the sublime is described as a mental representation of an object uncircumscribed by visual outlines. It is this movement of the sublime towards a representational freedom which lies behind the Romantic preoccupation with boundary

17

lines, edges and horizons. The hard-seen outline of Mont Blanc will become, for Wordsworth, Coleridge and Shelley, the source of a crisis of representation which poetry cannot resolve, but only register.

The progressive internalisation of the eye in the eighteenth-century sublime, which matches the progressive interest in the subject rather than the object, results in a preoccupation with the difficulty, the strangeness and even the failure of sight. While to be a sublime poet is to approach the rapture of the seer, to see, imaginatively and intensely, is to risk a kind of blindness. As the boundaries of the external world are pushed out towards infinity, and as writers come to advocate the freedom and obscurity of the act of seeing, the whole model of sight becomes self-defeating. To be raised, ravished, transported by an image of the infinite is also to be incapacitated by it. As visibility opens, both outwards and inwards, towards vision, in the development of the sublime, it opens towards its own opposite. It is for this reason that studies of the sublime return with unfailing pertinacity to the example of Milton, the great prototype of the sublime bard. It is not just that Milton's poetry funds the eighteenth century with innumerable sublime quotations; it is that the figure of the man himself serves to characterise and define the scope of his art. Milton is the poet who not only dares to contemplate infinite and timeless landscapes, but whose imaginative sight is directly related to the fact of his blindness. He is the poet, in Gray's 'The Progress of Poesy',

> . . .that rode sublime
> Upon the seraph-wings of Extasy,
> The secrets of th'Abyss to spy.
> He pass'd the flaming bounds of Place and Time:
> The living Throne, the saphire-blaze,
> Where Angels tremble, while they gaze,
> He saw; but blasted with excess of light,
> Closed his eyes in endless night.[55]   (95–102)

It is the fact that Milton 'saw' which leads to his 'endless night'. The poet who so hugely and movingly yearns to see secret landscapes achieves his aim, punishingly and rewardingly, when his eyes are closed 'in endless night'. The eighteenth-century obsession with Milton prefigures the influence which he is to hold over the Romantic poets. Blake's *Milton*, Keats's *Hyperion*, Shelley's *Prometheus Unbound*, are all attempts at the sublime mode which fail to lay the ghost of their predecessor, but which struggle anxiously against his influence.

The indeterminate and unbounded landscapes of the sublime are thus represented in terms of mystical abandonment, enthusiastic feeling, visual liberty, obscurity or blindness. Such landscapes confirm an image of space which is capable of being infinite, and capable, therefore, of holding the infinite presence of God. Yet the characteristic of these landscapes is desolateness, solitude, emptiness. An immense expanse of water or desert or mountain is sublime to the extent that its horizon seems unattainable and the mind is not distracted by any smaller lines or shapes. Yet, while these landscapes signify the vastness of the Deity for most eighteenth-century theorists, they are also able to signify something very different. Without the hidden pressure of the presence of God, an aesthetic of vastness becomes an aesthetic of the void. This danger is already hinted at in the way that the model of sight comes to be defined in terms of its opposite. If Milton sees the ways of God, precisely because he sees nothing bounded to the human eye, yet it would only take the loss of God for him to see nothing. If the abyss has no secrets, is it possible for the poet to spy in it?

Commonly in the eighteenth century, the language which is used to describe the unbounded landscape or obscure object of the sublime is a language of negatives. The relationship between the visually unbounded and the verbally negative is made plain in an extended passage of Lowth's *Lectures*. He writes that

nothing of this kind is nobler or more majestic, than when a description is carried on by a kind of continued negation; when a number of great and sublime ideas are collected, which, on a comparison with the object, are found infinitely inferior and inadequate. Thus the boundaries are gradually extended on every side, and at length totally removed; the mind is insensibly led on towards infinity, and is struck with inexpressible admiration, with a pleasing awe, when it first finds itself expatiating in that immense expanse.[56]

The 'continued negation' which culminates in the familiar mystical encounter with space, takes the form of a protestation of inferiority and inadequacy. This is a negation which affirms its opposite, by a process of default, or rather, belief. The sublime object is celebrated by the incommensurability of the description. Words are lame to undertake the far flights of the sublime, and as a result, Lowth insists on a negation, which is like a modesty trope. His passage is full of verbal defeats: the words 'inadequate', 'insensibly', 'infinity', 'inexpressible', 'immense'. But each of these negations is still a promise of its opposite: of what cannot be adequate, sensed, finite, expressible or measured. For Lowth, as for so many eighteenth-century authors, the sublime object comes to be expressed by a tactical failure of language compensated by religious faith.

It is this element of faith which gives to the language of difficulty, inadequacy and unattainability its hidden reward. Thus Lowth can claim, with a composure which is rarely felt in Romantic statements of the kind, that 'while the imagination labours to comprehend what is beyond its powers, this very labour itself, and these ineffectual endeavours, sufficiently demonstrate the immensity and sublimity of the object'.[57] There is a principle of compensation at work here, making even the ineffectualness of the imagination a 'sufficient' expression of the object. We feel the labour and the endeavour, and although these fall short of their object, they urge a leap of faith. Without that faith in the inexpressible 'immensity and sublimity of the object' the language of the sublime is *merely* ineffectual and insufficient.

Aesthetics of the sublime, in the eighteenth century, are not strictly means of judging artistic merit at all. They are celebrations of creativity, and of a creativity which always precedes its expression in words. Whether that creativity be located in the natural landscape, which shows forth the vastness of the Deity and is therefore confused with the creation, or whether it is located in the poet's enthusiasm, that emotional urgency which hurries the heart's feelings into words, or whether it is located in the imagination, which represents objects that are vaster or stranger than life, the art of the sublime springs from sources which lie behind and before language. It is not Longinus' 'certain Eminence or Perfection of Language', but rather his 'Image reflected from the inward

Greatness of the Soul' which becomes the key to an eighteenth-century aesthetic of the sublime. It celebrates a creativity which precedes and continually eludes the clutch of words and forms, and against which words and forms find the measure of their very poignant and expressive inadequacy.

At the heart of the sublime, therefore, there is a crucial but problematic break: the break between inspiration and work, between sensibility and style, between impression and expression, vision and text. Art is defined and authenticated by the first. The paradigmatic figure of the sublime poet is of one who stands solitary, powerless, silent and rapt before the object, the landscape or the idea, which first arrests him. It is this strong seeing which comprises his originality and power, and its communication is of secondary value. Hence the predominance of a vocabulary belonging more to theatre or oratory than to the facts of writing and reading, in the eighteenth-century sublime. What the hand has written is translated back to what the imaginative eye first sees. Communicating to others in words is thus not intrinsic to the act of creation, but is a kind of fallen and generous attempt to repeat the original vision. Longinus merely lends his support to this vocabulary of seeing when he writes, for instance, of how ' "the Imagination is so warm'd and affected, that you seem to behold yourself the very things you are describing, and to display them to the life before the Eyes of an Audience" '.[58] It is a metaphor of the theatre which clearly underlies his description of the warmed imagination. Although the poet here is describing his thoughts in words, he is presented as an actor-visionary, who sees things so intensely that he performs the act of seeing as if to the life. The emphasis is not on the words, nor on the objects seen, but rather on a special kind of seeing, which is then transmitted from poet to audience. The language of 'dramatic display',[59] which is so common in eighteenth-century theories of expression, locates the power of the poet's art in the quality of his vision, not the quality of his words. His creativity is defined in terms of a psychological performance.

By thus referring back from the poet's description to the original vision which instigates it, an aesthetic of the sublime focusses on a discrepancy between result and intention which, if it did not command our willing belief, might become troublesome. 'In the sublime', writes Thomas Weiskel, 'a *relation* to the object – the negative relation of unattainability – becomes the signifier in the aesthetic order of meaning.'[60] This is the principle behind Kant's comprehensive systematisation of the eighteenth-century sublime. He writes that we 'may describe the Sublime thus: it is an object (of nature) *the representation of which determines the mind to think the unattainability of nature regarded as a presentation of Ideas*'.[61] Once the limiting boundaries of the visible and sensible world are pushed out in the mind's representation of them, the fact of their being unattainable then becomes richly meaningful. This principle of defeat, of insufficiency and unattainability, makes the art of the sublime one in which verbal grasp always falls short of imaginative reach.

However, such a theory of original creativity is based on an essentially mystical presupposition that the unworthiness of language affirms the greatness of the object. It is for this reason that the sublime continually invokes the presence of God. Lowth can celebrate the insufficiency of language, because he takes for granted an object worthy of such failure. Just as the sublime poet's blindness is caused and justified by the divine brightness of the abyss, so the sublime poet's language is supported and 'graced' by the inexpressible fullness of God, or the godly imagination. Yet, once the presence of God fades from this aesthetic, the note of composure and optimism, which runs through most eighteenth-century descriptions of the sublime, gives way to something different.

It is perhaps Edmund Burke above all who hints at this alternative potentiality of the sublime before the Romantics confront it. His thesis is that 'whatever is in any sort terrible, or is conversant about terrible objects, or operates in a manner analogous to terror, is a source of the *sublime*'.[62] Among other commonplace examples of the sublime, Burke also gives the idea of '*general* privations', such as '*Vacuity, Darkness, Solitude* and *Silence*'.[63] He presents the terrifying sublime object as an hypostatised abstraction, and specifically one which designates the absence of something. It is this aspect of Burke's *Enquiry* which sounds strangely modern. A source of the sublime is the mind's terror when confronted with emptiness and absence, and this emptiness and absence point to no mitigating divinity. If Burke's *Enquiry* stands behind the development of the Gothic in the second half of the century, it also begins to define that distinguishing feature of the Gothic: the uncanny.

In his unfinished essay 'The "Uncanny" ' (1919) Freud defines it as everything 'touching those residues of animistic mental activity within us and bringing them to expression'.[64] The uncanny unleashes a primitive yet familiar fear, and specifically one which is no longer accounted for by any religious orthodoxy. It is a fear, therefore, of the empty spaces that haunt consciousness after the gods have disappeared. This is a fear which has been repressed in terms of individual development and surmounted in terms of cultural development. Its uncanniness is therefore directly related to its being unexplained by religious belief. It is broadly this element of uncanniness which can be detected in Burke's sublime of terror. The ideas of *'Vacuity, Darkness, Solitude* and *Silence'* cause terror because they are spaces which no longer simply proclaim the infinite spaciousness of God. Instead, they mark a kind of absence. It could be said that, when an aesthetic of the sublime begins to shed its theological support, it still confronts the Miltonic abyss, but finds instead that it is secretless and vacant.

It is this alternative face of the sublime which confronts Shelley. If the eighteenth-century sublime is an aesthetic which relies heavily on support from religious belief; which derives its vocabulary from the language of mystical transport; which transforms the large expanses of the universe into images of the Deity; which converts obscure sight into imaginative visionariness; which proclaims the written word inadequate by comparison to the godly imagining of the poet; then Shelley, who remains a radical and an atheist throughout his life, cannot subscribe but uneasily and anxiously to such an aesthetic. Walter Benjamin claims that the sublime comes to an end with the new capitalism of the city in the poetry of Baudelaire. Benjamin defines the sublime in his own terms as the 'aura', which is a kind of reciprocating but distancing effect in any object. 'To perceive the aura of an object,' he writes in the essay 'On Some Motifs in Baudelaire', 'we look at means to invest it with the ability to look at us in return.'[65] The aura is, as Geoffrey Hartman usefully explains, a form of 'presence' which has become 'displaced from its religious origin'.[66] No longer a believer, the poet still desires to find in the object of his gaze, a reciprocating presence.

However, it could be said that the 'aura' begins to fade before Baudelaire. Aesthetics of the sublime in the eighteenth century already contain the seeds of their own contradiction, in desiring to make art nature, and creativity the Creation. However, it is Shelley who is perhaps the first consistently unbelieving poet of the sublime. It is he who still looks on the landscapes of infinity, but who expresses the possibility, in his poems, that they do not 'look at us in return'. The characteristic of the Shelleyan sublime will be its unbelief, and its recognition, therefore, that what the human imagination confronts in its creative aspiration may be only a vacancy.

SHELLEY: FROM EMPIRICISM TO THE SUBLIME

The development of a theory of the sublime in the eighteenth century is marked by a gradual shift from an objective to a subjective discourse. In the first half of the century sublimity or grandeur is generally presented as a quality of the natural landscape. Such a landscape is characterised by its unbounded heights and depths, by a vastness which serves to overpower the representational capacity of the eye, and which thus affirms the invisible presence of the Deity. But in the second half of the century, emphasis is laid more and more on the subjective nature of the artist, who responds to the external landscape with a reciprocal inner largeness of soul or feeling. This subjective orientation calls attention to the emotional energy with which the artist sees, instead of categorising the object seen. But this interest in the psychological effect of creativity is one which opens up a problematic space between the moment of original vision and its communication in words. By insisting on the priority and authenticity of the artist's enthusiasm or emotional intention as opposed to their later representation in the work, theories of original genius in the eighteenth century insist on a division between creative sensibility and writing which is still present in Romantic aesthetic. In the eighteenth century this dissociation between feeling and writing is one which guarantees the originality of the artist precisely because the work is inadequate by comparison, but for the Romantics, and for Shelley in particular, it is a source of doubt and mistrust. Shelley's gradual development of an aesthetic of inspiration from the unlikely ground of his early empiricism is one which is always beset by uncertainty and scepticism, and these become the keynotes of his own sublime mode.

Roy Park writes of the nineteenth century, in *Hazlitt and the Spirit of the Age*, that 'in the absence of a philosophy capable of combating the dominant empirical epistemology of the Utilitarians the responsibility for the defence of the "existential", the "imaginative", or the "immaterial" passed to literature'.[1] Just such a defence is undertaken by Shelley in 1821, when he replies to Peacock's utilitarian attack on contemporary poets with his fine testament to the revolutionary potential of poetry in 'A Defence of Poetry'. But although the 'Defence' takes the form of an answer to Peacock's empirical utilitarianism, it must also be seen as the culmination of a long debate in Shelley's own writings between a philosophical empiricism and an aesthetic of creativity. If Shelley seeks to defend 'the "existential", the "imaginative", or the "immaterial"' in his answer to Peacock, something of the urgency and stress with which he does so derives from his own intellectual and philosophical sympathy for Peacock's position. In a sense, Shelley is answering his own empirical arguments against the fictionalising tendencies of metaphor and personification when he elaborates his vitally metaphorical aesthetic. Such an aesthetic defends poetry as a divine, mysterious, inspirational force, which cannot be reduced to the forms and models of art, for such 'Poetry is indeed something divine' (VII. 135). But although Shelley presents an aesthetic of dissociated inspiration and writing in the 'Defence', and although he continually resorts to a language of religious experience, this is not an easy adoption of the traditional sublime to replace his earlier empiricism. In spite of its tone of enthusiastic commitment and celebration, 'A Defence of Poetry' contains an essentially anxious and uncertain description of creativity, and one which is reached by way of a long debate in Shelley's own writings, between the conflicting claims of empiricism and poetry, radicalism and Christianity, reason and feeling. It is this debate which underlies and shapes that peculiarly hard-won aesthetic of inspiration in the 'Defence'.

The long and fervent 'Notes on Queen Mab' (1813) bear witness to the sheer breadth of reading which fed Shelley's youthful radicalism, and helped him formulate a theory of social revolution inspired mainly by Enlightenment *philosophes*, English empiricists and Godwin. Kenneth Neill Cameron has mapped this wide and unsystematic reading in *The Young Shelley: Genesis of a Radical*, where it lends support to his claim that the 'core of Shelley's poetry is his philosophy of social revolution'.[2] Although empiricism is only one aspect of this intellectual seed-time, it is the empirical emphasis on sense perception which seems to be the least assimilable influence on Shelley's early writing. When, in the letters of 1810–12, he turns from philosophical and political arguments to speculation on the workings of the imagination, Locke and Hume are the main obstacles in his mind. As a result, there is a conflict between Shelley the radical and Shelley the poet, and this conflict becomes evident from a very early date.

Shelley's clearest statement of allegiance to an empirical theory of knowledge is in the pamphlet which caused his dramatic expulsion from Oxford in 1811. *The Necessity of Atheism* (1811) was probably written jointly with Hogg,[3] although the fact that Shelley freely repeats its arguments in his own 'Notes on Queen Mab' and in *A Refutation of Deism* (1814) is evidence of his whole-hearted co-operation in the project. Significantly, the pamphlet is little more than an exposition of two arguments derived from Locke and Hume, but in Shelley's hands directed unapologetically against the arguments in favour of the existence of a God. The first method of attack derives from the Lockean principle that the 'senses are the sources of all knowledge to the mind, consequently their evidence claims the strongest assent' (v. 207). Belief is a passive, not an active response, and depends on sense perception which, in the case of the Deity, is manifestly lacking. The other method of attack restates Hume's sceptical theory of causation: that 'we can only infer from effects causes exactly adequate to those effects', and that, as a result, the idea of 'an eternal, omniscient, Almighty Being' is redundant, as its definition is one that 'leaves the cause in the obscurity, but renders it more incomprehensible' (v. 208). That all knowledge springs from sense perception and that the theory of a divine first cause simply anthropomorphises a source of ignorance, are arguments to

27

which Shelley returns throughout his writings. However, the context of this most explicit espousal of empiricism is revealing. To advocate an epistemology based on sense perception, as well as on a Humean scepticism towards the relation of cause and effect, is, for Shelley, the most efficient challenge to orthodox Christianity. 'Every reflecting mind must allow that there is no proof of the existence of a Deity' (v. 209), he resoundingly concludes. However, such a challenge need not only be directed against theological rationalisations of belief. It includes in its range of attack all forms of anthropomorphic imagining or personification, and Shelley elsewhere is soon shirking the logic of his own empiricism.

Although his poetic career has often been divided into an early period of political and philosophical radicalism and a later period of idealism or platonism, there is another debate which underlies Shelley's poetry and which is already in progress at this early date. The letters written during the years 1810–12, mainly to Elizabeth Hitchener, reveal a still passionate determination to attack orthodox Christianity, and particularly that of his correspondent. Such an enterprise is again carried out with much assistance from Locke. Shelley condemns all arguments based on feeling, rather than reason and sense perception, as justification for belief, and condemns the figurative propensities of language which support those arguments. However, in these letters he is also making the first tentative moves towards a description of creativity, and this results in a curiously contradictory and tortuous kind of reasoning. While his deep antagonism towards Christianity and its social institutions leads Shelley to make huge claims for reason and plain prose, these are claims which at other times he seems to regret. What these letters make clear is that there is already a tension in his thought between the cause of political radicalism, which requires the abolition of oppressive institutions like Christianity, and the cause of poetry, which allows deceptive and superstitious devices of language to flourish. The letters reveal that Shelley is not just debating the merits of his own radical atheism and his correspondent's orthodox belief, but that he is also conducting a more difficult debate between his radical empiricism and an aesthetic of poetry. His sense of unease about the reconcilability of the two kinds of discourse is hinted at in a letter to Godwin written in the summer of 1812. Here he claims of his past that 'I read Locke, Hume, Reid & whatever metaphysics came in my way, without however renouncing poetry' (*Letters*, 1. 303). This hint of unease underlies the many debates in the letters of 1810–12 concerning the merits of reason against feeling, of sense perception against belief, of plain prose against metaphors and personifications. Shelley's allegiance to the former is rarely unaccompanied by a note of regret.

This division of sympathies can be traced in his use of that key word of the sublime: 'enthusiasm'. He employs it, in the very early letters to Hogg, in the sense of religious or emotional fanaticism, as do Locke and Hume. Thus he confesses himself 'the wildest, most delirious of enthusiasm's offspring' (*Letters*, 1. 29), or elsewhere 'the most degraded of deceived enthusiasts' (*Letters*, 1. 44). In spite of the curious relish with which Shelley applies the word to himself, he intends its pejorative signification of irrational extremism to predominate. However, a year later, in his second letter to Godwin, which gives a history of his development from being a writer of wild romances to a sober reader of *Political Justice*, Shelley uses the word 'enthusiasm' to signify, almost regretfully now, that creative sensibility which gave rise to those writings. He tells Godwin, 'I was haunted with a passion for the wildest and most extravagant romances: ancient books of Chemistry and Magic were perused with an enthusiasm of wonder almost amounting to belief. My sentiments were unrestrained by anything within me.' The association of enthusiasm with superstitious belief is complicated by an association with creativity, however wild and foolish; with being 'the votary of Romance' (*Letters*, 1. 227). That Shelley's attitude to his youthful outpourings is not quite as superior and dismissive as he seems to claim, is comically betrayed by his then sending the famous author, the new 'regulator and former' (*Letters*, 1. 229) of his mind, copies of those enthusiastic romances, *St. Irvyne* and *Zastrozzi*. Behind this declaration of sobriety and rationality, there lurks a faint nostalgia for the imaginative enthusiasm of the past. When, in his next letter, Shelley addresses Godwin as 'my friend and my adviser, the moderator of my enthusiasm' (*Letters*, 1. 229), he reveals a quality of his own nature still strong enough to need to be repressed.

Thus enthusiasm is associated in Shelley's mind both with the folly of irrational belief and with the impulse to write. To be a 'votary of Romance' is to be a religious fanatic in the cause of the imagination. His adoption of Godwin as an intellectual mentor who will restrain and guide his thoughts is tinged with this odd pride and regret for the enthusiasm of the past. His use of the word thus becomes a kind of gauge of his contradictory allegiances, to metaphysics but also to poetry, to reason but also to feeling. In an early letter of 1811, Shelley advises Hogg to look up Locke on enthusiasm, which, 'whether in religion, politics or morality' is 'equally inexcusably fatuitous'. That Shelley is here blaming Hogg for an infatuation for his sister which he himself had engineered does not seem to daunt him. Hogg is 'prejudiced like Religions votaries who reason whilst they can, & when that ceases to be possible, they *feel*' (*Letters*, 1. 96). This is the height of folly because love, like religion and the composition of romances, springs from that enthusiasm which is antipathetic to reason.

The term thus comes to shelter a number of associated ideas: creativity, feeling, love, belief, which are all linked by their common opposition to reason, but which will return like the repressed in Shelley's later work. When he comes to write the Preface to *The Revolt of Islam* (1817), for instance, the term 'enthusiasm' is no longer caught in an opposition to reason. There Shelley claims that it is 'the business of the Poet to communicate to others the pleasure and the enthusiasm arising out of those images and feelings in the vivid presence of which within his own mind consists at once his inspiration and his reward' (*P. W.*, p. 33). He defines the purpose of poetry as a doubling of the original exchange between the mind and its vivid 'images and feelings'; an exchange which is itself already a kind of accomplished artistic work: 'at once his inspiration and his reward'. The role of enthusiasm, no longer fettered by the greater claims of reason, is that of a mediating strength of feeling which, in the long tradition of the sublime, makes communicating to others as nearly original as a secondary activity can be. It is as if Shelley works through his own Enlightenment in the early letters and prose, but comes in the end to proclaim a Romantic version of the sublime which will protect feeling and enthusiasm from empirical reduction.

However, the tensions and contradictions in the early letters are a witness to how costly such an aesthetic will be for Shelley. Writing to Elizabeth Hitchener in June 1811, he is still trapped in an opposition between the claims of empiricism, which he broadly calls reason, and the claims of a desired creativity. There is a polarisation of the two in this letter which reveals just how much is at stake on either side. Shelley writes:

> With pleasure I engage in a correspondence which carries its own recommendation both with my feelings & my reason. I am now however an undivided votary of the latter....Locke *proves* that there are no innate ideas...thus overturning all appeals of *feeling* in favor of Deity...To a belief in Deity I have no objection on the score of feeling, I would as gladly perhaps with greater pleasure admit than doubt his existence....My wish to convince you of his non-existence is twofold: First on the score of truth, secondly because I conceive it to be the most summary way of eradicating Christianity....Imagination delights in personification; were it not for this embodying quality of eccentric fancy we should be to this day without a God...this personification, beautiful in Poetry, inadmissible in reasoning... I recommend reason. – Why? is it because since I have devoted myself unreservedly to its influencing, I have never felt *Happiness*. I have rejected all fancy, all imagination. (*Letters*, i. 99–101)

In this passage, Shelley's espousal of Locke begins to seem less than happy. Because Locke has disproved the theory of innate ideas he has, according to Shelley, overturned all arguments for the existence of God which are based on '*feeling*'. This curious misrepresentation of Locke shows how far Shelley's reading of him has become confused with personal issues. Shelley presents himself as 'an undivided votary' of reason, because it is his intention to disprove the existence of God with the irrefutable argument of sense perception. But a little later he betrays how much might be lost with the loss of 'all appeals of feeling', and in a curious *volte-face* he admits his willingness to believe 'on the score of feeling'. The 'undivided votary' of reason seems to regret the very argument which has made him 'undivided'. However, empiricism still has on its side the merits of truth and the eradication of Christianity, both of which will be achieved, according to a rather hasty logic, if he can convince Elizabeth Hitchener of God's 'non-existence'.

This is a characteristically Shelleyan strategy, by which he invokes the arguments of empiricism in the cause of eradicating Christianity, only to regret that they are so effective. The source of this regret is made clear in the last part of the letter. Support for the existence of God derives, not only from a willingness to feel, but also from the poeticising imagination, and those devices of rhetoric which Locke condemned as 'perfect cheat'. The culprit is as much the poet as the believer. For the idea of God is supported by the delighting 'Imagination' and the 'eccentric fancy', which indulge what Shelley elsewhere calls 'the anthropomorphism of the vulgar' (*P.W.*, p. 814). Yet, he again betrays a divided allegiance in acknowledging that 'this embodying quality' is 'beautiful in Poetry'.

In this letter, the argument is wrecked upon an opposition which Shelley regrets even as he impresses it upon his reader. He makes a simple division between, on the one hand, atheism, reason, Locke's argument against innate ideas, truth and plain prose, and, on the other hand, religious belief, appeals of feeling, imagination, personification, beauty, poetry, happiness. As a result, his intellectual and political recommendation of the first is wretched: 'I have never felt *Happiness*.' His avowed rejection of all the personifying tendencies of the language of fancy and imagination betrays by its emphasis how far their attraction exceeds the evidence against them. What the letter reveals is just how much Shelley's use of Locke in the cause of 'eradicating Christianity' forced him to reject, and also how reluctant that rejection is. The 'undivided votary' of reason then goes on to insist on the unhappy division between what is 'beautiful in Poetry, inadmissible in reasoning'. The real debate in these letters is not so much between atheism and Christianity, but between the two kinds of discourse they presume. The problem which confronts Shelley at this stage, and which he will confront again in Peacock's 'The Four Ages of Poetry', is that the language of reason is progressive, while the language of poetry is reactionary. Ten years later he will answer Peacock with a defence of poetry as revolutionary *because* it is imaginative, but in 1811 he only regrets the opposition they present. However, it is worth noticing that, for all his allegiance to the cause of reason, atheism and literal prose in this letter, the capitalised personification of 'Poetry' quietly breaks the very rule he is at pains to establish. Even while denouncing all superstitious anthropomorphisms, Shelley carelessly allows this one of his own to stand.

It is this distrust of personification which lies at the heart of Shelley's opposition to the language of poetry, and it derives from his objections to the methods of religious reasoning. In particular, it derives from his objection to the language of the religious sublime, which affirms the nature of God by way of personified abstractions or negative attributes. In his 'Notes on Queen Mab' Shelley mocks this habit of substituting a word for a thing, a figure of speech for something which is absent. He complains that 'God is represented as infinite, eternal, incomprehensible; He is contained under every *predicate in non* that the logic of ignorance could fabricate' (*P.W.*, p. 814). He then quotes in support of this view a passage from d'Holbach's *Système de la Nature*, which parodies the traditional language of the religious sublime. 'En remontant de causes en causes,' he quotes, 'les mortels ont fini par ne rien voir; et c'est dans cette obscurité qu'ils ont placé leur Dieu (*P.W.*, p. 815). The traditional language of mystical rapture is turned against itself. This is not the obscurity of imaginative vision, which sees the unseeable, but merely intellectual obscurantism, which creates a darkness by its own sophistical reasoning, and calls it God. This defeat of the senses is not a proof of sublime vision, but of ridiculous ignorance. From an empirical point of view, as Shelley is quick to recognise, the language of the sublime is a piece of verbal trickery, which substitutes a negative word for a clear idea, and hallows a principle of obscurity in the place of clear sight. The 'logic of ignorance' fabricates a divine darkness because it cannot see, and then fixes it with a personifying language of negatives.

33

However, elsewhere, Shelley shows a susceptibility to the effect of the sublime in the natural world which challenges such rigid empiricism, and forces him to confront again the opposition between reason and poetry. During the summer of 1811 he was on holiday in South Wales, and from there wrote two letters to Elizabeth Hitchener which contain passages attempting to describe the effects of its wild and grandiose landscapes. In the first of these, provisionally dated 13 July 1811, Shelley breaks off a hectic argument on religious belief to write:

> This country of Wales is excessively grand; rocks piled on each other to tremendous heights, rivers formed into cataracts by their projections, & valleys clothed with woods, present an appearance of enchantment – but *why* do they enchant, *why* is it more affecting than a plain, it cannot be innate, is it acquired? – Thus does knowledge lose all the pleasure which invol[un]tarily [ari]ses, by attempting to arrest th[e] fleeting Phantom as it passes – vain al[most] like the chemists aether it evaporates under our observation; it flies from all but the slaves of passion & sickly sensibility who will not analyse a feeling. (*Letters*, 1. 119–20)

Once again his attempt to define feeling, the feeling of enchantment and of pleasure, stumbles against the arguments of Lockean empiricism: 'it cannot be innate, is it acquired?' However, it is precisely this analytical habit of mind which makes the reception and communication of pleasure difficult: 'Thus does knowledge lose all the pleasure.' Interestingly, it is the language of 'Chemistry and Magic', associated with his being a 'votary' not of reason but of 'Romance' (*Letters*, 1. 227), which serves to describe the 'Phantom' pleasure. Against his better reason, and against his knowledge that those who feel are mere 'slaves of passion & sickly sensibility', Shelley asserts that the landscape holds a magical presence, an enchanter, a Phantom, even a mere 'chemists aether', which the reasoner cannot arrest. A philosophical curiosity to discover why the landscape enchants is disenchanting. Only by forgoing the freedom to reason and analyse and by being a slave of passion may the 'fleeting Phantom' be held.

The language of enchantment, of magic and enthusiasm, works against the logic of the passage. Shelley regrets his freedom to reason, and desires to be a slave. The 'fleeting Phantom', which prefigures many later ghostly passings of inspiration in his work, eludes the grasp of the empirical and analysing mind, which is therefore left with a pleasureless and disenchanting freedom. This early ghost of Shelley's future aesthetic significantly arises out of a landscape which is 'excessively grand', and which reaches 'to tremendous heights'; a landscape of nearly defeating magnitude and superabundance. Shelley's insistence on the use of reason against the claims of feeling, of analysis against the forces of enchantment, fails to lay this Phantom of possible sublimity.

In a second letter of July 1811, Shelley again reveals a susceptibility to natural grandeur which poses a threat to his philosophic reasoning. He breaks off an argument on political justice and equality with the following paragraph:

> Nature is here marked with the most impressive character of loveliness and grandeur, *once* I was tremulously alive to tones and scenes – The habit of analysing feelings I fear does not agree with this. It is spontaneous, & when it becomes subjugated to consideration ceases to exist. But you do right to indulge feeling where it does not militate with reason, I wish I could too – This valley is covered with trees, so are partly the mountains that surround it. Rocks piled upon each oth[er t]o an immense height, & clouds intersecting them, in other places waterfalls midst the umbrage of a thousand shadowy trees form the principle features of the scenery. I am not wholly uninfluenced by its magic in my lonely walks... (*Letters*, I. 127–8)

Again it is the sight of natural 'loveliness and grandeur', of a landscape of sublime heights and depths, which releases in the poet a momentary regret for his loss of feeling, his loss of an aesthetic response: being 'tremulously alive to tones and scenes', which the habit of analysis has numbed. Reason and feeling, analysis and magic, remain in opposition. Nonetheless, the passage points to where, in the future, the elusive Phantom of creativity may be found. It is this landscape of sublime solitude and largeness which is capable of awakening in the poet a susceptibility to magic, enchantment, ghostliness, which usurp upon his better judgement, and permit an alternative means of seeing the world: one which is made strange by 'feeling'.

The expression of these early doubts and regrets seems to be fostered by a context which is traditionally that of the sublime.

The tension between what Shelley calls reason: his resolute atheism and the empirical arguments that support it, and what he calls feeling: a creative responsiveness to natural grandeur, the force of which eludes analysis, like ghosts the arresting hand, becomes extreme in these letters from South Wales. They contain the first tentative moves towards a theory of creativity which is in opposition to the demands of reason, and which celebrates in its place the elusiveness and unpredictability of the spirit of beauty in the world.

It is in the summer of 1816, during Shelley's visit to the Alps, that this preoccupation with the effect of natural grandeur becomes central once again, and in the letters written during the months of May, June and July of this year, Shelley begins to elaborate his own aesthetic of creativity. These letters show a marked change of direction in Shelley's thinking. He is no longer concerned to attack Christianity with the weapon of Lockean empiricism, and as a result he is to some extent freed from his earlier commitment to reason. Surrounded by the Alps, that self-conscious domain of the eighteenth-century sublime, and reliving the scenes of Rousseau's *Julie, ou la Nouvelle Héloïse* in their actual locations, he comes to need a description, not so much of how the mind knows, but of how it imagines. No longer in dispute with superstitious orthodoxies, Shelley turns his attention to the workings of the mind in creation without, now, having to be an apologist for reason. In the Alps he finds to hand, as it were, an aesthetic which traditionally authenticates extremes of emotion or feeling. However, he does not just succumb to a well-established fashion of semi-conversion and rapture on viewing the Alps, and to the familiar and sometimes tired vocabulary of admiration and enthusiasm which the experience provokes. Certainly, by 1816 Shelley had come across innumerable descriptions of the sublime in the works of Addison, Monboddo, Reid and Stewart, and he had also been greatly influenced by William Drummond's sceptical challenge to empiricism in his *Academical Questions*, and by Lowth's extended study of the biblical sublime in his *Lectures*. All these must have contributed to his loss of interest in empiricism, and to his new preoccupation with an aesthetic of grandeur and space. However, his own

36

descriptions of the effect of this 'scenery of wonderful su[blimity]' (*Letters*, I. 475) are a long way from simply affirming the presence of God in them.

Where Shelley once advised that the 'senses are the sources of all knowledge to the mind', he now champions the independent and active power of the 'imagination', which, he writes, 'surely could not forbear to breathe into the most inanimate forms, some likeness of its own visions' (*Letters*, I. 481). The imagination is no longer a regrettable source of epistemological confusion and superstitious ignorance; it is a transforming and enlivening force, which works like the breath of inspiration upon 'inanimate forms', and forces the external world into 'some likeness of its own visions'. Reality is no longer perceived passively, but is shaped by vision. Just how radical is this new allegiance to imaginative as opposed to empirical knowledge becomes evident in a later passage where Shelley describes the effect of reading Rousseau:

I read Julie all day; an overflowing, as it now seems, surrounded by the scenes which it has so wonderfully peopled, of sublimest genius, and more than human sensibility. Meillerie, the Castle of Chillon, Clarens, the mountains of La Valais and Savoy, present themselves to the imagination as monuments of things that were once familiar, and of beings that were once dear to it. They were created indeed by one mind, but a mind so powerfully bright as to cast a shade of falsehood on the records that are called reality.

(*Letters*, I. 485)

The 'sublimest genius' of Rousseau is characterised by its ability to people the scene with creatures of its own imagining. Such 'sensibility' is no longer slavish and sickly, but is a power capable of transforming the 'reality' that the mind merely records. By comparison to this new and 'powerfully bright' influence, the evidence of the senses seems false. In terms of Romantic poetic theory this is hardly new, but in terms of Shelley's earlier writings it has the freshness of something newly discovered.

Another feature of Shelley's description of the Alps in these letters is his frequent use of negative adjectives. While he once mocked the kind of reasoning which represents God by every '*predicate in non*', he now describes the sublime scene before him with emphasis on its defeating and privative appearance. He writes, for instance, that 'forests of impenetrable thickness & untrodden, nay, inaccessible expanse spread on every side' (*Letters*, 1. 475). The characteristic of the scene is its inaccessibility to the senses, and particularly to the sense of sight. The description works by what Lowth called a 'continued negation', which makes the object exceed the scope of human sight and human words. Expression only labours ineffectually after its object, and communicates it by default. This traditional method of the sublime throws into relief the difficulty of expression. Thus in another letter to Peacock, Shelley exclaims:

– But how shall I describe to you the scenes by which I am now surrounded. – To exhaust epithets which express the astonishment & the admiration – the very excess of satisfied expectation, where expectation scarcely acknowledged any boundary – is this to impress upon your mind the images which fill mine now, even until it overflows? (*Letters*, 1. 495)

The passage has the effect of a verbal swoon. There is the dramatic, even histrionic fear of failure, the sense of language being quickly exhausted by comparison to the richness of the object and the effect of boundaries and outlines opening out into infinite space. Shelley adopts with ease here the vocabulary of an aesthetic which has as its main aim to describe how the mind is raised, ravished and transported in its apprehension of divine grandeur. Characteristically, too, the purpose of his description is not to contain the scene in words, but 'to impress upon your mind the images which fill mine now'. Language is exhausted in order that a more original and psychological communication may take place, which is a transmission of the scene's emotional effect: 'the astonishment & the admiration'.

It is this deference to the earlier experience of being enraptured or overpowered which marks much of Shelley's language in these letters. For instance, on the day before the composition of 'Mont Blanc', he describes to Peacock the effect on his mind of first seeing the mountain:

The immensity of these aerial summits excited, when they suddenly burst upon the sight, a sentiment of extatic wonder, not unallied to madness – And remember this was all one scene. It all pressed home to our regard & to our imagination. . . .All was as much our own as if we had been the creators of such impressions in the minds of others, as now occupied our own. – Nature

was the poet whose harmony held our spirits more breathless than that of
the divinest. *(Letters,* 1. 497)

The state of spirit evinced by the word 'breathless', in its literal
meaning, as well as its literary meaning of 'speechless', is characteristic of the effect of the natural sublime. It is precisely powerlessness
which is expressive. Shelley then echoes the eighteenth-century
attribution of creativity to the creation, of art to nature. 'Nature
was the poet whose harmony held our spirits more breathless than
that of the divinest,' he writes. Creativity is transferred back to
another author: to the poet Nature whose first writings, which are
'impressions in the mind', have the effect of causing speechlessness
in the listener. Nonetheless, it is this overpowering of the mind by
some original and most natural 'harmony' which is paradoxically
pressing for communication. There is a doubling of roles here,
whereby the poet is so intensely a spectator and a listener that
he becomes a creator in turn: 'All was as much our own as if we
had been the creators of such impressions in the minds of others,
as now occupied our own.' It is by being the recipient of an earlier
and more original poetry, one which is communicated wordlessly
to the mind, that the poet becomes creative. This seems to echo a
much quoted passage from Longinus, which describes how 'the
Mind is naturally elevated by the true Sublime, and so sensibly
affected with its lively Strokes, that it swells in Transport and an
inward Pride, as if what was only heard had been the Product
of its own Invention'.[4] Shelley's change from passive to active
participation, from being possessed by the power of Nature to
making it his own, 'All was as much our own,' echoes a long
tradition of attributing art to nature in order to recover it as a
more authentic art. So here, what is first seen or impressed upon
the mind by Nature becomes the inspiration for a secondary
creativity, which seeks to turn powerlessness and breathlessness into
power, into speech.

It is in these letters of 1816 that Shelley outlines an aesthetic of
creativity which draws most closely on a vocabulary of the sublime,
and which diverges strongly from his earlier anti-Christian
empiricism. While he once regretted the personifying tendencies of

poetic language, he now celebrates Rousseau's imaginative peopling of the scene, and while he once mocked the method of proving the existence of God by way of negative attributes, he now stresses a similar insufficiency of language to account for the overpowering and unbounded nature of the landscape. His need to protect the imaginative and the immaterial leads him to employ a language which philosophically and politically he distrusts. Albert Gérard writes of the Romantics in general that they brought to bear a 'philosophy of creativity to epistemology', and thus 'endeavoured to formulate a general theory of knowledge which would take the poetic experience into account'.[5] The fact that Shelley remains an empiricist in matters of religious belief but derives his theory of creativity from the eighteenth-century sublime makes of his attempts to combine the two a peculiarly difficult process. Unlike Wordsworth and Coleridge, he never sheds his radical atheism, and his scepticism towards a creative force within the universe. But while he refuses to concede any epistemological evidence for the existence of a God, he is drawn to an aesthetic which idealises the immaterial and numinous properties of the landscape. The conflict between these two perspectives will become one of the distinguishing features of that poetry which is written in the manner of the sublime, and which has as its main theme the desire of the imagination to find a presence in the empty scene.

Shelley's most extended and persuasive account of the workings of the mind in creation, however, is to be found in 'A Defence of Poetry' (1821). His method of countering Peacock's mocking and witty dismissal of poetry as socially irrelevant is to give a description of poetry as a Power which exceeds the particular work and the particular poet. This essential poetry is always a force for change and renovation. That Shelley recognises the evasiveness of such a reply is made clear in a letter to Peacock, where he writes that 'I have taken a more general view of what is Poetry than you have, and [you] will perhaps agree with several of my positions without considering your own touched' (*Letters*, II. 275). Shelley's 'more general view' of poetry is one which raises it above the particular work and presents it instead as the original energy of creativity. By this method he can agree with Peacock's enlightened and progressive position, and yet celebrate poetry as the source of that progress. His general argument thus subscribes to Peacock's utilitarian claim that poetry should be socially useful and responsible, but contains the important corollary that, as Marilyn Butler writes, poetry achieves this 'when it is most imaginative'.[6] The 'Defence' is thus a tactical outdoing of Peacock's enlightened utilitarianism. Poems may be subject to all the mistaken and reactionary beliefs of their authors, but poetry itself is the very spirit of change and progress.

In a sense, Shelley is confronting in Peacock an empirical argument against poetry that is similar to his own empirical arguments against Christianity. Peacock makes a basic distinction between reason, which is the agent of the progressive 'sciences of morals and of mind',[7] and imagination, which is the agent of a fanciful, superstitious and generally reactionary poetry. Reason is progressive and enlightened while the poetic imagination, particularly that of contemporary poets, looks back towards 'barbarous manners, obsolete customs, and exploded superstitions'.[8] In Peacock's utilitarian scheme of things, the backwardness of the poet's mind is characterised especially by his habit of personifying inanimate objects and of seeing invisible spirits. Like Locke and Hume, as well as the younger Shelley, he associates the anthropomorphising language of poetry with the language of superstitious creeds, and especially, by discreet implication, Christianity. Like those too, he finds such an association to be most clearly fostered by the landscapes of the sublime. 'Rocks, mountains, seas, unsubdued forests, unnavigable rivers, surround [the poet] with forms of power and mystery, which ignorance and fear have peopled with spirits, under multifarious names of gods, goddesses, nymphs, genii, and daemons,'[9] he writes.

Shelley confronts in Peacock's work the same argument he himself once used to discredit Christianity: the argument that 'were it not for this embodying quality of eccentric fancy we should be to this day without a God' (*Letters*, I. 101). Here too the guilty ones are not the theologians but the poets, and particularly the

Lake Poets who, according to Peacock's ruthless logic, 'contrived, though they had retreated from the world for the express purpose of seeing nature as she was, to see her only as she was not, converting the land they lived in into a sort of fairy-land, which they peopled with mysticisms and chimaeras'.[10] The poet's enthusiasm to see what cannot be seen, and his desire to people the empty landscape with fictional presences, are in contradiction to modern enlightenment and scientific truth. The empirical model is for Peacock, as it was for Shelley, the model of progress, and consequently he banishes poetry, particularly the poetry of the sublime, from the republic of useful and progressive knowledge. To summon imaginary presences from the empty landscape is to propagate once more childish creeds and exploded superstitions. Peacock thus condemns the poet for the very reasons that an aesthetic of the sublime has celebrated him: he is a latter day enthusiast or fanatic.

Against Peacock's empirical mockery of contemporary poetry, Shelley issues two main arguments in its defence. The first simply includes the poet amongst those moralists, philosophers and teachers who contribute to the betterment of mankind. Shelley accepts the principle of political improvement as a criterion of poetic value, but adds that poetry legislates for the gradual liberation of the race because it works upon the individual moral sense, of which the 'great instrument' is 'the imagination' (VII. 118). He reclaims the imagination as a source of moral improvement, asserting that 'A man, to be greatly good, must imagine intensely and comprehensively' (VII. 118), and he thus links ethical responsibility with poetry at its very source. It is not the precise wording of poetry which bears responsibility for progress, but the energy of imagining, which is more truly the poet's role. Shelley's second argument works by redefining poetry as an original and strange Power, which eludes representation by the empirical senses, and which precedes the act of writing individual poems. It is this aspect of the 'Defence' which reveals how far the conflict with Peacock is once again a conflict between the principles of empiricism and an aesthetic of the sublime.

If one of Peacock's main objections to the poetic imagination is that it perpetuates the folly of religious belief, this association is one that Shelley's answer reiterates. Poets, in the widest sense which includes legislators, politicians and teachers as well as artists, are those who 'draw into a certain propinquity with the beautiful and the true, that partial apprehension of the agencies of the invisible world which is called religion' (VII. 112). This explicit link between poetry and religion shows a marked change from Shelley's earlier position. What poetry shares with religion, however, is not a common object, for Shelley still affirms that the object of poetry is 'beautiful' and 'true', but a common means of knowing the object, which is by a 'partial apprehension'. It is this need for an alternative epistemology which forces a liaison between poetry and religious belief. Throughout the 'Defence' Shelley is trying to find an alternative to that knowledge gained from the evidence of the senses, and he does so by insisting on a failure of apprehension which is akin to mystical possession. Thus he writes that poetry 'acts in a divine and unapprehended manner, beyond and above consciousness' (VII. 116), or, a little later, that 'Poetry acts in another and diviner manner,' because it 'awakens and enlarges the mind itself by rendering it the receptacle of a thousand unapprehended combinations of thought' (VII. 117). Elsewhere, he states unequivocally that 'Poetry is indeed something divine' (VII. 135), and, at the end, that 'Poets are the hierophants of an unapprehended inspiration' (VII. 140). To 'apprehend' in these contexts seems to mean either to arrest or to predict and Shelley's accumulated definitions of poetry are definitions which emphasise the failure of the mind to calculate or to hold its object. Like that earlier Phantom of pleasure in the landscape of South Wales, poetry is an elusive and invisible force, which acts like divine revelation, and cannot be arrested, seen or foreseen by the human mind.

Thus Shelley answers Peacock's commonsensical empiricism, that the poet should see nature only as it is and not as he imagines, with the claim that 'poetry defeats the curse which binds us to be subjected to the accident of surrounding impressions', and instead 'it spreads its own figured curtain, or withdraws life's dark veil from before the scene of things' (VII. 137). The action of poetry is a covering or an uncovering, but in either case it marks a dissatisfaction with the object as merely seen. Whether poetry adds its own figures and elaborations, or exposes an unfamiliar nakedness, it confuses the eye, and forces it to see differently. 'It compels us to feel that which we perceive, and to imagine that which we know' (VII. 137), Shelley claims. This is a fine and deft revision of Peacock's polarisation of reasoning and imagining, when he rejoices that in the moral sciences 'reason gains the ascendancy...over imagination and feeling'.[11] Instead, Shelley insists that the poet must perceive, not distinctly but feelingly, and must know, not passively but imaginatively. While he himself once lamented the irreconcilability of reason and feeling, of the empiricist's knowledge and the poet's imaginative fabrications, he now celebrates their confusion. Poetic creativity is a defeat and unfamiliarising of the senses.

However, if Shelley approaches the language of mystical rapture in his search for 'a theory of knowledge which would take the poetic experience into account', it is in his theory of poetry as inspiration that he sounds his most interesting and self-defining note. His tactics in the 'Defence' are generally to refer back from poetry as the written text to Poetry as the inspiratory source of all revolutionary activity, whether moral, legislative, philosophic or literary. He is concerned, not so much with the writing of poems but, in the tradition of the sublime, with the original impetus to write, which is described in terms of a mysterious and unpredictable Power. The exact provenance of this Power is ambiguous. It arises at times from within, like the colour of a flower, and at times passes from without, like the action of a wind. Much of the critical controversy over Shelley has centred on whether his theory of inspiration is platonic and thus locates inspiration outside man, or 'psychological and expressive',[12] as Abrams terms it, and thus locates inspiration within. However, it is not so much the exact provenance of inspiration which concerns me, as its relation to the poet and the poem. It is here that Shelley betrays an uncertainty and scepticism that are central to his theory of poetry.

To advocate an aesthetic of poetry in terms of the original Power which inspires it, is to isolate the written word from its source. Generally, in eighteenth-century theories of the sublime, words, by their very inadequacy and inferiority, signal the magnitude and superiority of their object. However for Shelley, the relation between inspiration and its expression in poems is not so optimistic and compensatory. He writes, for instance, that 'the mind in creation is as a fading coal, which some invisible influence, like an inconstant wind, awakens to transitory brightness...Could this influence be durable in its original purity and force, it is impossible to predict the greatness of the results; but when composition begins, inspiration is already on the decline' (VII. 135). It is not whether inspiration comes from within or without which defines it, but how it is related to the act of 'composition'. This relation is essentially one of decline and loss. Composition cannot recover the original brightness of inspiration, but rather begins to lose it from the start. Although the 'fading coal' of the mind is briefly fired again, as by 'an inconstant wind', composition itself is only gained at the expense of inspiration. Writing is thus by its very nature a process of loss. This famous metaphor for poetry is one that contains no reward or recompense for the fallen state of composition. Inspiration is a kind of god which is uncertain, inconstant and always in flight from words. It is the original Power of writing, but a Power which is forfeited in the very attempt to recover it.

This principle of loss is inherent in that other metaphor of inspiration as a wind. Shelley writes that the pleasure arising from 'evanescent visitations of thought and feeling' is 'as it were the interpenetration of a diviner nature through our own; but its footsteps are like those of a wind over a sea, which the coming calm erases, and whose traces remain only, as on the wrinkled sand which paves it' (VII. 136). This very Shelleyan image of creativity brings to the tradition of the sublime a perilousness and scepticism which is new. The wind that passes like a 'diviner nature' leaves no trace except a slight wrinkling of the sea-bed. The first imprint of the wind's footsteps is one which is erased by calm, and is only retained, differently, in the new, fine patterning of the sand. Instead of affirming the presence of the god, Shelley's metaphor emphasises its loss. Like that earlier Phantom of creative pleasure, this one too cannot be arrested by the senses.

Thus between the imprint on the sea's surface and the patterning of the sand, between inspiration and composition, there is the delay and distance of the sea. This brilliant image, by which inspiration is perilously translated into faint markings on the bed of consciousness, works by stressing forgetfulness and loss as the condition of the god's recovery in words: 'the coming calm erases'. Throughout Shelley's writings, the image of the sand and waves, which describes the receptivity of the mind in creation as if it were a natural page awaiting a kind of writing, contains this possibility of complete erasure. There is no certain passage from inspiration to composition. Instead, for Shelley, the mind records the traces of a god walking on the water only by a process of losing and forgetting. Poetry is only a secondary and different patterning of the sand, bearing witness to inspiration as to something which is always lost.

Shelley's aesthetic of original inspiration is thus different from those of many eighteenth-century precursors. It stresses doubt and loss instead of faith and compensation. If composition is always an inadequate representation of that Power which first inspires it, yet composition is all that remains to the poet. If writing is still a residual trace of the passing god, it is one which works by no principle of faith in that god. As a result, Shelley's aesthetic of poetry as inspiration is one which very quickly becomes a doubt and anxiety about composition. The distance between the wind's passing and its faint recovery in words is a distance which cannot be crossed in reverse. As a result, words remain isolated by a sense of their own loss. Without the continued pressure of inspiration, the sublime poem risks becoming ' "mere" rhetoric'.[13]

To define writing as a loss of vision, composition as a loss of inspiration, as Shelley does in the 'Defence', is to isolate the poem's rhetoric from the Power which makes that rhetoric full and authentic. On the one hand, he needs to assert the numinous properties of such a Power, which works mysteriously and incalculably, like divine revelation, but, on the other hand, he refuses to affirm it as an abiding presence. Thus the 'Defence' contains the curious paradox that, while Poetry in its ideal state is inspiration, poems are the loss of inspiration. The act of writing always relinquishes something that went before.

It is in his poems that Shelley plays out the implications of this divided aesthetic. Whether located within the poet, as an intuitional command, or outside, as a Power to be half apprehended or felt, inspiration is a Power which cannot be arrested or held in writing. It is a Power which declines, decays, vanishes. Writing only marks the fact that the god has passed. As a result, the Shelleyan sublime continually forces attention back towards the poor devices of composition, the remaining 'traces...on the wrinkled sand'. The breach between inspiration and composition is one which threatens the unbelieving poet of the sublime with a knowledge that the composition of poems may be a mere rhetorical fictionalising: a writing that is deserted and emptied of the gods. It is this knowledge that underlies those poems which seek to turn the inspirational origin of their writing into an object to be contemplated, questioned and imagined.

3

SCEPTICISM AND SUBLIME POWER:
'HYMN TO INTELLECTUAL BEAUTY' AND 'MONT BLANC'

In the summer of 1816, while Shelley was writing letters to Peacock about the effect on his imagination of the 'scenery of wonderful su[blimity]' (*Letters*, 1. 475) in the Alps, he also wrote two fine poems inspired by that scenery and related to those letters. 'Hymn to Intellectual Beauty' and 'Mont Blanc' are both poems which seek to address and know the presence of a hidden Power within the landscape. Such a Power defies perception by the senses but nonetheless commands the attention of the imagination. In both poems Shelley expresses dissatisfaction with the merely visible scene and seeks to apprehend some originating Power which lies beyond 'the records that are called reality' (*Letters*, 1. 485). He is thus writing very much in the tradition of the sublime. The infinite vistas of the Alps traditionally indicate the presence of a Deity whose nature exceeds the scope of human comprehension, but who may be affirmed by that very excess. The apparent emptiness of the scene is relieved by the mind's compensating sense of presence.

However, although Shelley is clearly drawing on this tradition of mystical rapture and collapse, the 'Hymn' and 'Mont Blanc' both express the difficulty of their aim. Theirs is a mode of address which questions the nature and the very existence of the object. The Power that may lie behind the vast landscapes of the Alps is one that the poet desires to imagine, but to imagine, with the bleak honesty of his unbelief, as a hard choice between something and nothing. These poems are not, therefore, affirmative addresses or prayers to the hidden Deity, but testing inquiries into the workings of the imagination as it confronts a landscape that is desolating in its emptiness. The Power which the imagination desires to meet is one which cannot answer for the scene of devastation all around, and which cannot totally alleviate the poet's apprehension of vacancy. As a result the two poems play uneasily between the imaginative realisation and the absolute remoteness of their object. The tension between the two is one of the main themes as well as one of the rhetorical problems of the 'Hymn to Intellectual Beauty' and 'Mont Blanc'.

Besides the well-established tradition of religious conversion and inspired writing associated with the landscape of the Alps, these poems are also indebted to the specific works of two poets whom Shelley read and respected throughout his life. The 'Hymn to Intellectual Beauty' is heavy with the mood of Wordsworth's 'Intimations of Immortality' ode, and 'Mont Blanc' often recalls Coleridge's poem on the same landscape, the 'Hymn before Sun-Rise in the Vale of Chamouni'. However, it is useful to look at the debt as one of dissent rather than of imitation. Consciously or unconsciously, Shelley's poems differ from their models, and it is this difference which helps define that mixture of daring and scepticism, of desire and disbelief, which shapes their writing. It is the point at which Shelley diverges from Wordsworth and Coleridge that marks out the path of his own aesthetic of the sublime; an aesthetic which cannot make up for the perennial divorce of inspiration and composition, of poetic origins and the poetic text. Such a divorce underlies the writing of these two poems and makes their landscapes the site of a new and peculiarly Shelleyan struggle, between Power and its interpretation in words.

Wordsworth's unfinished essay on 'The Sublime and the Beautiful' is one of his rare prose descriptions of the effect of the sublime. He defines it as that state which 'suspends the comparing power of the mind & possesses it with a feeling or image of intense unity, without a conscious contemplation of parts'.[1] This is probably indebted to Coleridge, who makes similar statements in his notes on German philosophy.[2] The sublime is a state of mind in which subject and object are fused; in which the imagination is fully identified with its object. It is for this reason

49

that Wordsworth condemns Burke's sublime of terror, as forcing a sense of self-preservation on the spectator which separates him from the terrible object.[3] Only when the mind achieves a sense of 'intense unity' with the external world is there an influx of power. Wordsworth also describes the effect of the sublime as a collapse or defeat of the mind before the object of its contemplation. He writes, not altogether lucidly, that 'Power awakens the sublime either when it rouses us to a sympathetic energy & calls upon the mind to grasp at something towards which it can make approaches but which it is incapable of attaining. . . or, 2dly, by producing a humiliation or prostration of the mind before some external agency.'[4] This effect of failure is the familiar accompaniment of the mind's sublime reach. To gain the unified consciousness which marks the sublime moment is to endure, paradoxically, 'a humiliation or prostration of the mind', which marks its inability to encompass the object. The sublime is characterised by a state of excess which is at once gain and loss, 'intense unity' and 'prostration'. But it is evident from the awkward and highly abstract language of the essay that Wordsworth is ill at ease with the sublime. He writes more assuredly in his own voice when, contrasting the beautiful and the sublime, he claims that the mind 'is more dependent for its daily well-being upon the love & gentleness which accompany the one, than upon the exaltation or awe which are created by the other'.[5] It is this preference for the quieter mood of the beautiful which points to the characteristic register of his poetry, but points also to Shelley's divergence from him.

Generally, Wordsworth shirks the crisis of 'exaltation or awe' attendant upon the sublime for the sake of the moral continuity, the 'daily well-being', of the beautiful. This evasiveness becomes apparent in the language of the 'Intimations of Immortality' ode, for instance, or of 'Tintern Abbey', where, as Geoffrey Hartman writes, 'while there is internal acceleration, the feeling of climax is avoided'.[6] As both these poems tell, the poet's sublime encounter with the natural world, an encounter which produces 'a feeling or image of intense unity, without conscious contemplation of parts', is one that belongs to the irrevocable past of childhood. Wordsworth's method is generally to modify sublime exaltation into calm regret: regret for the 'aching joys' (84) and 'dizzy raptures' (85) of boyhood in 'Tintern Abbey',[7] for instance, or regret for 'the visionary gleam' (56) of early childhood in 'Intimations of Immortality'.[8] Such loss is then converted into a promise of continuing creativity in the spirit of 'love & gentleness'. The adult poet finds, in place of passion and rapture, a milder sensitivity to the influence of the beautiful. This influence affords a continuing daily hopefulness of the heart and a poetry of equivalent calm and temperateness. Such a poetry is not subject to crisis and verbal collapse, in the manner of the sublime. It is this Wordsworthian spirit of regret and recompense which informs the last stanza of Shelley's 'Hymn to Intellectual Beauty'. But although the 'Hymn' addresses the quieter spirit of Beauty in the world, and reiterates a Wordsworthian regret for childhood rapture, the direction and tone of the poem press beyond these, and reflect a desire for the more extreme and critical registers of the sublime. As a result the poem is uncertain both of its tone and theme, as if its Wordsworthian influence were not fully assimilated to Shelley's own direction of thought.

The term 'Intellectual Beauty', as Kenneth Cameron defines it, means 'the beauty of the mind and its creations'.[9] By this time Shelley no longer distinguishes thoughts of the mind from external things. In the 'Essay on Life', written probably a year before, he refutes the empirical division of the world into mind and matter by adhering to what he calls 'the intellectual system' (VI. 195) of philosophy, which is an amalgam of William Berkeley and William Drummond. According to these, Shelley claims, the 'difference is merely nominal between those two classes of thought, which are vulgarly distinguished by the names of ideas and of external objects' (VI. 196). His philosophical concerns then characteristically shade into a concern with creativity. It is the child's emotional and imaginative engagement with the external world which is the origin and best exemplar of poetic perception. Only a few adults are able to retain this undifferentiating absorption in external objects: 'Those who are subject to the state called reverie, feel as if their nature were dissolved into the surrounding universe, or as if the surrounding universe were absorbed into their being' (VI. 195). It is this state of reverie, akin to the passionate sensibility of the child in Wordsworth's thinking, which frees the poet's perception from the dulling familiarity of Life. But although the spirit of Intellectual Beauty recalls this Wordsworthian identification of mind and things, the impulse of the poem is to look beyond it, to a relationship between the mind and its object which is flawed, difficult and dividing.

As Harold Bloom[10] and Judith Chernaik[11] point out, it is the 'Intimations of Immortality' ode which lies behind the composition of Shelley's 'Hymn', and the Wordsworthian intonations are clearest in the final stanza:

> The day becomes more solemn and serene
>   When noon is past – there is a harmony
>   In autumn, and a lustre in its sky,
> Which through the summer is not heard or seen,
> As if it could not be, as if it had not been!
>   Thus let thy power, which like the truth
>   Of nature on my passive youth
> Descended, to my onward life supply
>   Its calm – to one who worships thee,
>   And every form containing thee,
>   Whom, SPIRIT fair, thy spells did bind
> To fear himself, and love all human kind.

(P.W., pp. 529–31, lines 73–84)

The 'power' which Shelley addresses and invokes here is that of Intellectual Beauty, the 'SPIRIT fair'. Such a power was met most intensely in the poet's 'passive youth', but nonetheless that meeting gives the promise of continuing if calmer creativity: 'to my onward life supply / Its calm'. The end of the poem celebrates a Wordsworthian compensating tranquillity and, in the place of past ecstasy or reverie, a code of sympathy for mankind. Shelley's debt to Wordsworth is one which strangely affirms an 'autumn' of the spirit and equivalent loss of intensity, although the time of writing was midsummer and Shelley only twenty-four. The derivativeness of the last stanza, with its profession of maturity and resignation, emphasises, however, the very different tone of the rest of the poem.

This difference is highlighted by the fact that the 'Hymn' seems to address two separate powers. While the last stanza invokes the 'power' of Beauty itself, the first stanza claims that Beauty is only the 'awful shadow of some unseen Power' (1). The title, according to Kenneth Cameron, is confusing, because 'there can be no question but that the "Power"...is not intellectual beauty'.[12] This confusion in the poem concerning the precise nature of its object is a confusion which helps mark out the path of Shelley's divergence from Wordsworth. He writes:

> THE awful shadow of some unseen Power
> Floats though unseen among us, – visiting
> This various world with as inconstant wing
> As summer winds that creep from flower to flower, –
> Like moonbeams that behind some piny mountain shower,
> It visits with inconstant glance
> Each human heart and countenance;
> Like hues and harmonies of evening, –
> Like clouds in starlight widely spread, –
> Like memory of music fled, –
> Like aught that for its grace may be
> Dear, and yet dearer for its mystery.   (1–12)

Although this stanza is mainly expressive of the precarious and fragile spirit of Beauty, the tone of the first two lines is curiously portentous by comparison. Why Beauty should be an 'awful shadow' of 'Power' is not made clear, and the adjective seems more applicable to the hidden origin than to the delightful reflection. It is the 'unseen Power', and its difficult relation to the natural world, which seem more truly a source of awe. Not only is this Power described as at two removes, being neither world nor shadow, but it is also twice 'unseen', and thus doubly unavailable to the senses. Shelley presents both the Power and its shadow as invisible, yet the relation between them implies that Power is substantial compared to the shadow. In spite of the poem's inspired celebration of the manifestation of Intellectual Beauty in the natural world, it nonetheless strains after knowledge of a different and more remote Power; one which cannot be so pleasurably registered in the diversity of nature.

It is in stanza II that this straining to know something beyond Intellectual Beauty makes itself felt. Shelley writes:

> Spirit of BEAUTY, that dost consecrate
> With thine own hues all thou dost shine upon
> Of human thought or form, – where art thou gone?
> Why dost thou pass away and leave our state,
> This dim vast vale of tears, vacant and desolate?
> Ask why the sunlight not for ever
> Weaves rainbows o'er yon mountain-river,
> Why aught should fail and fade that once is shown,
> Why fear and dream and death and birth
> Cast on the daylight of this earth
> Such gloom, – why man has such a scope
> For love and hate, despondency and hope? (13–24)

It is the sheer precariousness of Beauty, the way it disappears without trace and leaves the world 'vacant and desolate', that causes the poet to search beyond. While Beauty shines on 'thought or form', it also deserts these and leaves, in form, a vacancy and desolation, and, in thought, a mental equivalent to that desolation which is 'fear and dream and death and birth'. It is this outer and inner emptiness which causes the poet's discontent. The spirit of Beauty cannot answer, for instance, 'why the sunlight not for ever / Weaves rainbows' because it is itself synonymous with the rainbows. The poet's questions thus implicitly require another voice to answer. Such a voice might remain after the spirit of Beauty has passed; remain in that landscape which no longer reciprocates the poet's humanising consciousness with an 'inconstant glance', an 'aura', but rather presents a kind of permanent blank to the eye. The voice of such a Power cannot be found in the transient diversity of the visible world, but in the spaces, both within and without, which the spirit of Intellectual Beauty leaves empty. Shelley's 'Hymn' is dissatisfied with the very object it seems to celebrate and address.

The desire for ulterior knowledge is then denied in stanza III. But the denial is worded in such a way as to suggest where such knowledge might be found:

> No voice from some sublimer world hath ever
> To sage or poet these responses given –

54

Therefore the names of Demon, Ghost, and Heaven,
Remain the records of their vain endeavour,
Frail spells – whose uttered charm might not avail to sever,
   From all we hear and all we see,
   Doubt, chance, and mutability.
Thy light alone – like mist o'er mountains driven,
   Or music by the night-wind sent
   Through strings of some still instrument,
   Or moonlight on a midnight stream,
Gives grace and truth to life's unquiet dream.   (25–36)

The poet's questions find 'No voice' to answer them. If a voice were to reply, it would be 'from some sublimer world' which is the domain of religion and superstition. For Shelley, however, the 'sublimer world' is empty and silent, and he mocks, here, the 'spells' which it traditionally contains. He seems to be using the term sublime with the accuracy of its eighteenth-century usage, as differentiated from the beautiful. The 'sublimer world' is one which no longer supports the eye with the various and delightful forms of Beauty, but which opens out beyond what can be seen, and merges into the region of the gods. The sublime voice is denied because it too closely approximates the voice of religion, specifically that, in the original version, 'of God and ghosts and Heaven'.[13] Shelley, it seems, is aware of the close association of the sublime and religious belief, and forcefully denies his interest in the second. Nonetheless, the poem pushes towards that region on the other side of Beauty which might contain some explanation of why the world becomes 'vacant and desolate'. Although Shelley takes pains to deny faith in the superstitious 'spells' of Christianity, and substitutes for it the 'Doubt, chance, and mutability' of nature, nonetheless he is still drawn to the 'sublimer world' as to the place which might hold a voice to answer his doubts and fears. He repudiates the creeds of religion, but still aspires to some explanation of the infinite and unvaried spaces that the spirit of Beauty cannot conceal. The 'Hymn' thus postulates two objects: the spirit of Beauty, which is mutable and transient, and the Power which originates it, which is vaguely located in the higher, emptier regions of 'some sublimer world'.

The very emphasis of Shelley's denial betrays the attraction of what he denies. Although celebrating Intellectual Beauty, the 'Hymn' expresses fierce regret for its transience and a desire to apprehend a more enduring and original force. It is this desire which is strangely in contrast with the Wordsworthian calm of the final stanza, and which may explain the tense register of stanza v. Shelley writes:

> While yet a boy I sought for ghosts, and sped
> Through many a listening chamber, cave and ruin,
> And starlight wood, with fearful steps pursuing
> Hopes of high talk with the departed dead.
> I called on poisonous names with which our youth is fed;
> I was not heard – I saw them not –
> When musing deeply on the lot
> Of life, at that sweet time when winds are wooing
> All vital things that wake to bring
> News of birds and blossoming,
> Sudden, thy shadow fell on me;
> I shrieked, and clasped my hands in ecstasy! (49–60)

Here he recounts, as he once recounted in a letter to his new mentor Godwin, his boyhood enthusiasm for romance and the supernatural. Such enthusiasm is spurred by his desire for an answering voice, for 'high talk with the departed dead'. But as in stanza III, his imaginative hope to find such a voice brings him into contact with the ruses of religion: the 'poisonous names' of Christianity. As in the earlier stanza, to seek a voice from some further world is to trespass in the kingdom of the gods, and these are emphatically denied: 'I was not heard – I saw them not.' There is no response, in this poem, from the second world beyond the grave.

However, from this denial of supernatural presences there results an encounter with the spirit of Beauty which is highly melodramatic: 'Sudden, thy shadow fell on me; / I shrieked, and clasped my hands in ecstasy!' Timothy Webb rightly warns against interpreting such lines with biographical literalism. They are, he suggests, 'ritual exclamations rather than symptoms of poetic collapse'.[14] The ritual quality, however, derives from the language of sublime rapture and defeat, which suggests an object of grander proportions than the 'SPIRIT fair' of the title. The words 'thy shadow' ambiguously address Beauty and the 'unseen Power' of which it is indeed only the 'shadow'. The encounter is an overwhelming and violent experience, which seems out of key with the message of the poem. The deliberate break between 'musing deeply' and feeling the sudden shadow fall upon him contradicts the spirit of equanimity and continuity which the poem advocates. In contrast to Wordsworth's discursive logic in 'Intimations of Immortality', Shelley presents an experience which halts the poet and disrupts the logic of the poem in an emotionalism which finds no adequate translation into words. The histrionic poses and inarticulate gestures: 'I shrieked,' 'With beating heart and streaming eyes' (63), are attempts to convey an experience of emotional transport which surpasses the scope of poetry. Thus the poet pleads: 'That thou – O awful LOVELINESS, / Wouldst give whate'er these words cannot express' (71–2). Such an admission of poetic collapse and inarticulateness which the power of Beauty must compensate clearly draws on the tradition of sublime rapture.

The 'Hymn to Intellectual Beauty' thus strains after knowledge of an object which lies beyond the frail appearances of Beauty and after a register which does not avoid but rather seeks the effect of climax and collapse. The poem is uneven in tone as a result. The Wordsworthian autumn of the last stanza remains in conflict with the Shelleyan high noon of the two preceding stanzas, and the poet's final optimistic resignation to a life of 'calm' and human 'love' fails to answer the ringing plea that the shadow of Beauty should not disappear and leave the world inexplicably vacant:

> Depart not as thy shadow came,
> Depart not – lest the grave should be,
> Like life and fear, a dark reality.   (46–8)

The 'unseen Power' which casts the shadow of Beauty upon the world cannot be known or heard, but cannot quite be relinquished either, 'lest the grave should be...a dark reality'. In the essay 'On Life', Shelley writes that 'there is a spirit within...at enmity with nothingness and dissolution' (VI. 194). It is this fear of 'nothingness' which haunts the 'Hymn' in spite of its own scepticism of finding any communicable voices in the 'vacant and desolate' spaces that Intellectual Beauty leaves behind. Significantly, it is this desolation which provides the setting and the object of the second poem written in the summer of 1816.

Behind the composition of 'Mont Blanc' it is possible to trace a number of influences. Shelley's discussions with Peacock of the previous year on Zoroastrian mythology and his heady conversations with Byron during these weeks on what Byron ruefully termed 'metaphysics, mountains, lakes, love unextinguishable, thoughts unutterable'[15] clearly indicate some of his preoccupations at the time of writing. However, one of the most interesting influences is that of Coleridge's 'Hymn before Sun-Rise, in the Vale of Chamouni'. This poem appeared in the eleventh number of *The Friend* of which, Charles Robinson has shown, Shelley or Byron almost certainly possessed a copy in Geneva.[16] There are a number of clear verbal echoes of the 'Hymn' in 'Mont Blanc', but the comparison is again more significant for the differences it brings to light. If Shelley acknowledges Coleridge as his precursor in the Vale of Chamouni and as his precursor as a poet of the sublime, he does so in a spirit of opposition.

Coleridge's own attitude to the sublime tends to be allied to an attitude of religious faith. In a letter to Thelwall of October 1797, he wrote: 'My mind feels as if it ached to behold & know something *great* – something *one & indivisible* – and it is only in the faith of this that rocks or waterfalls, mountains or caverns give me the sense of sublimity or majesty!'[17] He defines the sublime in nature very much as an index of faith, faith in 'something *one & indivisible*'. It is just such an aching for faith which lies behind the hectic rhetoric of the 'Hymn before Sun-Rise'. As Norman Fruman has shown, contrary to the assertions in its notes, the poem was not composed in the Vale of Chamouni at all,[18] and, as De Quincey pointed out, is in part an unacknowledged translation of a poem by Friederica Brun. It may be this knowledge of second-hand spontaneity which gives the poem its curiously exaggerated tone and explains Coleridge's defensive attitude to it. He reports in a much later letter that Wordsworth 'condemned the Hymn in toto . . . as a specimen of the Mock Sublime', but still defends the poem against this charge as an honest expression of his own 'strong devotional feelings gazing on the Mountain'.[19] Coleridge's compulsive and lasting dishonesty about the composition of the poem betrays perhaps his own uncertainty concerning its merit. Certainly Wordsworth rightly detected in it a straining for effect which is false, while Shelley, in his own poetic reply, implicitly condemns in it a religious orthodoxy which is glib.

It is the ease with which Coleridge personifies the object of his address which above all differentiates it from Shelley's object. The landscape of the 'Hymn before Sun-Rise' is one which is quickly transmuted into a living presence that can be known by faith. Coleridge writes:

> I gazed upon thee,
> Till thou, still present to the bodily sense,
> Didst vanish from my thought: entranced in prayer
> I worshipped the Invisible alone.[20]　　　　　(13–16)

The poem achieves the wish expressed in Coleridge's letter to Thelwall as the sublime landscape becomes the sign of an invisible presence, and sight: 'I gazed' gives way to faith: 'I worshipped.' As the poem progresses, Coleridge transforms the unresponsive silence of the scene: the fact that the mountain rises from its 'silent sea of pines, / How silently!' (6–7), into the sound of a 'sweet voice' (27), and finally into a deafening chorus which repeats, as if in opposition to some lingering doubt, the name Coleridge wishes to hear:

> GOD! let the torrents, like a shout of nations,
> Answer! and let the ice-plains echo, GOD!
> GOD! sing ye meadow-streams with gladsome voice!
> Ye pine-groves, with your soft and soul-like sounds!
> And they too have a voice, yon piles of snow,
> And in their perilous fall shall thunder, GOD!　　　(58–63)

The poem exorbitantly proclaims the resolution of all uncertainty and doubt in this litany of faith. Yet, while Coleridge's intention is, as his footnote claims, to emphasise incredulously: 'Who *would* be, who *could* be an Atheist in this valley of wonders!' his poem fails to convince. He protests too much, and the result is a kind of hectoring which betrays, by its very insistence, a fear of untruth or failure. The obsessive naming of God exacts belief by verbal force, not by imaginative conviction. Shelley's 'Mont Blanc' is the reply of one who scandalously described himself in the hotel register at Chamouni as Democrat, Philanthropist and Atheist, and who, against all the converting potential of the sublime scenery and of Coleridge's sublime 'Hymn' to it, gave as his resolute destination, 'L'Enfer'.[21]

On the day when Shelley composed 'Mont Blanc' he wrote the following passage in his diary letter to Peacock:

I will not pursue Buffons sublime but gloomy theory, that this earth which we inhabit will at some future period be changed into a mass of frost. Do you who assert the supremacy of Ahriman imagine him throned among these desolating snows, among these palaces of death & frost, sculptured in this their terrible magnificence by the unsparing hand of necessity, & that he casts around him as the first essays of his final usurpation avalanches, torrents, rocks & thunders – and above all, these deadly glaciers at once the proofs & the symbols of his reign. (*Letters*, I. 499)

The deity in Shelley's thoughts at the time of writing 'Mont Blanc' is not the God of Christianity, but one more in keeping with his own perception of the landscape: the god of storm and pain of Zoroastrian mythology. Peacock identifies Ahrimanes as 'the principle of evil' in contrast to Oromazes, 'the principle of good',[22] and Shelley's description of the landscape around Mont Blanc is clearly influenced by the pessimistic and inhuman attributes of such a god. Instead of finding, in this traditional location of the sublime, evidence of an infinitely benign and creative Power, Shelley finds evidence of a careless and death-dealing tyrant, whom he presents as something much less than human when he writes, in the same letter, that one 'would think that Mont Blanc was a living being & that the frozen blood forever circulated slowly thro' his stony veins' (*Letters*, I. 500). The sublimity of this landscape recalls for Shelley a 'sublime but gloomy theory' of progressive desolation and destruction. However, it is necessary to take account of the fact that the description in this letter is very much sensitised to Peacock's imagination: 'Do you...imagine him' and the passage should not be read as an explanation of the Power in 'Mont Blanc'. Shelley's overt personification of the mountain for Peacock's benefit is interesting rather for the contrasting relief into which it casts the poem. There are no mythological presences in 'Mont Blanc', no gods either of good or evil. In fact, Shelley seems to be at pains to avoid the 'vulgar mistake' of personifying the mountain as 'endowed with human qualities and governing the universe as an earthly monarch governs his kingdom' (*P.W.*, p. 812).

Nonetheless, the problem of personification is central to 'Mont Blanc'. Whereas Coleridge is keen to personify the mountain almost from the start, Shelley still distrusts the habit of substituting a word for a thing and thus creating a presence from devices of rhetoric. Personification, he once lamented, is 'beautiful in Poetry, inadmissible in reasoning' (*Letters*, 1. 101). When he comes to write poetry which is concerned with the question of whether there is a hidden presence or Power in the landscape the tension between his scepticism and his poetic need becomes extreme. It is useful to distinguish two kinds of personification with reference to 'Mont Blanc'. According to Patricia Meyer Spacks, personification in the sublime lyric of the later eighteenth century stresses 'function rather than appearance'.[23] It thus intends a transformation of inanimate objects into active daemons or ghosts or spirits. Wordsworth's famous attack on 'personifications of abstract ideas'[24] in the Preface to *Lyrical Ballads* is an attack on their use as merely rhetorical devices, unsupported by belief in this capacity for transformation. However, personification also occurs on a purely verbal level, whenever, according to Donald Davie, 'an abstraction . . . can govern an active verb'.[25] It is part of Shelley's purpose in 'Mont Blanc' to refuse to personify the mountain as an animate and wilful spirit, capable of deliberated action, and therefore merely a debased kind of God. Nonetheless, it is the purpose of the poem to address the landscape as a possible sign of some greater Power which the poet desires to realise as a voice. On the one hand, such a Power has no proper name and no creative will, but on the other hand, if that Power is nothing, the whole poem risks becoming a mere short circuit of rhetoric, a kind of empty speech. For Shelley, composition still desires to recover the fullness of inspiration, which is the lost Power of its own writing.

A number of critics define the Power of 'Mont Blanc' as philosophical Necessity. Both I. J. Kapstein[26] and C. E. Pulos,[27] for instance, present it as the concept of Necessity which Shelley derives from Hume, and give interpretations of the poem which centre on its philosophical meaning. However, as so often with Shelley, his philosophical concerns are yoked to aesthetic concerns, and his epistemological investigations have less to do with the mind than with the imagination. In 'Mont Blanc' his quest to find the Power which impels all things with relentless and indifferent strength is also a quest for the original Power of his own writing. 'Mont Blanc' might be interpreted as a poem which confronts the problem of its own divided aesthetic, in confronting a landscape which divides the presence of Power from 'the human mind's imaginings'. This familiar landscape of the sublime is one which presents Shelley, not with signs of the Deity, but with the equivalent of his own imaginative scepticism. In 'Mont Blanc' he confronts the landscape of religious conversion, he describes an autobiographical experience of awe, fear and enlightenment and he uses the language of exalted and personifying address. He too is writing a kind of hymn or ode to the genius of the place. However, unlike Coleridge, Shelley questions the model within which he writes and, as a result, the language of 'Mont Blanc' comments anxiously on its own workings. The Power of the mountain is addressed within a framework which has long presumed a divine model for that Power; a model which the atheist must reject. But while Shelley the sceptic denies the presence of a creative God behind the landscape, Shelley the poet yearns for licence to imagine an alternative origin of things, which is the origin also of his own creativity. Thus 'Mont Blanc' follows the direction of the 'Hymn to Intellectual Beauty' in being a venture into the 'sublimer world' which the spirit of Beauty has deserted, and which might thus be merely 'desolate and vacant' to the imagination.

In Section 1 Shelley gives a description of the mind's relation to the external world which is very much in the spirit of the Intellectual Philosophy as formulated in the essay 'On Life'. He writes:

THE everlasting universe of things
Flows through the mind, and rolls its rapid waves,
Now dark – now glittering – now reflecting gloom –
Now lending splendour, where from secret springs
The source of human thought its tribute brings
Of waters...   (*P.W.*, pp. 532–5, lines 1–6)

There is no hierarchical discrimination between the status of the mind and that of the everlasting universe of things. The convoluted and interchanging action of mind and things in this passage expresses that 'undifferentiated unity, neither thought nor thing, and yet both',[28] which Wasserman attributes to the Intellectual Philosophy. These eleven lines have been much analysed as holding the key to Shelley's philosophical position in the poem. Certainly they contain a didactic and neat statement of epistemology, which turns the whole external scene into a metaphor for the interdependent relation of mind and universe. However, in tone and terminology, they are somewhat out of step with the rest of the poem. After Section I the register shifts from that of philosophical debate to the register of address and prayer, and the poem becomes properly an ode. As a result, the once reciprocal relation of mind and universe gives way to a new preoccupation with the object that lies behind the 'everlasting universe of things' and that cannot be apprehended by a play of sense impressions like the refracted light of water upon the sides of the Ravine. The relation of the mind to this hidden object is a relation of uncertain surmise and question. By turning from philosophical statement to the mode of address, Shelley presents the object of that address as separate and estranged, and 'Mont Blanc' ends, not by affirming, but by putting that object in question.

Thus Section II, although seeming to follow logically from what has gone before, is in fact startlingly different in tone and emphasis:

Thus thou, Ravine of Arve – dark, deep Ravine –
Thou many-coloured, many-voicèd vale,
Over whose pines, and crags, and caverns sail
Fast cloud-shadows and sunbeams: awful scene,
Where Power in likeness of the Arve comes down
From the ice-gulfs that gird his secret throne,

> Bursting through these dark mountains like the flame
> Of lightning through the tempest... (12–19)

The new mode of address here presents the scene as mildly personified. It is addressed as 'thou' and described as 'many-coloured, many-voicèd'. But although the outward scene assumes the status of a half-animate presence, this is not the main object of the poet's interest. As in the 'Hymn to Intellectual Beauty', the visible properties of the scene, its transient and ephemeral 'cloud-shadows and sunbeams' which represent the spirit of Beauty in the world, only serve to point the poet towards another object which is more steadfast and original: towards 'Power'. The very richness and multiplicity of the 'universe of things' is, for Shelley, no more than a sign or displaced attribute of Power, which 'in likeness of the Arve comes down / From the ice-gulfs that gird his secret throne'.

The landscape is thus a signpost towards some hidden presence that is not named or perceived, but which appears 'in likeness' of the river or 'like' lightning. The comparison measures the difference as well as the similarity between the Power and the visible scene. The place conveys the presence of a tyrant or a Jove, but it also affirms that his nature is 'secret' and hidden high among 'the ice-gulfs'. Thus Shelley's description of Power is one which finds it estranged and unknown. The heights and depths of the Ravine bear the message of an original Power, but for Shelley the message is perilously separated from its object. It is this separation which informs the writing of 'Mont Blanc' and which threatens its sublime mode with a 'collapse into "mere" rhetoric',[29] into a language empty of presences.

This separation of the Power from its visible manifestations in the scene has the effect of turning the landscape of the poem into a baffling wilderness. When the infinite spaces of the sublime are deserted of the gods, or of the Power which originates them, they become, for the sceptical poet, indeed a desert. It is this alternative which Shelley acknowledges in those curiously discrepant lines which follow his description of the Ravine. The various and fluctuating Beauty of the scene becomes held in suspension, in a 'strange sleep / Which when the voices of the desert fail / Wraps all in its own deep eternity' (27–9). An earlier draft of these condensed and somewhat unassimilated lines shows how far the effect of 'deep eternity' in the landscape is one which entails the sinister failure of all sound and colour in the scene:

<blockquote>
and the sleep
The sudden pause which does inhabit thee
Which when the voices of the desart fail
And its hues wane, doth blend them all & steep
Their tumult in its own eternity...[30]   (32–6)
</blockquote>

If the passage strangely echoes the Simplon Pass episode in *The Prelude* which Shelley could not have known, it does so because it similarly translates 'tumult' into a stillness which has the character of 'eternity'. By this change the multiplicity of the 'many-coloured, many-voicèd vale' gives way to a sense of 'eternity' which, by contrast, is silent and unvarious.

There is a disturbing, self-defeating quality about Shelley's lines. The sense of 'eternity' is gained by the failing and waning of all 'voices' and 'hues'. This apocalyptic vision of the scene as timeless and permanent is one which comes very close to presenting a blank and empty prospect to the mind. The Ravine is like a 'desert' in the sense that it is emptied of its semi-animate voices and colours, and has become vast and formless. Its 'deep eternity' springs from that 'strange sleep' which seems to confuse an inner with an outer scene, and which points, therefore, to an association between consciousness and the landscape of 'eternity' which Shelley will develop in later poems, particularly *The Triumph of Life*. To apprehend the 'deep eternity' of the scene it seems necessary to have all voices fail and colours wane, and to apprehend, in their place, a desert. The implications of these lines are as yet un-accommodated within the poem, but they prefigure the way in which the desert comes to be Shelley's characteristic landscape of the sublime, because it is the landscape of lost presences or absent Power.

After this brief and pessimistic apocalypse, Shelley turns to the Ravine again in order to seek the specific origin of his art. The

Ravine contains 'the still cave of the witch Poesy' (44) from which emanate 'Ghosts of all things that are' (46). Kapstein's claim that the ghosts might be taken to stand for 'words'[31] certainly seems the most likely explanation of what emanates from the cave. However, Shelley's concern is not with these but with a hidden and unreflected presence. His thoughts go

> Seeking among the shadows that pass by
> Ghosts of all things that are, some shade of thee,
> Some phantom, some faint image; till the breast
> From which they fled recalls them, thou art there!   (45–8)

As Kenneth Cameron writes: 'The power, not the cave, is the essential creative force.'[32] But what the passage expresses is that the presence of such a Power, which the poet addresses as 'thou', is in a paradoxical relation of loss to the words in which it might be externalised. The poet goes in search of the origin of poetry, but finds that it lies outside the writing of poems. It is only by losing hold of words altogether that he can affirm the presence of their origin: 'till the breast / From which they fled recalls them, thou art there!' It is only when shades, phantoms and images are recalled to their invisible platonic source that the source itself is known. But this characteristically divided aesthetic of Poetry and poems, inspiration and composition, works only to beggar the poet of the means of art. There is no image to reflect the hidden origin. Its only true expression is imagelessness, or a recall of all images to their source. The triumph of the last acclamation 'thou art there!' is in fact a kind of despair of ever being able to *say* precisely where. Without 'some shade', 'Some phantom, some faint image', the poet can see and can say nothing. It is only in the revolutionary drama of *Prometheus Unbound* that Shelley overcomes this inevitable loss, by having words returned to their source and uttered again like the unexternalised language of the heart. In 'Mont Blanc' the search for the natural origin of words is one which ends abruptly where words end: 'thou art there!'

After this crucial break, the poet begins to speculate again on the imagined origin of the scene. As in the 'Hymn to Intellectual Beauty', it is Wordsworth who suggests a means of recovering

66

imaginative vision from despair: 'Some say that gleams of a remoter world / Visit the soul in sleep' (49–50). According to these, sleep contains the potential for dream; for 'gleams of a remoter world' which extends beyond the boundaries of what is visible. But Shelley answers this Wordsworthian intimation with an alternative description of sleep: 'does the mightier world of sleep / Spread far around and inaccessibly / Its circles?' (55–7). He brilliantly suggests that the 'remoter world' contains no gleams, but only this endless repetition of limits. Such a sleep turns the unbounded vistas of the sublime into an infinite regress of boundaries which are both inaccessible and yet imprisoning. Like the earlier 'strange sleep' of the 'desert', this sleep also opens upon a prospect of mere endlessness, which parodies the liberating infinity of the sublime. In this nightmarish space the imagination is merely lost, and its disorientation is finely emphasised in the lines which follow: 'the very spirit fails, / Driven like a homeless cloud from steep to steep / That vanishes among the viewless gales!' (57–9). This landscape of infinitely receding horizons makes the spirit feel 'homeless'. By going beyond the horizon of each 'steep' the spirit loses direction and purpose, and goes nowhere. Shelley is aware of how the landscape of infinite space may become, without a presence to fill it, an unhomely and unfocussed place; indeed uncanny.

However, in spite of this bleak alternative to the traditional responsiveness of the sublime landscape, Shelley continues to seek, although despairingly now, some Power to explain the desolation before him:

> Is this the scene
> Where the old Earthquake-daemon taught her young
> Ruin? Were these their toys? or did a sea
> Of fire envelop once this silent snow?
> None can reply – all seems eternal now. (71–5)

Such a landscape traditionally compels speculation about first causes, and, in spite of his atheism, Shelley's questions are also teleological. His poem goes in search of origins as obsessively as Coleridge's, but the search is continually thwarted. Once again 'the voices of the desert fail', and the poet confronts an unresponsive

67

landscape: 'None can reply – all seems eternal now.' Just as earlier the failure of voices in the desert led to a sense of 'deep eternity', so here the silence of the landscape usurps the prerogative of the absent Deity in being 'eternal'. Shelley grimly associates the emptiness and silence of the scene with that eternity which should belong to the Power within it. As in the 'Hymn to Intellectual Beauty' there is no mythological or divine voice to answer his quest for origins. Instead, his imagination meets a silence which has the quality of being itself 'eternal'.

However, it is precisely from this denial of answers that Shelley affirms a different kind of voice:

> The wilderness has a mysterious tongue
> Which teaches awful doubt, or faith so mild,
> So solemn, so serene, that man may be,
> In such a faith,[33] with nature reconciled;
> Thou hast a voice, great Mountain, to repeal
> Large codes of fraud and woe; not understood
> By all, but which the wise, and great, and good
> Interpret, or make felt, or deeply feel. (76–83)

These lines contain Shelley's manifesto for an alternative and nearly silent voice, which will repeal the evils of contemporary politics and religion, and whose message is 'social and political as much as metaphysical'.[34] However, it is not the precise message of this voice as its relation to the poet which is of interest. Having denied that any mythological deity can reply to his questions, Shelley finds in the scene a voice which perfectly answers to his desire, precisely because it does not answer. It is a voice without speech; it communicates no dogma or creed. Such a voice is known by 'faith' that so far differs from itself as to be also 'doubt'. The voice of enlightened revolution is one which speaks mysteriously and indirectly to those few who would 'Interpret, or make felt, or deeply feel.'

Shelley is presenting the voice of political revolution as the Power of original inspiration, which speaks first to the heart and then compels its difficult transmission in poetry. The poet is merely an interpreter of this first language which belongs, in the tradition of the sublime, not to art but to nature. It is the task of the human poet to feel and repeat its silent communication. However, because this voice cannot be anthropomorphised as a presence, its relation to the poet is precarious and doubtful. Although the poet seeks for a voice to precede his own and to give it the authority of a more natural speech, he nonetheless acknowledges its infinite distance from himself, and its inability to speak apart from himself. The tongue of the wilderness is 'mysterious' and the voice of the mountain is 'not understood / By all', until voiced again. This sublime but desolate and empty landscape has a voice which cannot speak except by being spoken of by the poet. By interpretation and feeling, the poet makes the voice of nature his own, and reclaims the hidden Power of the scene from its infinite remoteness. Shelley's manifesto for revolutionary change is one which advocates a return of language to its source, a return of art to nature, so that composition might be very nearly inspiration once again. It is in *Prometheus Unbound* that this promise is realised. But in 'Mont Blanc', the poet's desire to interpret the voice of the mountain is still threatened by the knowledge that there might be no voice there to precede and to authenticate his own.

It is this knowledge which underlies the desolate vistas of Section IV. Here Shelley admits that the original Power for which he seeks is infinitely distant:

> Power dwells apart in its tranquillity,
> Remote, serene, and inaccessible:
> And *this*, the naked countenance of earth,
> On which I gaze, even these primaeval mountains
> Teach the adverting mind. (96–100)

In the Scrope Davies manuscript Shelley writes of the Power that it is 'Remote, sublime, and inaccessible', thus revealing how, in his thoughts, sublimity is associated with a landscape of absolute remoteness. Power is unknown, distant and indifferent. This is the language, as Timothy Webb points out, of the Lucretian gods,[35] and it is a language which sceptically contradicts our expectations of the scene. This Power is neither the beneficent Creator, nor the tyrannical Ahrimanes, but an absolutely remote and unknown presence. The sublime scene, for Shelley, is one which opens up distances that, like the endless circles of sleep, are 'inaccessible' to the mind. The Power that dwells in this scene is incommunicable and 'apart'.

Once again Shelley's poem presents the alternative face of the sublime. This vast space is not the natural home of the Deity, but a desert, a wilderness, an endless prospect of desolation: 'a flood of ruin / Is there, that from the boundaries of the sky / Rolls its perpetual stream' (107–9). While the effort of theories of the sublime in the eighteenth century was to push out the boundaries of the visible world in acclamation of God's grandeur, Shelley finds in the natural horizon, the 'boundaries of the sky', a limit for which the sceptical imagination is grateful. When, elsewhere, he imagines the 'remoter world' that exceeds the visible horizons of the scene, he finds a space which is bewildering, unhomely and unimaginable.

Yet it is the purpose and greatness of 'Mont Blanc' to dare the unimaginable. In Section v Shelley resumes his quest for origins; for that Power which, although so infinitely apart, might nonetheless be apprehended by the imagination. This is Shelley's most daring and most bleak comment on the mind's relation to the origin it would claim for its own. He writes:

> Mont Blanc yet gleams on high: – the power is there,
> The still and solemn power of many sights,
> And many sounds, and much of life and death.
> In the calm darkness of the moonless nights,
> In the lone glare of day, the snows descend
> Upon that Mountain; none beholds them there,
> Nor when the flakes burn in the sinking sun,
> Or the star-beams dart through them: – Winds contend
> Silently there, and heap the snow with breath
> Rapid and strong, but silently! Its home
> The voiceless lightning in these solitudes
> Keeps innocently, and like vapour broods
> Over the snow. The secret Strength of things
> Which governs thought, and to the infinite dome
> Of Heaven is as a law, inhabits thee!
> And what were thou, and earth, and stars, and sea,
> If to the human mind's imaginings
> Silence and solitude were vacancy? (127–44)

Although Shelley affirms the presence of the Power, it remains inaccessible to the human mind. Its place is dark, unpeopled, silent and secret. Shelley's language is still pulling in two directions at once: towards presence and absence. He claims that 'the power is there', but only where 'none beholds'. Against the repeated address and invocation he stresses the absolute remoteness of the Power, which exists by deprivation of all knowledge or sense of it. The tension between these two perspectives: between personifying the Power as 'thou' and placing it irrecoverably beyond human apprehension, is then repeated, not resolved, in the last question:

> And what were thou, and earth, and stars, and sea,
> If to the human mind's imaginings
> Silence and solitude were vacancy?

In these lines Shelley neither affirms nor disproves the nature of his object. Instead, he puts it in question once again, and the question, significantly, is an aesthetic one. The last lines reveal that the Power he seeks has to do, not so much with philosophical or political systems, but with 'the human mind's imaginings', and it is in relation to those imaginings that it exists.

This last question, in its fine openness, presents a choice which has informed the whole poem, and in which the meaning of the whole poem is staked. This is the choice between 'thou' and 'vacancy', between an anthropomorphic presence and nothing. If the 'Silence and solitude' of the sublime landscape that Shelley confronts in 'Mont Blanc' is a 'vacancy' to the mind, then to address Power as 'thou' is a piece of empty rhetoric. It is the personification of an absence, and a substitution of 'a word for a thing' (*P.W.*, p. 812). However, the question also implies that the loss of 'thou' is a loss of 'earth, and stars, and sea'. All these, it seems, would fail if the mind acknowledged its object to be 'vacancy'. To face the sublime landscape as a silent and solitary void is to face the loss of all the world besides, and leave to the imagination an eternal desert. Just as in the 'Hymn to Intellectual Beauty' the poet seeks an 'unseen Power' to explain the 'vacant and desolate' world which the spirit of Beauty has left behind, so in 'Mont Blanc' the Power which Shelley desires to find is one which, although remote and inaccessible, might keep him from the horror of imagining nothing. The last question, like a palimpsest, offers the choice of two imaginings to the sceptical poet of the sublime: he can imagine 'thou' or nothing.

'Mont Blanc' thus follows the wishful direction of the 'Hymn to Intellectual Beauty' in its search for Power; its search for a presence to make the wilderness imaginable. Such a Power is one that the sceptic denies, but the poet fears to lose. In the end, the presence of a 'thou' in the landscape becomes a last and precarious prop of 'the human mind's imaginings'. It is a way of still resisting 'vacancy'. Nonetheless, the greatness of 'Mont Blanc' stems from the difficulty with which its own 'imaginings' are achieved. It is because Shelley presents the landscape of the sublime as, at times, a desert of sleep, a wilderness without a voice, an eternity from which there is never a reply, that the affirmation of the end remains so bleakly and dearly won. Shelley's poetry of the sublime is one that cannot avoid knowing that the place of Power might be a 'vacancy', and that the origin of all things might be nothing: be perfect 'Silence and solitude'. However, if the poet is to imagine and to write, he must still seek for the Power and the voice that precede his own, and that make his rhetoric full and authentic. It is in *Prometheus Unbound* that Shelley finds an optimistic and therefore revolutionary answer to the finely weighed question at the end of 'Mont Blanc'.

4

THE POLITICS OF CREATIVITY:
PROMETHEUS UNBOUND

Shelley began the composition of his great lyrical drama *Prometheus Unbound* in the autumn of 1818. This grand political reworking of the Prometheus myth is set in landscapes of mountains and ravines which distinctly recall the landscapes of the 1816 Hymns. Such a setting also indicates a continuing preoccupation with an aesthetic of infinite space. The landscapes of Acts I and II are desolate, rugged and vast. They present a prospect of bleak heights and depths which, in the manner of the sublime, defy easy perception by the senses. But as in the Hymns, the very desolation of the place is one which then compels a sense of presence and it is the imaginative struggle to find presences and voices in the scene which provides the dramatic action of the work. However, in *Prometheus Unbound* the desire to meet hidden powers and voices in the sublime landscape is linked to a political idealism which is new, and which makes of this work Shelley's most consistently optimistic expression of the revolutionary purpose of writing.

Acts I and II consist mainly of dialogue between the two central protagonists, Prometheus and Asia, and the inorganic presences of the Earth, the Phantasm of Jupiter, the Furies and Demogorgon, with whom communication is difficult. These are not so much autonomous and realised characters as strange and distant voices or images, which Prometheus and Asia hardly hear or see, and which they only partly understand. In fact, Shelley seems at pains to undermine their status as dramatic characters by presenting them as scarcely embodied voices, which are either incommunicably remote or subjectively near. In *Prometheus Unbound* Shelley is still working within the terms of an aesthetic which would make silence, space and emptiness into interpretable voices. As a result

73

much of the dramatic interest of the play centres on the question of communication. This is not so much a drama of character and action, as of voices and the mind's imaginings. It is, therefore, as many critics have pointed out, hardly drama at all. But this very failure is consistent with Shelley's revolutionary purpose in the work.

Revolutionary action in *Prometheus Unbound* is finely linked to the activities of perceiving and imagining. As M. H. Abrams writes in *Natural Supernaturalism*, 'Shelley's ruling figure for the advent of the renovated world is that of an instantaneous and radical alteration of sight.'[1] This alteration of sight is one of the persistent themes and one of the aesthetic problems of the work. Characteristically, sense perception gives way to another kind of perception, which is internal and relative. The empirical eye gives way to feeling and interpretation. Thus, while the political message of *Prometheus Unbound* is the inevitable fall of tyranny and liberation of the race, the dramatic interest of the work centres on how those events may be imaginatively motivated and apprehended. Since the action of the play is necessary and foredoomed, because it is in the control of Demogorgon, the element of struggle is confined to how the hidden powers and voices of that action can become known to the mind. As a drama of the inevitable, *Prometheus Unbound* raises again the problem of imaginative perception and communication which preoccupied Shelley in 1816.

In this play, Shelley again goes in search of origins. This search is mainly conducted by Asia, who goes on a journey to the centre of the earth in order to address and question the gloomy Power that resides there. It is this encounter with Demogorgon which brings about the fall of Jove and liberation of Prometheus, and it is an encounter which takes the form of a perfectly internalised dialogue. Demogorgon exists by way of a mixed scepticism and desire of the imagination which is very much Shelley's own. It marks the culmination of a long debate in his writings between intellectual atheism and poetic need.

The process of this debate can be landmarked by two passages from Shelley's prose writings. In the first of these, the 'Notes on

74

Queen Mab' of 1813, he asserts unequivocally: 'Religion is the perception of the relation in which we stand to the principle of the universe. But if the principle of the universe be not an organic being, the model and prototype of man, the relation between it and human beings is absolutely none' (*P.W.*, p. 811). At this stage he denies any possibility of a relation between the inorganic principle of the universe and the human mind, on the grounds that what is not conceived as an organic and human being cannot be conceived at all. There can be no 'relation' with a Power that is not anthropomorphic. But although Shelley continues to deny the anthropomorphism of this Power, his position does shift somewhat. In the second passage, from the 'Speculations on Metaphysics', which may have been written as late as December 1819[2] while Shelley was finishing *Prometheus*, there is a noticeable revision of his earlier claim. Here he writes that

it will be objected, the inhabitants of the various planets of this and of other solar systems; and the existence of a Power bearing the same relation to all that we perceive and are, as what we call a cause does to what we call effect, were never subjects of sensation, and yet the laws of mind almost universally suggest according to the various disposition of each, a conjecture, a persuasion, or a conviction of their existence. (VII. 59)

He answers the hypothetical objection by claiming that conjectures, persuasions and convictions are no less valid activities of the mind than is sensation. The existence of an original Power can be affirmed, if tentatively, by these alternative kinds of perception. It is through these, therefore, that a relation between the unknown, inorganic Power and the human imagination might be saved. In *Prometheus Unbound* Shelley is returning to the unanswered question of 'Mont Blanc', but in a different form and with a different purpose.

The form of *Prometheus Unbound*, which Shelley denominates '*A Lyrical Drama*', is an expression of the conflict which informs it. In October 1818, Shelley refers to the work as 'a lyric & classical drama' (*Letters*, II. 43) and six months later commends it again to Peacock as 'a drama, with characters & mechanism of a kind yet unattempted' (*Letters*, II. 94). His designation of the work as both lyrical and dramatic is informed by a sense of its peculiar merits and innovations as well as of its debt to classical drama. In later letters, however, he seems at pains to deny the work's derivativeness, but his protestations of originality sound oddly defensive. The terms he uses to defend the work from charges of imitation are revealing. He writes, for instance, to Thomas Medwin in July 1820, that ' "Prometheus Unbound" is in the merest spirit of ideal Poetry, and not, as the name would indicate, a mere imitation of the Greek drama, or indeed if I have been successful, is it an imitation of anything.' It is the quality of 'ideal Poetry' which distinguishes *Prometheus* from its classical predecessors, and also from Shelley's other play, *The Cenci*, which in the same letter Shelley describes as 'a composition of a totally different character' (*Letters*, II. 219). His emphasis on the poetic and ideal nature of *Prometheus*, although false as a means of distinguishing it from Aeschylus, is interesting because it points to a tension in the work which is not just an accident of its form, but springs from its theme. The 'ideal Poetry' of *Prometheus Unbound* consists of a lyricism which pulls against the dramatic properties of the work, and tends to transpose action into the register of song. The denomination of the work as a lyrical drama points to a tension between the demands of dramatic representation, which externalises and visualises character and event, and the demands of the sublime lyric, which internalises character and event and makes them merely objects of the poet's imaginative perception. While the events of *Prometheus Unbound* are, on the one hand, conducted by autonomous and visible agents, they are also, on the other hand, conducted by shadows, voices, creatures of 'the human mind's imaginings'.

Shelley probably derives his distinction between drama and lyricism from Schlegel's *Lectures on Dramatic Art and Literature* which he was reading in March 1818,[3] about six months before commencing work on *Prometheus*. Schlegel's definition of dramatic literature centres on a distinction between theatrical and poetic interest. He writes that 'a dramatic work can therefore be considered in a double point of view, how far it is *poetical*, and how far it is *theatrical.* –'[4] The difference between the two proves to be a distinction between an external, empirical mode of representation and an internal, sublime mode. Thus he writes, in language which prefigures some of the language of Shelley's 'Defence', that for drama to be 'poetical it is necessary that it should be a mirror of ideas, that is, thoughts and feelings in their character necessary and eternally true, which soar above this earthly life', while 'without them a drama becomes altogether prosaic and empirical, that is, composed by the understanding from the observation of reality'.[5] According to Schlegel, the ideal nature of Greek drama, and of Aeschylus in particular, consists of its representation of high and abstract ideas, which, in their very elevation 'above this earthly life', require a correspondingly sublime language. He directs his reader to Kant's definition of the sublime in the *Critique of Judgement*, and then describes the poetry of Aeschylus as betraying 'a sublime and serious mind'.[6] It seems likely that Shelley's title '*A Lyrical Drama*' is based on Schlegel's oppositions between poetic and theatrical writing, and therefore between a sublime and an empirical representation of the world. While *Prometheus Unbound* is a manifesto for revolutionary change and for the establishment of an earthly utopia, it proposes such events in terms of a change in the poet's manner of seeing the world and of expressing it in poetry.

Prometheus Unbound opens with a scene which distinctly recalls 'Mont Blanc'. The landscape which confronts Prometheus is rugged and desolate, and significantly 'without herb, / Insect, or beast, or shape or sound of life' (I. 21–2); without, that is, the modifying and varying spirit of Beauty. Instead, Prometheus is bound to a precipice, and looks out on a frozen and broken landscape which gives the eye no change or rest. The precipice is 'eagle-baffling', and 'Black, wintry, dead, unmeasured' (I. 20–1). If, as Abrams claims, the eagle soaring above the abyss is a symbol of consolation in the face of political despair for a number of Romantic poets, particularly for Wordsworth and Schiller,[7] Shelley's eagle, which is baffled by the void beneath and cannot sustain its flight above it, must represent Prometheus' failure of hope at this point. Like the speaker of 'Mont Blanc', Prometheus faces a landscape of unchanging and immeasurable space, which mirrors his imaginative hopelessness, but in which he still desires to find a responsive and powerful voice. Like the poet of the earlier poem, he addresses and questions the landscape around him, in the hope of finding in it a voice powerful enough to instigate change. Where the poet of 'Mont Blanc' found in the mountain a voice not easily understood, but worthy of revolutionary interpretation and deep feeling, so Prometheus seeks, in his dialogue with the Earth, a voice, among the many confusing voices that he hears, which has the force of action.

Although Act I recalls the predicament of the speaker in 'Mont Blanc', in showing the protagonist before a desolate and unpeopled landscape with which he nonetheless desires to communicate, it also differs from 'Mont Blanc' because Prometheus does in fact conduct a dialogue with inorganic presences. He addresses the Earth, the Phantasm of Jupiter and the Furies, and they do reply. The fact that Shelley is writing a drama, not a lyric, means that the dialogue Prometheus desires is possible from the start. The voices which he seeks take shape as dramatic characters, who act and speak. Thus, although the plight of Prometheus is to be alone and hopeless, before a landscape which mirrors the failure of social change as well as the failure of imaginative communication with it, the form of the work permits a dialogue with that landscape which alleviates its strangeness and inhumanity. Prometheus addresses the Earth, and she replies to his questions.

However, the form of this dialogue between the two characters poses a difficulty. After Prometheus has asked for the words of his curse to be echoed by the Mountains, Springs, Air and Whirlwinds of the Earth, she answers his request with the following speech:

> The tongueless caverns of the craggy hills
> Cried, 'Misery!' then; the hollow Heaven replied,
> 'Misery!' And the Ocean's purple waves,
> Climbing the land, howled to the lashing winds,
> And the pale nations heard it, 'Misery!'   (I. 107–11)

The effect of Prometheus' curse was to rouse the world to an awareness of misery, but of a strangely vicarious and reflected kind. Although nature is capable of a kind of speech: a crying, replying, howling, it is speech devoid of human purpose, being 'tongueless' and 'hollow'. This language of nature is only an echo which reverberates in its mute and senseless spaces like the word ' "Misery!" ' Such a language originates elsewhere and is merely reiterated by the natural world. Although the landscape is as if capable of speaking and feeling, it in fact merely reproduces speech and feeling at a remove from its origin. This effect of distance is emphasised by Prometheus' response. He says 'I heard a sound of voices: not the voice / Which I gave forth' (1. 112–13). The Earth's description is distanced and estranged from Prometheus' understanding, and reaches him only as a kind of expressive inarticulateness: 'a *sound* of voices'.

This difficulty of communication is precisely the point. The dialogue with the Earth only serves to make more obvious the distance between the two speakers. Prometheus as the representative of man, 'the type of the highest perfection of moral and intellectual nature' (*P.W.*, p. 205) as Shelley describes him, cannot commune directly with powers that are not sentient. Nonetheless, Prometheus' desire for communication refuses to concede that the relation between the inorganic Earth and himself is therefore 'absolutely none' (*P.W.*, p. 811). Instead, he persists in seeking an intelligible response: 'Why scorns the spirit which informs ye, now / To commune with me?' (1. 124–5). The interchange which follows does not resolve the difficulty, but shows how the difficulty itself can lead to a new kind of intelligibility.

A few lines later Prometheus' reproachful questions begin to find a reply:

> Why answer ye not, still? Brethren!
> *The Earth.*   They dare not.
> *Prometheus.* Who dares? for I would hear that curse again.
> Ha, what an awful whisper rises up!
> 'Tis scarce like sound: it tingles through the frame
> As lightning tingles, hovering ere it strike.
> Speak, Spirit! from thine inorganic voice

79

I only know that thou art moving near
And love. How cursed I him?
The Earth.   How canst thou hear
Who knowest not the language of the dead?
Prometheus. Thou art a living spirit; speak as they.
The Earth. I dare not speak like life, lest Heaven's fell king
Should hear, and link me to some wheel of pain... (1. 130-41)

The dramatic fact of the Earth's cowardice in the face of Jupiter's power to link her 'to some wheel of pain' is translated into another drama, which is one of communication. It is not just that she fears to speak; it is that her speech, 'the language of the dead', is unintelligible to Prometheus. Although on one level the Earth intends not to answer Prometheus because she fears the consequences, on another level that intention is formed by the impossibility of answering him in any language he might understand. As so often in *Prometheus Unbound*, the political action of the play is linked to the problem of perception and effective speech. Shelley's reminder here that the voice of the Earth is 'inorganic' raises the old problem of whether the natural landscape can have any voice which is communicable to man. As in 'Mont Blanc' the answer to such a problem is found by shifting the onus of intelligibility from the external voice to the listener's internal interpretation of it.

In his book *Shelley's Later Poetry*, Milton Wilson writes of the dialogue between Prometheus and the Earth that she 'communicates with him sympathetically, not verbally, and he gradually becomes more and more attuned to what she is saying'.[8] This process of attunement is described in terms of the failure of sense perception. No longer even 'a sound of voices', what Prometheus now hears is 'scarce like sound'. Instead, it is akin to something felt: ''Tis scarce like sound: it tingles through the frame / As lightning tingles, hovering ere it strike.' What might be externally audible is transposed into something felt internally, and felt, significantly, as lightning, which cannot be foretold or contained. The difficult communication of the Earth is thus described in terms of imminent inspiration, and Prometheus' understanding of it in terms of imaginative receptivity. The revolutionary regenerator of mankind learns to be a sublime poet, able to interpret and to feel the landscape as a voice. That Shelley intends an association between the image of lightning and poetic inspiration is made clear in the Preface, where he writes in defence of his own originality, that 'a number of writers possess the form, whilst they want the spirit of those whom, it is alleged, they imitate; because the former is the endowment of the age in which they live, and the latter must be the uncommunicated lightning of their own mind', and later that in his own age the 'cloud of mind is discharging its collected lightning' (*P.W.*, p. 206). In both examples lightning represents the peculiar nature of creativity, which cannot be imitated and cannot, in its action, be forestalled.

Thus Prometheus learns to understand the voice of the Earth by internalising her meaning. Such internalisation represents a marked shift from a dramatic and external mode of communication to a lyrical and internal one. Far from exploiting his new licence to anthropomorphise inorganic objects as characters, Shelley's drama makes dialogue with them difficult, and substitutes for mutual interchange this internal and obscure apprehension of their speech. It is the very difficulty and distance of the Earth's voice which makes it the more powerfully expressive. Thus Prometheus claims: 'Obscurely through my brain, like shadows dim, / Sweep awful thoughts, rapid and thick' (1. 146–7). The familiar language of the sublime: 'obscurely', 'dim', 'awful', describes a kind of communication which is no longer based on sense perception, and which takes the form of private intuition rather than public dialogue. Prometheus, at this point, is less a participant in a drama of interacting characters, than a sublime poet, attending to the voice of his own inspiration. This internalising of the object solves the technical difficulty deriving from the fact that, as Wasserman puts it, 'only a single language is available to Shelley and his reader, and yet the reader must accept the explicit statement that Earth's language is really different from Prometheus' '.[9] The difference of her language is preserved in the strangeness of Prometheus' response to it.

The shift from dramatic dialogue to solitary apprehension marks one of the basic themes of *Prometheus Unbound*. Political liberation is a liberation of the imaginative eye from what Shelley calls in the 'Defence' 'the accident of surrounding impressions' (VII. 137), and such a liberation is the prerogative of the lyrical poet. The close association between dramatic action and lyrical eloquence in *Prometheus Unbound* reflects the association between Shelley's politics of revolutionary change and his aesthetic of private and inspired writing. The work attempts to unite the two, not merely in its polemic but in its actual workings.

In Act I the Earth continues to resist Prometheus' wish that the words of his curse be externalised by her, claiming that, while his words are not spoken, they are preserved by 'Mountains, and caves, and winds, and yon wide air, / And the inarticulate people of the dead' (I. 182–3) as 'a treasured spell' (184). Such words are a source of secret consolation, of 'secret joy and hope' (185), but they are ineffective. This dissociation of the word from the speaker gives it a magical and mysterious property. In the 'Hymn to Intellectual Beauty' Shelley wrote that 'the names of Demon, Ghost, and Heaven' (27) are

> Frail spells – whose uttered charm might not avail to sever,
> From all we hear and all we see,
> Doubt, chance, and mutability. (29–31)

Here too he is using the word 'spell' in the sense of words divorced from their utterance. Only in being uttered is their capacity to resolve doubt, chance and mutability tested. Similarly, the binding 'spells' (83) of the spirit of Beauty are messages which are silent and strange, but which compel from the poet a reciprocating action of fear and love. In keeping Prometheus' words secret and unspoken, the Earth prevents them being efficacious, and prevents them being translated into a code of moral and revolutionary action.

This break, between the words of the curse which have become 'a treasured spell' and the speaker of the curse, is a variant of Shelley's aesthetic of divorced inspiration and composition, voice and interpreter. Only by being resolved into poetic utterance can the mysterious Power of speech be put to use. Yet here Prometheus wishes the spell to be uttered, not so that it can be the source of revolutionary action, but so that it can be revoked.

This is why he must not repeat the curse himself, although the Earth implies that he has forgotten it: 'Thy curse, the which, if thou rememberest not...' (1. 180). Because the words of the curse were spoken in hatred and revenge they cannot be the impulse behind revolution. They are a false inspiration, and their power as spells must not be harnessed to the act of speaking, but be exorcised. As Prometheus no longer has the will to hate, he cannot repeat or even remember his curse. But in order that the words should not remain a falsely 'treasured spell', they must be externalised in some way.

Such a refusal to activate words by speaking them is one of the main themes of Act 1. When Prometheus later confronts the figure of the crucified Christ, he refuses to repeat his name: 'Thy name I will not speak, / It hath become a curse' (1. 603–4). As Susan Hawk Brisman writes, 'Jesus represents for Prometheus the fate of the savior turned symbol, the reduction of a creed to a watchword.'[10] Curses and spells in this play are both forms of speech which have become dissociated from the impulse of the heart. They are forms of speech which must be repealed without being repeated. For Prometheus to utter the cursed name of the founder of Christianity is to invest it with power once more, and thus to perpetuate in words the tyranny that Christianity has become. For similar reasons, the Furies refuse to put into words their knowledge of the course of the revolutionary war, because 'to speak might break the spell / Which must bend the Invincible' (1. 535–6). Unuttered words have a kind of defeating magic. They are spells in the sense that they are unwilled formulas, and also in the sense that they hold the mind paralysed, or spellbound, by their power. The mind of Prometheus is subdued by this unspoken, secret knowledge, which has the quality of being unchanging and unchangeable for as long as it is not harnessed to speech.

It is this discrepancy between the unspoken and the spoken which may partly explain the much disputed meaning of the 'two worlds of life and death' (1. 195). Although the Earth refuses to utter the curse herself, she urges Prometheus to search the second world beneath the grave, and there to 'Call at will / Thine own

ghost, or the ghost of Jupiter' (1. 210–11). The characteristic of
the world beneath the grave is that it contains a shadowy replica
of everything in the upper world, but in a state of unsubstantiality
and namelessness. Everything in this lower world is impressionistic,
because it has not been utilised by the creative will, which is the
will not only to act, but to name. Paul Dawson writes that the
'elaborate and powerful conception of the double worlds' is 'a
piece of machinery' for which Shelley has no more use in the rest
of the play, and which is therefore dramatically unaccounted for.[11]
However, if the passage is read as referring to the inevitable divorce
between the spell and its utterance, between the image and its
expression in words and action, it could be seen to stand at the
heart of Shelley's drama.

Significantly, the second world contains not only the shadowy
doubles of all living things, but also

> Dreams and the light imaginings of men,
> And all that faith creates or love desires,
> Terrible, strange, sublime and beauteous shapes. (1. 200–2)

Such language is reminiscent of 'Mont Blanc', where the poet
would substitute for the object of faith, the object of 'the human
mind's imaginings'. This world beneath the grave protects all the
transient phantoms of what is dreamed, imagined, believed or
desired. Here the objects of the poet's imaginings as well as of the
fanatic's faith are saved from vacancy, and each can be summoned
in speech. Such a place is thus the repository of all the objects of
thought before they are yoked to words. It is not absolutely separate
from the world of the living, but may be crossed by those who
dare to match their dreams to words, or their ideals to action.
Both Prometheus and Asia desire to cross into the world beneath
the grave in this play. The separation between the two is crucial
to the dramatic and the imaginative action of the work.

Prometheus, however, desires to recover the 'treasured spell' of
his words, not in order to activate but to negate it. The Earth tells
him:

> Ask, and they must reply: so the revenge
> Of the Supreme may sweep through vacant shades,

84

> As rainy wind through the abandoned gate
> Of a fallen palace.   (I. 215–18)

In language which tells of the inevitable fall of the tyrant, and of revenge as already meaningless and too late, the Earth informs Prometheus how his words may be reiterated without power. By summoning the Phantasm of Jupiter to repeat the curse, Prometheus ensures that utterance and utterer remain separate, and therefore that a false intention does not become effective speech again. Revenge is shown to be empty by being expressed by an empty speaker. When the Phantasm of Jupiter appears, it asks:

> Why have the secret powers of this strange world
> Driven me, a frail and empty phantom, hither
> On direst storms? What unaccustomed sounds
> Are hovering on my lips, unlike the voice
> With which our pallid race hold ghastly talk
> In darkness?   (I. 240–5)

The status of the Phantasm is, as a number of critics have shown, a reflection of Prometheus himself. Wasserman writes that Shelley intends an 'actual identification of the execrating Prometheus with Jupiter, the god he made in his image'.[12] The Phantasm is thus a projection both of the tyrant Jupiter and of the hatred which affirms tyrants as a legitimate object of opposition. Both kinds of projection are capable of being repealed.

But the Phantasm is also an empty echo of another's speech. Like the earlier tongueless and hollow reverberations of the landscape, the 'unaccustomed' speech of the Phantasm is speech dissociated from human will and purpose. Once again Shelley is undermining the dramatic autonomy of such a character by making it a frail embodiment of another's words, and as such, an embodiment of words which have become senseless. This characteristic is made clear in Prometheus' greeting of the Phantasm as a 'Tremendous Image' (I. 246). Such an appellation is resonant of that faculty of the poet which can create a world of shadowy presences from its dream or belief or imagining. The Phantasm is a tremendous image of the Promethean mind, because it has been imagined out of hatred and uttered as a curse. Thus the Phantasm is presented

85

as a mere fantasy of power, and as a mere configuration of vengeful words. As it begins to recite the curse, Prometheus reads the processes of his own past mind in its appearance:

> I see the curse on gestures proud and cold,
> And looks of firm defiance, and calm hate,
> And such despair as mocks itself with smiles,
> Written as on a scroll: yet speak: Oh, speak!   (I. 258–61)

Thus the dialogue between Prometheus and the Phantasm is collapsed into an internal and solitary confrontation between Prometheus and the embodied words of his curse. The dramatic irony of having Jupiter curse himself is underlaid by this other theme of having Prometheus meet his own words in objective form. Shelley's claim in the essay 'On Life' that the 'difference is merely nominal between those two classes of thought, which are vulgarly distinguished by the names of ideas and of external objects' (VI. 196) justifies his dramatic embodiment of the human mind's imaginings as a character who speaks. However, the subjective status of the Phantasm as an 'Image' is one which Prometheus desires to revoke, and he does so by reversing the normal process of creativity. Instead of internalising the words of the Phantasm as his own, to be interpreted and felt, he externalises them in an 'empty voice' which remains alien and inhuman, informed by 'no thought' (I. 249). Prometheus' curse is a miscreation, which although dramatically substantiated as the Phantasm, in fact remains a senseless formula of words, removed from poetic utterance and therefore from revolutionary action.

Prometheus' third meeting in Act I, with the Furies, is similarly a mistaken imagining. The Furies are only helpless externalisations of what Prometheus can 'know' (I. 459) and think (I. 475) and 'imagine' (I. 478). 'The Furies', writes Schlegel, referring to Aeschylus, 'are the dreadful powers of conscience, in so far as it rests on obscure feelings and forebodings, and yields to no principles of reason.'[13] The Furies of Shelley's play, however, are not emanations of guilt, but of despair; the despair, as Cameron argues, afflicting those 'radical intellectuals' who have witnessed 'the failure of the French Revolution'.[14] It is only this despair, and

Prometheus' consequent susceptibility to endure mental agony, which gives substance to the Furies. In a brilliant antithetical simile, Shelley describes the Furies, not as dramatic agents but imaginative projections of Prometheus' sufferings. They tell him:

> As from the rose which the pale priestess kneels
> To gather for her festal crown of flowers
> The aëreal crimson falls, flushing her cheek,
> So from our victim's destined agony
> The shade which is our form invests us round,
> Else we are shapeless as our mother Night. (I. 467–72)

Their transient natures are no more than a false imagining of the tortured mind; a fiction of despair and dread. Like much of the characterisation of this play, they are internalised and presented as fleeting embodiments of an inner trauma. Even while they appear to be the agents of pain, the language reveals that they are inversely created by pain, although this is a miscreation. It is the mind of Prometheus which acts, by giving the 'shade' of 'agony' to otherwise 'shapeless' things. Such a creation is a perversion, but it is nonetheless only a close variant of that ideal creativity which is the poet's, whose language 'rules with Daedal harmony a throng / Of thoughts and forms, which else senseless and shapeless were' (IV. 416–17). If the Furies are a reflection of everything Prometheus imagines with fear or dread or pain, their status is nonetheless equivalent to what he can imagine with hope and power.

Thus revolutionary action in this work is an act of mind, not of hand, and essentially it is an act of the imagination. The dramatic struggle is not a struggle between equal protagonists, but a mental struggle between two kinds of imaginative projection: one pessimistic and the other optimistic. Prometheus is the revolutionary by dint of being the creator, but the creator capable of both good and ill, where good and ill are created by the same imaginative processes of finding shapes and voices in apparent vacancy. Whether the object be the Earth, or the Phantasm of Jupiter, or the Furies, each is an imagining out of nothing, but each is not therefore good. The responsibility remains with the poet to choose amongst the 'Terrible, strange, sublime and beauteous shapes' of the mind.

87

Thus, although Act I of *Prometheus Unbound* repeats the question of 'Mont Blanc', the question whether the poet can imagine sufficiently strongly to fill sublime landscapes with presences, there is an added dilemma in the case of the poet who would be a revolutionary. Prometheus imagines the Phantasm and the Furies, but he must reject them as the creations of pessimism and hatred and pain, which are antithetical to revolutionary change. Although there is a shift from dramatic action to internal lyricism, from dialogue to monologue, from apparently autonomous characters to imaginative fictions, this is not because Shelley is avoiding the political theme of the work, but because he is characteristically seeing politics as a poetic issue. If the Earth, the Phantasm and the Furies are merely versions of what Prometheus can surmise, on a stage which is in fact the theatre of his own mind, they are also aspects of a moral and political choice which he, the imaginer, must make. So although Act I of *Prometheus Unbound* dramatises the problems of poetic imagining and communicating, it also presents imagining and communicating as political events for which Prometheus is responsible.

After Prometheus has retracted the curse and endured the onslaught of the Furies his dramatic role is practically at an end. In Act II it is Asia, his counterpart and the representative of love, who continues the work of revolution. She does so by returning to the second world beneath the grave from which Prometheus summoned the Phantasm, and confronts there the figure that lies at the heart of Shelley's drama: 'Demogorgon, a tremendous gloom' (I. 207). Both the location and the nature of Demogorgon may owe something to Schlegel's definition of tragedy, as polarising liberty and necessity. In the *Lectures on Dramatic Art and Literature* he writes that while

the feeling of internal dignity elevates the man above the unlimited dominion of impulse and native instinct, and in a word absolves him from the guardianship of nature, so the necessity which he must also recognize ought to be no mere natural necessity, but to lie beyond the world of sense in the abyss of infinitude; and it must consequently be represented as the invincible power of fate. Hence it extends also to the world of the gods.[15]

Schlegel's passage turns upon his characteristic opposition of sense perception and sublime vision. Necessity dwells in that place which is so seductive to the Post-Miltonic imagination: 'the abyss of infinitude'. The way towards Demogorgon goes down through the 'void abysm' (II. iii. 72) in Shelley's work, and the nature of Demogorgon correspondingly repudiates sense perception.

But Demogorgon must also owe something of its nature to Shelley's earlier definitions of the philosophical concept of Necessity. In the 'Notes on Queen Mab' he wrote that the 'idea of necessity is obtained by our experience of the connection between objects, the uniformity of the operations of nature, the constant conjunction of similar events, and the consequent inference of one from the other' (*P.W.*, p. 809). This is an almost verbatim rendering of Hume. However, Shelley then goes on to enlist such a concept in the cause of eradicating Christianity. 'The doctrine of Necessity tends...utterly to destroy religion' (*P.W.*, p. 811), he writes, and adds, in language that foreshadows the great debate between Asia and Demogorgon, that 'the doctrine of Necessity teaches us that in no case could any event have happened otherwise than it did happen, and that, if God is the author of good, He is also the author of evil; that, if He is entitled to our gratitude for the one, He is entitled to our hatred for the other' (*P.W.*, p. 812). The actual passage in *Queen Mab* to which this philosophical Note is appended points up the difficulty of describing Necessity in verse. There it is addressed as 'Spirit of Nature!' and as 'mother of the world!' (*P.W.*, pp. 762–800, VI. 197–8), descriptions which attribute to it benign and procreative qualities that are strangely out of tune with the philosophical Notes. That Shelley is aware of the difficulty is evident, however, in his attempt to retract the personification he has initiated. He writes:

> all that the wide world contains
> Are but thy passive instruments, and thou
> Regard'st them all with an impartial eye,
> Whose joy or pain thy nature cannot feel,
> Because thou hast not human sense,
> Because thou art not human mind. (VI. 214–19)

These lines exhibit the old tension in Shelley's thought, between a desire for personification which is 'beautiful in Poetry', and a distrust of it as 'inadmissible in reasoning' (*Letters*, I. 101). He needs to affirm that Necessity is able to regard the world, but blindly 'with an impartial eye', and he needs to address the concept as 'thou', but only one which is senseless and mindless. This tension also informs the description of Demogorgon in *Prometheus Unbound*. In the later work Shelley is still slipping into the form of address which must anthropomorphise its object, but he is still presenting Demogorgon, like the Power of 'Mont Blanc', as a bleak and non-sentient alternative to the God of Christianity.

In his book *Red Shelley*, Paul Foot argues that Demogorgon is, as the etymology of its name suggests, the 'people-monster'[16] or the masses, and that Asia is therefore the political 'agitator'[17] who rouses the people to action. Such an interpretation is persuasive, but works only by isolating Demogorgon from its earlier manifestations, and by skirting the problem of the language Shelley uses to describe the encounter. Asia's journey into the realm of Demogorgon follows the indications of a dream, and is described as the movement of music. The subtle interweaving of dreams between Asia and Panthea results in the telepathic message being externalised by Echoes in the natural world, who then sing to direct Asia towards Demogorgon. The precise wording of the songs is important. The Echoes sing:

> O, follow, follow,
> As our voice recedeth
> Through the caverns hollow,
> Where the forest spreadeth;
> (*More distant.*)
> O, follow, follow!
> Through the caverns hollow,
> As the song floats thou pursue... (II. i. 173–9)

The way is not only described in the song, but it *is* the song: 'As the song floats thou pursue.' The movement of poetry is the movement towards revolutionary consciousness, so that the song here is perfectly translatable into action. Unlike the curse, which is

90

divorced from the intention of the utterer, and is treasured in secret and isolation from action, the song of the Echoes is 'in step' with Asia's actual movements.

This correspondence of song and action, of figurative and literal footsteps, is then stressed in the description of their mutual destination. The Echoes tell that

> In the world unknown
> Sleeps a voice unspoken;
> By thy step alone
> Can its rest be broken;
> Child of Ocean! (II. i. 190–4)

The dramatic direction of events, from world to underworld, is transposed into an aesthetic direction, from song to mysterious voice. The Echoes are personifications of a lyricism which leads, by the familiar route of the sublime, to 'a voice unspoken'. As in 'Mont Blanc', the presence which lies behind the empirical landscapes of the senses, in the infinite abyss of space, is characterised by a kind of voice: 'a voice...not understood / By all' or, as here, 'a voice unspoken'. In both works, the voice which is sought lies beyond the efforts of speech; beyond the receding echoes of song. Thus the journey of Asia and Panthea, which is a journey following the signposts of a lyric, might be interpreted as a mythological and dramatic crossing of that space which divides the original voice of inspiration from its difficult recovery in composition. Demogorgon is not only the unknown force of the masses or the Humean concept of Necessity; it is also the mysterious origin of song, which the poet desires to interpret or to feel.

This aspect of Demogorgon is made clearer in Act II, scene iii, where Asia and Panthea reach the entry to the underworld. Panthea explains that

> Hither the sound has borne us – to the realm
> Of Demogorgon, and the mighty portal,
> Like a volcano's meteor-breathing chasm,
> Whence the oracular vapour is hurled up
> Which lonely men drink wandering in their youth,
> And call truth, virtue, love, genius, or joy... (II. iii. 1–6)

The realm of Demogorgon is the place from which prophetic

91

inspiration, 'the oracular vapour', derives. It is the source of all that men call 'truth, virtue, love, genius, or joy'; of all that, in Shelley's broad definition of the word, marks out the poet. The '*Song of Spirits*' which describes the downward journey to this source describes it in terms of vision and poetry. The way leads

> To the deep, to the deep,
> Down, down!
> Through the shade of sleep,
> Through the cloudy strife
> Of Death and of Life;
> Through the veil and the bar
> Of things which seem and are
> Even to the steps of the remotest throne,
> Down, down! (II. iii. 54–62)

This is a journey which goes, in Schlegel's words, 'beyond the world of sense' to 'the abyss of infinitude'.[18] It is a journey not so much of time and space, however, but of perception, which penetrates beyond the visual barriers implied by the words 'shade', 'cloudy', 'veil' and 'bar', in order to reach its strangely unvisual destination: 'the steps of the remotest throne'. The object of the journey is known only as this metonymy of Power, which is a presence but defies visual representation. If perception is cleared of the confusions of the upper world, it achieves in their place a vision of something more enduring but more strange. This 'radical alteration of sight',[19] which characterises the politically motivated journey of Asia and Panthea, is an alteration which brings sight close to sightlessness. In 'the gray, void abysm' they learn to see, in the spirit of Milton, by being almost blind.

The journey to Demogorgon is thus an education in perception. It is also, as the second stanza tells, a journey *of* necessity, undertaken as 'steel obeys the spirit of the stone' (II. iii. 70). It is finally, however, a journey of poetic creativity:

> In the depth of the deep,
> Down, down!
> Like veiled lightning asleep,
> Like the spark nursed in embers,
> The last look Love remembers,
> Like a diamond, which shines

92

On the dark wealth of mines,
A spell is treasured but for thee alone.
Down, down! (II. iii. 81–9)

The 'voice unspoken' of Demogorgon is signposted by a succession of similes that become well-tried images of creativity in Shelley's work. The 'veiled lightning' is a commonplace of inspiration, while 'the spark nursed in embers', or in *'ashes'*[20] according to an earlier version, points to those 'Ashes and sparks, my words' (67) which prophesy revolution in the 'Ode to the West Wind', or to the 'fading coal' of the 'mind in creation' in the 'Defence'. The Power which originates revolutions is *like* the elusive Power which originates poetry. The dramatic way down to Demogorgon is thus a journey towards the tenor of these similes for poetry; a journey towards that which is like 'lightning', a 'spark', a 'last look', 'a diamond'. In this play it is the vitally metaphorical song which conducts events, and it is the language of poetic lyricism which can move revolutions.

Demogorgon itself is like a kind of secret poetry: 'A spell is treasured but for thee alone.' This exactly echoes the 'treasured spell' of Prometheus' curse. It is a form of words which utterance must release into action. Asia's journey in search of this 'spell' thus parallels Prometheus' search in the world beneath the grave for the form of words he wishes to repeal. The important difference between them is that Prometheus was motivated by hate, and must therefore refuse to utter the spell, whereas Asia is motivated by love, which alone can initiate revolutionary action. She, unlike Prometheus, will give a voice to the 'voice unspoken', and thus bring world and voice, spell and utterance, together, in a unity which has the power of bringing down tyrants and gods.

It is in Act II, scene iv, which constitutes the philosophical and dramatic climax of the work, that Shelley shows Asia releasing the 'spell' of Demogorgon by speaking it. Characteristically this scene, which catalyses Shelley's mythological revolution, presents a drama not of action, but of perception and communication. In the abyss, Asia and Panthea struggle to see the object which defies their sight, even as Shelley struggles with the spirit of the poet who has already preceded him in that place. The scene opens with the following interchange:

> *Panthea.* What veilèd form sits on that ebon throne?
> *Asia.* The veil has fallen.
> *Panthea.*　　　　　　I see a mighty darkness
> Filling the seat of power, and rays of gloom
> Dart round, as light from the meridian sun.
> – Ungazed upon and shapeless; neither limb,
> Nor form, nor outline; yet we feel it is
> A living Spirit.　　　　　　　　　　　　　(II. iv. 1–7)

Shelley's problem is how to portray a presence which has neither empirical nor religious status, but which is nonetheless a figure of universal Power. Demogorgon is not, as Wasserman emphasises, 'a God that Shelley has been tricked into admitting'.[21] At the same time, Demogorgon is something more than vacancy. As in 'Mont Blanc', Shelley's presentation of the unknown Power shifts brilliantly between something and nothing. At first the obscure form seems to be clarified with the lifting of the veil, but what Panthea then sees is contradictory. Although she claims to 'see', she then admits that the form is 'Ungazed upon', and finally asserts that 'we feel'. The Miltonic denials of light and shape compel this alternative perception, by which sight is internalised as feeling.

For all its Miltonic echoes, this description of Demogorgon is typical of Shelley's methods. He describes a presence which is very nearly an absence. The form of Demogorgon is a 'darkness' which, if it were not 'mighty', might be nothing. It is then described obliquely, through metonymy: 'ebon throne', and 'seat of power', or contradictorily: 'rays of gloom', or by a simile which cancels its own similitude: 'rays of gloom / Dart round, as light from the meridian sun'. Nonetheless, in spite of this nearly negating language, something is still saved to the understanding in that 'yet we feel'. The eclipse of the visible characteristically serves to authenticate what might be felt. Although Shelley cannot risk letting his dramatised god-term trick him into creating a dramatisation of God, neither is he willing to dispense with the god-term altogether. The Miltonic abyss still contains a presence for the

94

mind's imaginings, or at least contains the possibility for the mind to imagine a presence.

In the subsequent dialogue between Asia and Demogorgon, this shift from the object perceived to the perceiver becomes the very question at issue. Asia learns, in the questions and answers which follow, not to seek the epistemological status of the Power of the universe, but rather to take responsibility for her own imagining of it. At first, when Asia asks: 'Who made the living world?' (II. iv. 9) and 'Who made all / That it contains?' (9–10) and 'Who made that sense which...Fills the faint eyes with falling tears...?' (12, 15), Demogorgon gives the answers which Coleridge triumphantly celebrated in the 'Hymn before Sun-Rise'. It answers 'God' (9), 'Almighty God' (11), 'Merciful God' (18). Asia's questions create their orthodox answers. However, when she then asks 'who made terror, madness, crime, remorse...?' (19), the answer becomes evasive: 'He reigns' (28). This is not only, as Milton Wilson claims, a dramatisation of the old challenge to theological orthodoxy, which discovers in it the contradiction of ascribing 'the creation of evil to a beneficent God'.[22] Demogorgon's evasive answer also reflects the genuine perplexity of Asia's mind in seeking to give a name to the author of evil. What is being played out in this dialogue is not only an old theological debate, but the dilemma facing the sceptical mind. As soon as Asia dares to ask who created evil; as soon as she thus dares to utter a kind of scepticism, the naming of God becomes difficult. 'He reigns' marks a dissatisfaction with the anthropomorphism of the earlier answers, in favour of a more obscure attribution of authority. Demogorgon only gives the replies which Asia's questions make necessary. 'I spoke but as ye speak' (II. iv. 112), it tells her. Just as in Act I Prometheus comes to be attuned to the meaning of the Earth's voice by internalising it as his own obscure thoughts, so here Asia slowly begins to understand that the answers she receives from Demogorgon are in fact her own. Demogorgon is able to make intelligible her own confused forebodings only when she first expresses a desire to know. As she begins to understand its tactics, she frames her questions accordingly:

do thou answer me
As mine own soul would answer, did it know
That which I ask.   (II. iv. 124-6)

Shelley's techniques here are again to collapse the conventions of dramatic dialogue into monologue. Asia questions the unseen Power, but receives only the responses of her own soul. Demogorgon is not a divine authority, making its doctrines known to the world through Asia. It is not the voice of revelation, but the voice of her own heart, which answers just so much as she dares to ask. In going in search of the mysterious spell of Demogorgon, Asia is only going in search of her own language, which has become divorced from speech. The 'voice unspoken' is in fact her own. To interpret Demogorgon as Necessity or the masses is to give it an objective reality which Shelley seems at pains to undermine in this scene. Although Demogorgon certainly is the catalysing force of revolution, such a force is contained in words, specifically those words which, in their perfect correspondence to the heartfelt energy and enthusiasm of the speaker, distinguish the sublime poet as the unacknowledged legislator of the world.

Thus the character of Demogorgon is mediated through the words and feelings and imaginings of Asia. What she cannot know or imagine cannot be communicated to her by it, so that when she asks who is 'the master' (II. iv. 114) of Jupiter, she receives an expression of her own present ignorance:

If the abysm
Could vomit forth its secrets...But a voice
Is wanting, the deep truth is imageless...   (II. iv. 114-16)

The master of Jove is, of course, Demogorgon, as events will tell, but such a Power remains 'imageless' until it lies in Asia's capacity to imagine it. In this famous description of the abyss, Shelley is not claiming that 'a voice / Is wanting' because such a place is now empty, nor is he claiming that the abyss contains a secret and unknown presence which refuses to speak. Instead, he is asserting that imagelessness only corresponds to a failure to imagine, and that therefore 'a voice / Is wanting' only until Asia dares to raise her voice. The abyss is voiceless and imageless for as long as Asia's consciousness is unawakened to its revolutionary potential, when it will supply a voice and image of change. The dialogue ends with the answer to her final question: 'When shall the destined hour arrive?' (II. iv. 128). The form of the answer, however, is not as she expects, in words, but in action. Simply by formulating a desire for the renovation of the world, Asia has instigated it. The hour arrives as soon as she has desired it, and has expressed that desire in words. Demogorgon is only a projection of this capacity to imagine with hope, and by naming, to make that hope a reality.

Thus in Acts I and II of *Prometheus Unbound* Shelley is using his aesthetic of divided inspiration and composition, voice and speech, or of the secret spell and its speaker, in order to express a theory of political revolution which depends on the reconnection of the two. He therefore translates dramatic action into lyricism and song, and translates political events into events of uttering, questioning and naming. *Prometheus Unbound* is a drama about revolutionary speech. In it, Shelley supersedes the uncertainty and pessimism which inform the last section of 'Mont Blanc', where imaginative recovery of the Power of the mountain is threatened by 'Silence and solitude', and instead proclaims a triumphant reciprocity between Asia's imaginings of change and the capacity of Demogorgon to effect that change. By presenting Demogorgon's 'voice unspoken' as merely the correlative of Asia's own speech, and its strange spell as merely the knowledge which she has not yet uttered, Shelley optimistically brings about a reunion between the two parts of his aesthetic of poetry, in order to proclaim its indispensability to the task of revolution.

The problem with *Prometheus Unbound* as drama is that the struggle is resolved by the end of Act II, and that the subsequent two acts merely celebrate the events which Prometheus and Asia have brought about. The fall of Jupiter at the beginning of Act III is inevitable and expected. However, the meaning of the fall is again made subtly relative to the consciousness which experiences it. In his shock at meeting Demogorgon instead of his expected child, Jupiter asks the predictable question: 'Awful shape, what art thou? Speak!' (III. i. 51) and receives for answer: 'Eternity.

Demand no direr name. / Descend, and follow me down the abyss' (III. i. 52-3). Jupiter confronts the same mysterious Power as Asia, but knows it, not as the Power of change and revolution but as the Power of unchanging 'Eternity'. The 'name' is dire enough and, as in 'Mont Blanc', suggests the endlessness of the abyss when the imagination fails. It is this alternative aspect of Demogorgon which Yeats in his essay on *Prometheus Unbound* finds unacceptable. He writes of Shelley's play that 'Demogorgon made his plot incoherent, its interpretation impossible; it was thrust there by that something which again and again forced him to balance the object of desire conceived as miraculous and super-human, with nightmare.'[23] But this possibility of nightmare is one which always besets Shelley's apprehension of eternity, and is not a contradiction of it. The very nature of Demogorgon is to be both a dream of good, for Asia, and a nightmare of endlessness, for Jupiter. This is not an incoherence, but an ambivalence which is everywhere apparent in Shelley's presentation of origins. Demogorgon is the Power of social revolution when conceived by Asia, but it is also vacancy when conceived by Jupiter. Consciousness shapes eternity to its own desire, and Shelley's purpose in *Prometheus Unbound* is to deny any 'miraculous and superhuman' agency in human affairs, but rather to load the imagination with all responsibility for the object it encounters. Thus Jupiter finds in Demogorgon an eternity of darkness and unchangingness, which is the equivalent of his own consciousness.

The fall is then commented on by two bystanders who emphasise this hopelessness:

> *Ocean*. He sunk to the abyss? To the dark void?
> *Apollo*. An eagle so caught in some bursting cloud
> On Caucasus, his thunder-baffled wings
> Entangled in the whirlwind, and his eyes
> Which gazed on the undazzling sun, now blinded
> By the white lightning, while the ponderous hail
> Beats on his struggling form, which sinks at length
> Prone, and the aëreal ice clings over it.   (III. ii. 10-17)

The image of the eagle poised over the abyss, but then falling 'baffled', recalls the parallel situation of Prometheus in Act I. In both cases, the despair of the two protagonists is reflected in this figurative failure to sustain flight above 'the dark void'. The imagery makes the point that Prometheus and Jupiter are aspects of each other; the latter is created in the image of the former's despair, and that despair, whether of gods or men, finds its natural equivalent in the abyss of infinity, or, as Shelley more often terms it, eternity. This is the other face of Demogorgon, which presents itself to those who fail to hope or to imagine sufficiently well. In this work it is only Asia, the spirit of love, who ventures into the abyss of Demogorgon and finds in it a promise of change. As the Earth tells in a later song, Jupiter goes into the nothing which he is, while

> from beneath, around, within, above,
> Filling thy void annihilation, love
> Burst in like light on caves cloven by the thunder-ball.
>
> (IV. 353–5)

After the fall of Jupiter, the rest of *Prometheus Unbound* consists mainly of a hymn of the Earth. It is appropriate that this play, which is so much about the revolutionary force of language and poetry, should celebrate the fall of tyranny and the establishment of an earthly utopia with a lyricism which is at last liberated from the demands of dramatic presentation. Act IV is, unapologetically, a song, or rather a series of songs, which describe the new world of freed love and creativity. If *Prometheus Unbound* is a drama which pushes in the direction of lyricism throughout its first three Acts, that lyricism is achieved in Act IV. Characteristically, the triumph of the revolutionary spirit is a triumph of the poetic spirit. These last lyrics in a sense celebrate the Power of writing lyrics. The leisured songfulness of Act IV thus marks the triumph of the play's main theme, which is the liberation of the human mind's imaginings from despair; that despair which, in the wake of the French Revolution, has reinstated tyranny and doomed all idealists to a Promethean suffering on the edge of the abyss.

In the last song, Demogorgon recounts the events which have brought about this new order of the world, and reiterates the morality which directs the Shelleyan revolution to its different conclusion:

> To suffer woes which Hope thinks infinite;
> To forgive wrongs darker than death or night;
> To defy Power, which seems omnipotent;
> To love, and bear; to hope till Hope creates
> From its own wreck the thing it contemplates;
> Neither to change, nor falter, nor repent;
> This, like thy glory, Titan, is to be
> Good, great and joyous, beautiful and free;
> This is alone Life, Joy, Empire, and Victory. (IV. 570–8)

The sheer energy and profusion of these last lyrics is a tribute to the message they reflect. Political hopefulness, for Shelley, is an act of the imagination, and its realisation in deeds is an act of language. The task of the political liberator of mankind is not so much to fight but to hope, and to create the object of that hopefulness even in the face of despair and vacancy. In *Prometheus Unbound* it is not so much Prometheus as Asia who liberates the world, by finding in the darkness and silence of the abyss a voice to express her hope, and a Power to bring it to effect. The nature of that voice and of that Power is attested to and celebrated in the lyricism of the final act. After *Prometheus Unbound*, however, the coincidence of voice and song, Power and writing, of inspiration and composition, is rarely again so persuasive, so certain and so hopeful.

5

INSPIRATION AND THE POET'S SKILL: 'ODE TO THE WEST WIND' AND 'TO A SKYLARK'

In *Prometheus Unbound* the theme of political change is linked to the theme and practice of hopeful creativity. This is a drama not of event, but of perception and speech, in which the main protagonists, Prometheus and Asia, struggle to realise their political aims in a language which harmonises voice and speech, desire and the language of desire. The aim of the work is to bring about the new world by creating it in words; the words of a poetry which most perfectly coincides with what Duff referred to as 'the natural dictates of the heart, not fictitious or copied, but original'.[1] False creativity is one in which utterer and utterance are divorced from each other, as Prometheus is divorced from the words of hate and despair repeated by the Phantasm and the Furies. Such a divorce hinders the task of revolution. But true creativity is one in which utterer meets utterance as Asia meets Demogorgon and internalises its voice as her own: 'my heart gave / The response thou hast given' (II. iv. 121–2).

As a result of this concern with the approximation of voice and speech much of the writing of *Prometheus Unbound* is in the form of an address. Prometheus and Asia converse with the other characters by addressing them as presences, whose voices are less heard than felt, and whose communication surfaces in the consciousness of the protagonists like something they already know. The prevalence of this kind of address is important. The lyricism Shelley adopts and celebrates is a lyricism reminiscent of the form of 'Hymn to Intellectual Beauty' and 'Mont Blanc', because it is a lyricism which draws on the formal conventions of the ode.

In *The English Ode from Milton to Keats* George Shuster

confesses the difficulty of defining the ode. His own definition is therefore of very broad compass. He writes that it is 'a lyric poem derived, either directly or indirectly, from Pindaric models. These models were poems of praise, worship, reflection, commemoration, and patriotic sentiment. In addition they were . . . written in lengthier, more complex stanzas than those selected for ordinary lyric use.'[2] However, even this definition is too narrow to apply to the two odes Shelley wrote in the autumn of 1819 and the summer of 1820 respectively. The 'Ode to the West Wind' and 'To a Skylark' are not written after the Pindaric model, but in relatively short lines and strict rhyme and metre. Shelley blurs the difference between the ode and the lyric proper.[3] Of this later Romantic form Shuster writes 'that it is a lyric of an especial solemnity; that it is characterized by a note of address couched in relatively august terms; and that it is written round a "universal" theme'.[4] All that remains in this definition to distinguish the Romantic ode from other kinds of poetry which may share its solemnity and universality is the 'note of address'. This element is now of central importance. But it is also, for Shelley, a source of difficulty. The classical ode uses the form of address for the practical reason of its being generally sung or recited to someone.[5] However, when this context is removed, and the object of the ode is created imaginatively within the poem itself, the address is no longer a practical convention but a self-conscious and figurative strategy.

Another reason why 'the note of address' in the ode becomes problematic for Shelley stems from the fact that the ode is also traditionally associated with the prophetic writings of the Old Testament. This Hebrew derivation is important because it roots the English ode in writings widely considered to be the origin and epitome of the sublime, and it charges the note of address with a specifically religious significance. John Dennis had early linked the sublime with 'Sacred Poetry',[6] and the association becomes one of those fruitful commonplaces of aesthetic thinking for more than a century after him. In the *Lectures on the Sacred Poetry of the Hebrews*, Robert Lowth writes of this Hebraic poetry that 'as some of these writings exceed in antiquity the fabulous ages of Greece, in sublimity they are superior'.[7] This notion is still being repeated by Coleridge when he claims: 'Could you ever discover anything sublime, in our sense of the term, in the classic Greek literature? I never could. Sublimity is Hebrew by birth.'[8] Thus the ode carries a long history of association both with the writings of the Old Testament and with an aesthetic of sublimity. In his *Dictionary* Samuel Johnson defines the greater ode by 'sublimity, rapture, and quickness of transition',[9] and Lowth, after him, writes that of 'all the different forms of poetical composition, there is none more agreeable, harmonious, elegant, diversified and sublime than the ode'.[10] In the eighteenth century, as Shelley must have been well aware, 'sublimity was regarded almost universally as the essential characteristic of the lofty lyric',[11] and sublimity was regarded as the special prerogative of religious poetry. The habitual circularity of the reasoning only emphasises its popularity. The ode is defined by sublimity, and the sublime is defined by the workings of the ode. Practice and theory extend mutual compliments.

However, from this long convergence of aesthetic theory and practice two important facts about the language of the ode emerge. The first of these is the predominance in the ode, at least 'when it rises to any uncommon strain of sublimity', of 'frequent personifications'.[12] The second fact about the language of the ode, as a form privileged to reflect the workings of the sublime, is its principle of insufficiency before the natural expression of the speaker. As Lowth writes, with an unfailing confidence of novelty, in sublime writing 'is displayed all the genuine force of nature and passion, which the efforts of art will emulate in vain. Here we behold the passions struggling for vent, labouring with a copiousness of thought and a poverty of expression, and on that very account the more expressly displayed.'[13] These two features of the language of the ode are oddly conflicting. On the one hand, the use of 'frequent personifications' creates innumerable ghostly presences, which makes for a kind of linguistic plenitude. On the other hand, what the ode celebrates or addresses remains beyond the reach of its rhetoric which is therefore, paradoxically, poor and empty. While the ode rejoices in verbal artifice, it also denigrates all 'expression' before the 'copiousness of thought' which it forfeits. As a result, the rhetorical richness of the ode is a form of compensation for this loss. Such a conflict, translated into the conflict between wind or bird and its expression in poetry, becomes one of the thematic resources of Shelley's own odes.

In his article 'The Sublime Poem: Pictures and Powers', Martin Price writes that in general the 'moment of the sublime was a transport of spirit, and at such a moment the visible object was eclipsed or dissolved. The dissolution of the image threw the mind back on itself; typically, the failure of the image was expressed in a figure which played upon words that no longer sufficed.'[14] He links the principle of linguistic insufficiency in the sublime poem with the eclipse of the visual object. The sublime poem puts in question the value of visual representation, and therefore exploits a language which falls short. However, when the religious origins of the sublime are replaced by an aesthetic origin, this failure of verbal representation is no longer registered as evidence for the magnitude of the Deity, but as evidence of a creativity which continually out-distances the text. In these two odes by Shelley the language of negation or accumulated metaphor is not a language which belongs to some economy of compensation and rewards. Because the original inspiration of wind or bird is beyond representation in words, the poet's verbal address to it risks being merely poor and empty. But these poems also verge on the knowledge that if the original Power is imageless, it is also nothing if not images and words. While the sublime ode in Shelley's hands advertises the insufficiency of its rhetoric, it also contains the knowledge that there might be nothing else.

This element of imaginative risk is not generally recognised by those critics who condemn the Shelleyan sublime for being mawkish, careless and vague. Donald Davie, for instance, in *Purity of Diction in English Verse*, opposes Shelley's sublime mode to his urbane mode to the detriment of the former, and his criticism is dressed in terms which recall the criticisms of Leavis and Eliot. Such criticism emphasises the failure of Shelley's verse to deal in tangible experiences. Davie writes that Shelley's 'sublimity is peculiarly indefinite and impalpable'. He adds that 'his poetry is certainly sensuous; but the sensuousness is not of a sort to bring into poetry the reek and grit of common experience. For Shelley goes as far as poetry can go, while it uses intelligible language, in cutting the hawsers which tie his fancies to the ground'.[15] Both the 'Ode to the West Wind' and 'To a Skylark' have suffered from the kind of interpretation which accuses Shelley of doing the very thing he celebrates, which is to cut 'the hawsers which tie his fancies to the ground'. Such a grounding metaphor of poetry betrays the values of its writer. Davie is an empiricist in criticism because he assumes a basic reference between words and the 'reek and grit' which keeps poetry earthbound, and by metaphorical extension, earthy. Shelley's version of the sublime, however, as Davie points out, is one which breaks that reference. His poetry plays upon the anxious deficiencies of the text in relation to the elusive object it would display, and thus makes the relation between words and object perilous.

Leavis' criticism of Shelley has been answered by many scholars, but it is illuminating to turn to it again in order to reinterpret the Shelleyan sublime as neither religious consolation nor escapist nonsense. To condemn Shelley as Leavis does, and with the weight as of an accepted fact, for 'his weak grasp upon the actual',[16] is to presume an empirical model of 'the actual' and then to use that model as a value judgement. The authority of Leavis' criticism of Shelley in *Revaluation* rests on his frequent recourse to the verb 'to grasp' as an activity appropriate to the poetic intelligence. He writes, for instance, of 'a mind as little able to hold an object in front of it as Shelley's was',[17] and later condemns *The Triumph of Life* because 'in spite of the earnest struggle to grasp something real...the poem itself is a drifting phantasmagoria', which fails 'to place the various phases or levels of visionary drift with reference to any grasped reality'. Such failure, he adds, in words which exactly describe the intention of the sublime, 'is the more significant because of the palpable effort'.[18] Leavis writes of the activity of the creative mind in these passages as a handling of things rather than a writing of words. The opposite of this mental 'grasp' on reality is therefore described as an empty gesticulation, a helpless waving. Leavis complains of a passage from *The Cenci* that it 'does not grasp and present anything, but merely makes large gestures towards the kind of effect deemed appropriate'.[19] Here 'large gestures' are presented as the ineffectual opposite of 'grasp'. Leavis' description of the way poetic language works presupposes a ruling metaphor of hand and object, where the one seeks to acquire the other.

It is not surprising, therefore, that a poet whose frequent concern is with the failure of the creative mind to reach its object should not measure up to Leavis' standard. Shelley's own descriptions of the working of creativity are essentially anti-tactile. They emphasise a failure either to arrest or to apprehend the Power of inspiration as it passes. Those 'large gestures' which Leavis derides in fact beautifully describe a characteristic of the Shelleyan sublime: that its language generously reaches towards its object, but also fails to grasp it. Such a language both promises and loses its object. Its gestures in this sense are neither ineffectual nor, as Leavis implies, purely for effect. Instead, they are a measure of the poem's movingly inadequate reach. The workings of the sublime are still in radical antithesis to the values of empiricism, and Leavis' condemnation still serves usefully as a contrast to what Shelley celebrates in his odes: that insufficiency of language which, in his version of the sublime, goes unrewarded, and which thus acknowledges failure and loss as the ever-present potential of poetry.

Shelley wrote his 'Ode to the West Wind' in the autumn of 1819, and it was published in the *Prometheus Unbound* volume by Ollier in 1820. According to Shelley's own note to the poem, it 'was conceived and chiefly written in a wood that skirts the Arno, near Florence, and on a day when that tempestuous wind, whose temperature is at once mild and animating, was collecting the vapours which pour down the autumnal rains' (*P.W.*, p. 577). In a letter to the Gisbornes of 6 November 1819, he writes that 'I like the Cascini very much where I often walk alone watching the leaves & the rising & falling of the Arno. I am full of all kinds of literary plans. –' These 'literary plans' are put in opposition to the 'great sandy desert of Politics' (*Letters*, II. 150) to which his interests inclined in the autumn of 1819. However, this is not to say that the poems of the time are devoid of political interest. Like the 1816 Hymns and *Prometheus Unbound*, the 'Ode to the West Wind' is an invocation of that Power which is the source of all activity, political as well as literary. 'Politics', as Timothy Webb asserts, 'were probably the dominating concern in Shelley's intellectual life.'[20] Although in this ode Shelley draws more heavily than in the earlier works on the forms and language of religious experience so closely connected with the ode, his own purpose remains heterodox. The Power of the wind, as Webb insists, is not 'a personal deity',[21] for all the poem's invocations of it as 'thou', but an anonymous and unknown Power. However, there is a note of unease and uncertainty in the poem's presentation of that Power which makes it not so optimistic a manifesto as its high and energetic rhetoric suggests.

The poem opens with a direct address to the wind which is sustained throughout. The impulse of the verse is towards its object as a presence, and one which is described, in Harold Bloom's terms, as a relational 'Thou'[22] from the start: 'O WILD West Wind, thou breath' (1). This apostrophe acclaims the object as present and living. 'It is especially the apostrophe,' writes Irene H. Chayes, 'which may be part of meditation or encomium, that brings together an inner state of mind and an external object and makes possible a dramatic confrontation.'[23] The element of address gives to the wind the almost objective status of a dramatic character, who enters into a form of imaginative dialogue with the speaker of the poem. However, such faith in the wind's reciprocity is matched by an equal doubt as to the means of representing the wind's communication in words. As always for Shelley, 'dramatic confrontation' with the invisible Power takes the form of an overwhelming question as to how such a Power can be imaged if it is imageless, or imagined if it is unimaginable. The language of the 'Ode to the West Wind' acts out this problem of gain and loss.

O WILD West Wind, thou breath of Autumn's being,
Thou, from whose unseen presence the leaves dead
Are driven, like ghosts from an enchanter fleeing,

Yellow, and black, and pale, and hectic red,
Pestilence-stricken multitudes: O thou,
Who chariotest to their dark wintry bed

The wingèd seeds, where they lie cold and low,
Each like a corpse within its grave, until
Thine azure sister of the Spring shall blow

Her clarion o'er the dreaming earth, and fill
(Driving sweet buds like flocks to feed in air)
With living hues and odours plain and hill:

Wild Spirit, which art moving everywhere;
Destroyer and preserver; hear, oh, hear!

(*P.W.*, pp. 577–9, lines 1–14)

The wind is hailed first as 'breath', the 'breath of Autumn's being'. Such an address personifies the wind as living from the start, but living in a special sense, for it is the life-breath of the season. This is not a pictorial allegory of Autumn, but a similitude which characteristically evades visual definition. The wind is like Autumn's 'breath' by way of a metonymical association of 'breath' with life and voice, an association which Shelley explores more fully in *Adonais*. Such an association likens the wind to a force which is life-giving and creative. The angle of the metaphor is not where we might expect; it is not in a playful visibility of things which are invisible, like Keats's Autumn 'sitting careless on a granary floor' (14).[24] Instead, the comparison centres on the connotations of breath as creative energy, and specifically that energy which makes poems. Shelley's wish to erase all pictorial reference is stressed in the next line, where the wind is described negatively as an 'unseen presence'. In the tradition of the sublime, such an adjective serves as a denial of sense perception, and as a denial, therefore, of the means by which the mind might grasp its object. Typically, Shelley uses the harsher English negative which suggests an actual *un*doing of sight. Thus in the first two lines the wind is hailed as a presence which slips the evidence of the eye, and which must therefore command some alternative relation to the poet who addresses it.

108

In contrast to the wind, however, the natural objects which it controls or enchants are strongly visible. This contrast has platonic overtones which are reminiscent of Shelley's description of the cave of Poesy in 'Mont Blanc'. There the shadowy 'Ghosts of all things that are' become visible in contrast to the dark 'breast' of the Ravine 'From which they fled'. In both passages the visible ghosts are described as fleeing from an invisible and magical presence which controls them. Significantly too, the relation between the Power and its externalised phantoms is, in both passages, a relation of enchantment, witchery or magic; terms used reluctantly and wishfully in the early transitional letters of 1810–12, where the 'enchantment' (*Letters*, 1. 119) of the natural sublime still seemed anathema to the rule of reason and empirical evidence. But in the 'Ode to the West Wind' the leaves are 'like ghosts from an enchanter fleeing', and thus in a relation to the wind which is terrifying and magical, as well as difficult to perceive. Shelley's platonic imagery is associated with a mysterious and counter-empirical creativity. The relation between cause and effect, Power and its visible manifestations, is a relation of enchantment rather than of empirical knowledge. The wind is a magician as well as a revolutionary, and thus conflates two kinds of discourse which predominate in Shelley's works: the aesthetic and the political. Although 'the deity' of this ode is certainly 'a radical one and the heaven to which it looks forward...nothing less than a social and political revolution',[25] it is also an aesthetic one, and the revolution it promises must be accomplished in the words of the poem which it inspires.

The nature of the wind is thus both mysterious and uncertain, and the struggle to identify its nature in words or metaphors ends with an invocation which re-routes its identity back towards the poem which would express it: 'Wild Spirit, which art moving everywhere; / Destroyer and preserver; hear, oh, hear!' To address the source of creativity, the west wind of inspiration, is to become self-conscious of the means of address which the poem provides. What the wind might hear has already been uttered by the poet. The plea 'hear, oh, hear!' is a plea that the utterance of the poem might be united to the original breath of the wind, in order to bring about the Promethean renovation of the world in words. Yet the very retrospective nature of the plea that the wind should hear the poet's words as its own betrays a disjunction between the two which the poet regrets. The poem searches for the nature of the wind as that breath which originates its own speech, but which is therefore lost as breath as soon as it has become speech. The revolutionary promise of the ode is accompanied by this awareness of imaginative failure in the very act of speaking.

In stanzas II and III Shelley continues his search for what the wind is like, and repeats his plea that these utterances be heard. Wasserman writes that 'the first three stanzas of the *Ode* define the domains and powers of the petitioned god by describing the wind's effect on leaf on the land, on cloud in the air, and on wave on the sea'.[26] The controversial simile in the second stanza, describing how 'Loose clouds like earth's decaying leaves are shed, / Shook from the tangled boughs of Heaven and Ocean' (16–17) and the subaqueous 'woods' (39) in the third stanza, both extend the original reference of 'the leaves dead' to these other leaves in the sky and in the sea. In each stanza it is the relation of the wind to all these leaves which is the point at issue. Furthermore, the similes which Shelley elaborates put emphasis on the verbs rather than the nouns. 'Loose clouds' are like 'decaying leaves' not in point of colour or shape or texture, but because both are 'shed'. As Harold Bloom puts it, 'Shelley does *not* necessarily compare clouds and leaves, but he *does* compare the process of shedding.'[27] To rely on the visual aspect of such imagery is to be baffled by Shelley's seemingly vague and eccentric analogies. To attempt to 'grasp' their workings as objects of sight or touch, as Leavis does, is to misunderstand the aesthetic purpose behind them. For clouds are like leaves, not in appearance but in their similar subjection to the action of the wind, which is therefore known to be one and the same Power in all its natural manifestations.[28]

In stanza III Shelley writes:

> Thou
> For whose path the Atlantic's level powers

Cleave themselves into chasms, while far below
The sea-blooms and the oozy woods which wear
The sapless foliage of the ocean, know

Thy voice, and suddenly grow gray with fear,
And tremble and despoil themselves: oh, hear!   (36–42)

The woods of the ocean experience a kind of autumn as the wind passes. Significantly, however, theirs is a collaborative act of self-destruction: they 'tremble and despoil themselves'. The influence of the wind on the natural world is described in terms of that reciprocity which the poet desires. The leaves are not only passive to the influence of the wind, but respond to it in a series of active verbs: 'wear', 'know', 'grow gray', 'tremble and despoil themselves'. This description of the underwater leaves seems to prefigure that image of poetry as the trace of the wind's footsteps in the 'Defence'. It is not only the surface of the Atlantic which cleaves into 'chasms' before the wind, but also 'far below' the passing of the wind is felt as a collaborative change of season in the 'sapless foliage'. Behind the three different descriptions of the landscapes of earth and air and sea is the reiterated 'Thou' of the wind, to which all are linked in their co-operative act of change, and to whose invisible presence all visibly bear witness. Thus the many colours of the landscapes in these three stanzas: 'Yellow', 'black', 'pale', 'hectic red', 'dark', 'azure', 'living hues', 'blue', 'bright', 'dim', 'Black', 'blue', 'crystàlline', 'azure', 'gray', all these are the various effects of the wind which is 'unseen'. The very visual rhetoric of the poem is an attempt to record and to arrest that object which is not visible and which moves 'everywhere'.

It is in stanza IV that Shelley associates the relation between wind and world with himself. He writes:

If I were a dead leaf thou mightest bear;
If I were a swift cloud to fly with thee;
A wave to pant beneath thy power, and share

The impulse of thy strength, only less free
Than thou, O uncontrollable! If even
I were as in my boyhood, and could be

The comrade of thy wanderings over Heaven,
As then, when to outstrip thy skiey speed
Scarce seemed a vision; I would ne'er have striven

As thus with thee in prayer in my sore need.
Oh, lift me as a wave, a leaf, a cloud!
I fall upon the thorns of life! I bleed!

A heavy weight of hours has chained and bowed
One too like thee: tameless, and swift, and proud.   (43–56)

The conditional tense becomes the measure of the poet's aspiration to speak, not so much of the wind but like the wind. He identifies himself with the three orders of the natural world, with the land, the sky and the sea, in a wish to share their common collaboration with the wind's energy. To be 'a dead leaf', 'a swift cloud' or a 'wave' might be to rejoice in its 'strength'. Such aspiration then leads to a Wordsworthian recollection of 'boyhood', as of a time when the natural and human worlds came so close as not to have needed the mediation of 'prayer'. As in the essay 'On Life', Shelley's desire for that perfect collusion between the self and the surrounding universe shifts into the Wordsworthian key of regret. 'If even / I were as in my boyhood' shows where the conditional tense becomes a measure not only of reach but also of loss. To be human and adult is to know the failure of aspiration and the impossibility of realising it again.

Wasserman interprets these lines as a celebration of the poet's human freedom to 'give himself to the uncontrollable, necessary workings of the Power and once again be "*as* a wave, a leaf, a cloud" – not dehumanized, but as receptive to the Power as they'.[29] He interprets the poem as an optimistic mythology, by which the indifferent Power and human will may coincide in order to effect change. This is to be predisposed in favour of the poet's aspiration, but to ignore the principle of loss which impels such aspiration. It is because the poet can no longer be as in his boyhood that he has recourse to 'prayer'. This struggle to speak, to address the wind, is born of the knowledge of something that is gone, of his 'sore need'. The very language of aspiration is thus condemned to be a substituted 'prayer' for a reality which both adulthood and the words of poetry forfeit.

Yet even here there is a kind of gain. If this substitution of the poem's words for a literal comradeship is an intimation of loss, it also represents the gain of 'prayer'. If the poet were able to share the strength of the wind as a natural object or as a child, there would be no struggle to speak: 'I would ne'er have striven / As thus with thee in prayer in my sore need.' The poem's prayer is thus directly linked with the poet's 'sore need' of inspiration. Its composition is only gained where that inspiration is lost. Thus although this stanza seems to mime the upward direction of the poet's desire to be 'a wave, a leaf, a cloud', and thus at one with the wind, such desire is predicated upon the very earthbound and human condition of the poet who speaks. This contrary gravity is then given expression in the last lines of the section. These, as Timothy Webb has argued, are 'a highly-stylised cry of despair which must be seen as the culmination of a long tradition of prophetic poetry'.[30] The Daedalian energy of the sublime ode is rarely unaccompanied by the complementary fate of Icarus. However, while it is necessary to rescue these lines from accusations of egocentricity and melodrama, it is also important to retain the sense of failure and loss which they express. The poet cannot transcend the condition of his own 'life' at the end, because it is the condition which has made the writing of his poem possible. These lines point to the similarly stylised ending of *Epipsychidion* where the poet falls explicitly by the weight of his own 'words':

> The wingèd words on which my soul would pierce
> Into the height of Love's rare Universe,
> Are chains of lead around its flight of fire –
> I pant, I sink, I tremble, I expire!
>
> (*P.W.*, pp. 411–24, lines 588–91)

This interpretation of the 'Ode to the West Wind' as a poem which is based on the paradoxical movements of the Shelleyan sublime and which comments on these in its own workings finds its clearest support in stanza v:

> Make me thy lyre, even as the forest is:
> What if my leaves are falling like its own!
> The tumult of thy mighty harmonies
>
> Will take from both a deep, autumnal tone,
> Sweet though in sadness. Be thou, Spirit fierce,
> My spirit! Be thou me, impetuous one!

113

Drive my dead thoughts over the universe
Like withered leaves to quicken a new birth!
And, by the incantation of this verse,

Scatter, as from an unextinguished hearth
Ashes and sparks, my words among mankind!
Be through my lips to unawakened earth

The trumpet of a prophecy! O, Wind,
If Winter comes, can Spring be far behind?   (57–70)

Here there is an attempt to reassert the desired identification of the poet with nature, but it is an identification now complicated by a third term: that of the lyre. The visual likeness of lyre and forest and poet is secondary to the fact of their common relation to the wind, which is a relation of collaborative sound. They each temper the 'harmonies' of the wind to 'a deep autumnal tone'. The relation of the wind to its objects is the relation of the player to the instrument, or of breath to sound, a relationship that for Shelley is perilously separate but that he always desires to make one. In 'A Defence of Poetry' Shelley refers to the common Romantic image of the lyre in a context which is pointedly anti-empirical. There he writes that

there is a principle within the human being, and perhaps within all sentient beings, which acts otherwise than in the lyre, and produces not melody, alone, but harmony, by an internal adjustment of the sounds or motions thus excited to the impressions which excite them. It is as if the lyre could accommodate its chords to the motions of that which strikes them, in a determined proportion of sound.   (VII. 109)

The mind is not passive, but actively attuned to the influence of these Humean 'impressions'. It is this attunement which provides the partial resolution of the final stanza. The poet no longer asks to be borne beyond life and poems by the wind, but asks to be able to channel the Power of the wind through his own tuned strings; through the self which proclaims its readiness to be inspired and prophetic.

This assertion of the creative self is evident in the new demand to the wind: 'Be thou, Spirit fierce, / My spirit! Be thou me, impetuous one!' The 'Spirit' of the wind is reclaimed as the 'spirit' of the poet, so that the unattainable, mysterious divinity of the poem is mirrored in man. It was during this autumn of 1819 that Shelley wrote to Leigh Hunt on the subject of his *Nymphs* and *Story of Rimini* in language which identifies this secondary 'spirit' as the 'Imagination' (*Letters*, II. 152). As in all the earlier poems which play upon Shelley's sceptical version of the sublime, it is the imagination which alone mirrors the unknown Power, but ambiguously. For although 'spirit' reflects 'Spirit', the poet's desire to make them the same still acknowledges their difference. Such ambiguity is present in the overtly political exhortation of the 'Ode to Liberty', which was also published in the 1820 volume. There the liberating upward flight of the poet's song:

> My soul spurned the chains of its dismay,
> And in the rapid plumes of song
> Clothed itself, sublime and strong...
>
> (P.W., pp. 603–10, lines 5–7)

leads to the revolutionary imagining of a world in which

> human thoughts might kneel alone,
> Each before the judgement-throne
> Of its own aweless soul, or of the Power unknown! (231–3)

The juxtaposition of these last alternatives fails to resolve the problem of the relationship between the inner 'soul' and 'the Power unknown'. The two are yoked together, but are also kept apart by the choice they represent. As in the 'Ode to the West Wind', the Power that governs the aesthetic and political universe of man's 'thoughts' cannot be definitively placed either within or without the human mind. The poet's plea to the wind to be his own 'spirit', therefore, springs from the difference which, so often in Shelley's work, makes the former remote and inaccessible.

This last stanza also contains a poetic restatement of the divorce of inspiration and skill which besets the very writing of the poem. The spirit of the wind is still divided from the letter of the poem: from the 'dead thoughts' which are like 'withered leaves', from the incantated 'verse', and from the 'words' which are as 'Ashes and sparks'. The 'social and political revolution'[31] to which the poem incites is based on a typically Shelleyan politics, which is a politics not of action but of writing. All the autumnal leaves of the poem are now related to these literary 'leaves', which might rekindle from an 'invisible influence, like an inconstant wind' (VII. 135), the flame of revolutionary change. The words of the poem are the incendiary material, 'Ashes and sparks', from which the wind of inspiration might make fire. The 'Ode to the West Wind' ends by substituting for the passionate and unmediated collaboration of wind and world, or wind and child, the mediating poem. Such 'verse' is merely an 'incantation', a word that suggests the 'spell' of a language which is broken from its living source. Both the poet's 'thoughts' and his 'words' are dead. Yet, what the adult poet knows is that the wind is nothing now, if not mediated through his 'lips' and expressed in his 'words'. The religious address of the 'Ode to the West Wind' plays anxiously upon the fact that the wind cannot be gained until it is lost in words.

It is in 'To a Skylark' that Shelley elaborates even more self-consciously the problem of addressing a numinous presence in the language of poetry. This poem most effectively corroborates Davie's criticism that 'Shelley goes as far as poetry can go...in cutting the hawsers which tie his fancies to the ground.' The poem's fancy, the skylark, remains brilliantly ungrounded. It is perhaps this dissociation of the bird from the rhetoric of the poem which prompts Leavis' predictably adverse criticism. He writes of Shelley that 'being inspired was, for him, too apt to mean surrendering to a kind of hypnotic rote of favourite images, associations and words'.[32] As a value judgement, this is based on an assumption about Shelley's methods of composition which Leavis has derived from the effect of hypnosis which the poem creates. The poem is not carelessly inspired, but it is about Shelley's theory of inspiration. Leavis' objection that 'the poem is a mere tumbled out spate ("spontaneous overflow") of poeticalities, the place of each one of which Shelley could have filled with another without the least difficulty and without making any essential difference'[33] is an evaluation which assumes an ease and indifference about composition for which he has no grounds, as concerns either Wordsworth or Shelley. Instead, it could be said that the effect of 'a mere tumbled out spate' is precisely what a lark's song requires. As Judith Chernaik suggests, there is 'a conscious imitation of the pure spontaneity that the bird's song represents'.[34] This skilful imitation extends even to the subtle form of the stanzas, the first four lines of which 'shift from two to three real stresses, and from masculine to feminine rhyme, with all the agility of the bird they celebrate'.[35]

This ode is in fact a conscious and skilful expression of that divided aesthetic which is the ruling motif of so much of Shelley's work. Far from being the 'tumbled' statement of a certain kind of Victorian Romanticism, 'To a Skylark' is a vitally metaphorical description of the bird in terms of the reach and limits of metaphor. While the 'Ode to the West Wind' desires the presence of the wind mainly by way of urgent apostrophes, 'To a Skylark' seeks to approach the nature of the bird by a succession of likenesses, each giving way to the next. The effect of rush is not due to a carelessness in composition, but to this self-denying quality of the language, which places the bird always just beyond the reach of what it is like.

In his 'Memoirs of Percy Bysshe Shelley', Peacock quotes the first and fourth verses of Wordsworth's poem 'To the Cuckoo', and writes that 'Shelley was fond of repeating these verses, and perhaps they were not forgotten in his poem *To a Skylark*.'[36] Wordsworth's poem was no doubt very much in Shelley's mind at the time of composing his own. Both poems require what Martin Price has called a 'dissolution of the visible in the audible'.[37] 'No bird, but an invisible thing, / A voice, a mystery' (15–16)[38] writes Wordsworth, and Shelley similarly claims, 'Thou art unseen, but yet I hear thy shrill delight' (*P.W.*, pp. 602–3, line 20). But the two poems are also significantly different. Wordsworth turns the invisibility of the bird into moral and philosophical abstractions: it is a 'voice, a mystery' (16) or later 'a hope, a love' (23). Shelley's poem by contrast is full of pictures which are like the bird but none of which definitively holds it.

From the start, the skylark is greeted as no bird, but some unnamed force that is expressed in song:

HAIL to thee, blithe Spirit!
  Bird thou never wert,
That from Heaven, or near it,
  Pourest thy full heart
In profuse strains of unpremeditated art.

Higher still and higher
  From the earth thou springest
Like a cloud of fire;
  The blue deep thou wingest,
And singing still dost soar, and soaring ever singest.   (1–10)

The instantaneous and heartfelt song of the bird is without pre-meditation or skill. The bird is thus the sublime poet *par excellence;* one who expresses 'the natural dictates of the heart, not fictitious or copied, but original',[39] where originality serves as the antithesis of that creative delay occasioned by the human poet's recourse to skill or imitation. In Shelley's terms the bird represents that simultaneity of voice and utterance, voice and action, which is the ideal of the Promethean poet. The bird's 'full heart' translates without delay into 'unpremeditated art', and the bird's 'singing' is simultaneous with 'soaring'. However, the poem is not really about the bird, but about the poet who addresses it. From the start, this bird is in retreat from the speaker, flying 'Higher still and higher', and thus mapping out its distance from the poet on the ground. This is the space that confronted the poet of the 'Hymn to Intellectual Beauty' and 'Mont Blanc' and which Asia alone in *Prometheus Unbound* has crossed. The distance between the bird and the poet is the distance between vision and expression, between inspiration and writing, which the poet's attempt to write only makes more acute.

As in the 'Ode to the West Wind' the unseen nature of the bird is described in language that is highly visual. Shelley writes:

In the golden lightning
  Of the sunken sun,
O'er which clouds are bright'ning,
  Thou dost float and run;
Like an unbodied joy whose race is just begun.

The pale purple even
  Melts around thy flight;

118

> Like a star of Heaven,
> In the broad daylight
> Thou art unseen, but yet I hear thy shrill delight,
>
> Keen as are the arrows
> Of that silver sphere,
> Whose intense lamp narrows
> In the white dawn clear
> Until we hardly see — we feel that it is there.　　(11–25)

It is as if the poet were constructing a series of pictures in which to contain the bird; as if to frame it in these beautiful settings of late afternoon, evening and dawn were to arrest its flight. But these are like pictures from which something is always missing. In contrast to the visual and colourful nature of the scenes, the bird remains 'unbodied'. It is imagined against the 'blue deep', 'the golden lightning' of sunset, 'bright'ning' clouds, 'pale purple even', but it is imagined as something devoid of shape or colour. Typically the landscape of the poem, even in its visual abundance, is privative. The skylark is 'Like a star of Heaven' only when 'broad daylight' eclipses both. The comparison works, not by way of the traditional associations of a star, but by way of its visual absence: it is 'unseen'. It is as if, despite the visual superfluity of these stanzas, the poet desires to see less. Thus in the fifth stanza the bird's song is compared to a gradual narrowing and disappearance of the visible object. The 'silver sphere' of star or moon vanishes in the 'white dawn', and only by vanishing from sight becomes known as feeling. By rejecting any visual manifestation of the bird in the natural world, Shelley revises the source of Coleridge's dejection in that ode,[40] and affirms that 'we hardly see — we feel that it is there'.

However, to feel the bird as a source of creativity is not necessarily to be able to represent it in words, and it is this secondary activity of writing which threatens an aesthetic of unpremeditated inspiration with failure. In subsequent stanzas the problem of writing about the bird comes to the fore:

> What thou art we know not;
> What is most like thee?
> From rainbow clouds there flow not

> Drops so bright to see
> As from thy presence showers a rain of melody. (31–5)

The poet's imaginative relationship to the bird is assessed by images of what is 'most like' it. But as so often in Shelley's metaphors, the similarity is hard to find. Here, the bird's song is like 'Drops so bright to see', as if iconographically visible. But such visibility is deceptive. Finally, it is not the appearance or the sound of the lark's song which is like bright rain, but its profusion, for both song and rain flow abundantly from their hidden source. The bird itself remains hidden to the gaze, and is known only by the song which emanates from it.

It is this hiddenness which lies behind all the similes of the bird that follow:

> Like a Poet hidden
> In the light of thought,
> Singing hymns unbidden,
> Till the world is wrought
> To sympathy with hopes and fears it heeded not:
>
> Like a high-born maiden
> In a palace-tower,
> Soothing her love-laden
> Soul in secret hour
> With music sweet as love, which overflows her bower:
>
> Like a glow-worm golden
> In a dell of dew,
> Scattering unbeholden
> Its aëreal hue
> Among the flowers and grass, which screen it from the view!
>
> Likes a rose embowered
> In its own green leaves,
> By warm winds deflowered,
> Till the scent it gives
> Makes faint with too much sweet those heavy-wingèd thieves...
>
> (36–55)

In the first of these verses there is a characteristic inversion of roles. The poet hopes to sing like the skylark which sings 'Like a Poet'. This idealisation of the Poet, as one hidden by the sheer force of his enlightened thought, represents the presence of imaginative Power to which the 'unbidden' hymns bear witness. The inversion is reminiscent of Shelley's statement to Peacock that 'Nature was the poet whose harmony held our spirits more breathless than that of the divinest' (*Letters*, 1. 497). The ode addresses the bird as the source of creativity of which Shelley's own is a strenuous imitation. The similes which follow all repeat this preoccupying theme of effective and superabundant self-expression. Thus the music of the maiden 'overflows', the glow-worm is 'Scattering' its hue and the rose 'gives' out its overpowering scent. In each case the hiddenness of the subject, which is 'secret', 'unbeholden', 'embowered', is accompanied by unhindered profusion in the verb. 'The poem's central image', writes Harold Bloom, 'is of an abundance of joy and song so great that it must *overflow*.'[41] The bird's expression is one which occurs at the heart's bidding, without that delay which would force the poet to differentiate the bird from the song. As a result, it is described as a secret origin which coincides with the moment of song. The series of similes which describe the bird in these stanzas present it as at once unseen and self-expressive, hidden and outflowing, as at once the origin and the embodiment of song. The skylark stands for that eclipse of the Poet in his hymns which is the sign of a sublime and revolutionary poetry.

However, although Shelley addresses this ideal in 'To a Skylark', the address itself shows where the ideal fails. In the thirteenth stanza Shelley ceases to accumulate images of what the bird is like, and instead contrasts the lark's outpouring with faulty human song:

> Teach us, Sprite or Bird,
> What sweet thoughts are thine:
> I have never heard
> Praise of love or wine
> That panted forth a flood of rapture so divine.
>
> Chorus Hymeneal,
> Or triumphal chant
> Matched with thine would be all
> But an empty vaunt,
> A thing wherein we feel there is some hidden want. (61–70)

To compare the bird's song with human creativity is to find the second sadly wanting. There is a flaw or 'hidden want' in the poetry of the world which makes it empty by comparison to the lark's. This emphasis on the insufficiency of human poetry not only expresses its general failure to match the expressiveness of the bird, but also marks the failure of this particular poem to achieve its object. 'To a Skylark' is an address to the bird which is all the more urgent for feeling this 'hidden want'. It might be said that the poem wants the very object of which it speaks. In his biography *Shelley: The Pursuit*, Richard Holmes dismisses the poem as sentimental, because written at a time of 'nagging domestic difficulties'. The sentimentality seems to him to lie in 'the idea of escape into a world of immortal and effortless creativity'.[42] But the point about 'To a Skylark' is that such an escape is impossible. The poet remains on the ground, matching human art to the 'flood of rapture' which only the bird can show. The idea of escape is lost in the very act of writing. Unlike the bird, the poet knows the disjunction between the source of his inspiration, the lark, and the skilful composition of his poem about it. He does not escape with the bird, but knows instead the absences and contradictions that flaw human art.

It is, therefore, to this sad music of humanity that the poem turns in its last stanzas. It turns to an art that is earth-bound in its emotional contradictions and frustrated aspiration:

> We look before and after,
>   And pine for what is not:
> Our sincerest laughter
>   With some pain is fraught;
> Our sweetest songs are those that tell of saddest thought.
>
> Yet if we could scorn
>   Hate, and pride, and fear;
> If we were things born
>   Not to shed a tear,
> I know not how thy joy we ever should come near.   (86–95)

The lines imply that the distance between bird and poet remains uncrossed, and that the object of the poem's address remains beyond human reach: 'I know not how thy joy we ever should come near.' Judith Chernaik writes that the lyric as a whole represents Shelley's 'consummate poetic rendering of the power of joy'.[43] But it is difficult to read these lines in such a way. Instead, they seem to express the loss of that joy as well as the poignant complexity of human life and art which such a loss only makes more dear: 'Our sweetest songs are those that tell of saddest thought.' It is not perhaps strange that some of the most beautiful lines of the poem are these of regret and failure at the end. Shelley employs the counter-gravity of the sublime ode here to express that failure which is the very condition of writing. To write with art is to lose that creativity which alone belongs to nature. Yet, paradoxically, to write is the only means of saving nature from its own exalted inexpressibility. Shelley's poem both loses and saves the song of the lark.

Shelley's last address to the bird does not collapse the distance between bird and poet, between the 'blithe Spirit' and the man, between natural inspiration and human skill, but it does contain a note of characteristically Shelleyan prophetic hope. At the end, the poet asks:

> Teach me half the gladness
>   That thy brain must know,
> Such harmonious madness
>   From my lips would flow
> The world should listen then – as I am listening now.   (101–5)

This learned 'gladness' might, proleptically, bring about a transference of Power from the bird to the poet. If this transference could be effected, the poet would stand in the same relation to the world as the bird stands to him: the relation of speaker to audience. 'All was as much our own as if we had been the creators of such impressions in the minds of others, as now occupied our own' (*Letters*, 1. 497), Shelley wrote in 1816 concerning the effect of the landscape of the Alps. In 'To a Skylark' he is affirming that same doubling of roles, but in a tentative and prophetic future conditional tense.

Yet, although the ideal seems to be posited after the end of the poem, after the last 'now', in fact that ideal either has or has not been achieved in the song which is finished. The poem seems to be posing as prolegomena to another speech: 'The world should listen then,' but its real reference is retrospective and reinforces that desire of the poet's that his own words be as inspired as the song of the lark. Whether the poem has achieved that objective is the question it finally asks.

In both the 'Ode to the West Wind' and 'To a Skylark' Shelley is employing the mode of address to explore the distance between heaven and earth, inspiration and composition, which lies at the heart of his aesthetic of poetry. To resolve that distance is to achieve the language of simultaneous feeling and expression, which is the language of revolutionary change. However, in these two odes the distance between the poet and the wind or the poet and the skylark is one which cannot be crossed, but which remains as a flaw in the very writing of the poem. The revolutionary optimism of *Prometheus Unbound* has abated somewhat, and in its place Shelley laments the fallen nature of human song, which seeks to match its ideal but is always saddened by a 'hidden want'. It is this sense of something wanting which predominates in the poetry written after 1820 and which emphasises that aspect of Shelley's version of the sublime which makes it so often an aesthetic of imaginative despair and loss.

6

SHELLEY'S LEISURE FOR FICTION: *ADONAIS*

In the 'Ode to the West Wind' and 'To a Skylark' Shelley emphasises the distance and delay which his aesthetic of inspiration contains. To seek to translate the inspiration of wind into composition is to know that nature's voices are different from man's writing. By addressing the wind or bird the poet substitutes his own writing for their inspirational energy, and implicitly loses the object he would gain. As A. E. Powell points out, the 'poetic moment' for Shelley is uncompromisingly 'the moment of vision'.[1] But vision cannot be made into poems without loss, and after the radical hopefulness of *Prometheus Unbound* Shelley's poetry becomes progressively more conscious of this loss. *Adonais*, Shelley's elegy for the dead Keats, is the poem which most brilliantly and intricately plays upon the theme of loss as one appropriate both to the subject matter of which he writes and to the act of writing itself.

It was in March 1821 that Shelley sent his publisher Ollier the first part of 'A Defence of Poetry', which was the only part he finished. Three months later he was engaged in the composition of his elegy on the death of Keats. The theme of loss which underlies Shelley's aesthetic of inspiration as it is expounded in the 'Defence' also underlies the composition of *Adonais*. This is a poem which laments the loss of Keats, but which expresses that loss in terms of the lost voice or breath that first created poems. Such creativity is therefore not only Keats's but Shelley's own. The meaning of Keats's death is closely linked to the death of grief and the death of inspiration which mark the writing of this poem. Keats stands to the poet in the same relation as did the west wind and the skylark. But in *Adonais* there is a concentration

125

on the theme of loss which makes it, even more than the two odes, a poem conscious of its own writing as a form of defeat.

In 'A Defence of Poetry' Shelley wrote that 'when composition begins, inspiration is already on the decline, and the most glorious poetry that has ever been communicated to the world is probably a feeble shadow of the original conception of the Poet' (VII. 135). In *Adonais* the problem of human loss and human sorrow is linked to the problem of composition as an impoverished rhetoric. Shelley's elegy admits the fact that to write is to forgo the real nature of grief. Samuel Johnson points to this dilemma facing the elegist in his famous criticism of *Lycidas*, of which, he complains, 'the diction is harsh, the rhymes uncertain, and the numbers unpleasing'. The main force of his criticism, however, is not technical but moral. The poem, he adds, 'is not to be considered as the effusion of real passion; for passion runs not after remote allusions and obscure opinions'. Altogether, his condemnation of *Lycidas* as an over-elaborate and abstruse piece of writing depends on his dictum: ' "Where there is leisure for fiction there is little grief." '[2] Johnson condemns *Lycidas* for the reason that its complex rhetoric is dishonest, because to write a 'fiction' is necessarily to have ceased to grieve. The statement highlights a recurrent preoccupation and paradox of elegiac poetry. The poet is forced to consider how the contrived and leisured work of art can recapture the natural impulse of grief. The very form of the elegy, in a long tradition that stems from the elegies of Bion and Moschus which Shelley knew well, is based on certain mythological and rhetorical conventions, and yet the elegy is also expressive of the personal feelings and circumstances of the individual poet. It is both a highly formal, traditional genre and one which expresses a strong emotional commitment to the subject. The elegist is both mourner and poet, both grief-stricken and able to compose. He must have both ' "grief" ' and ' "leisure for fiction" '.

However, it is a characteristic of eighteenth-century aesthetics to oppose these two in a scale of values which credits feeling above art, original genius above imitative skill, vision above writing. The aim of such an aesthetic is to reunite the two, while still preserving their different status. The paradox inherent in this theoretical enterprise is revealed by Lowth in his *Lectures on the Sacred Poetry of the Hebrews*, where he writes of biblical elegiac writings: 'As in all other arts, so in this, perfection consisted in the exact imitation of nature.' He adds that 'funeral dirges were therefore composed in general upon the model of those complaints which flow naturally and spontaneously from the afflicted heart: the sentences were abrupt, mournful, pathetic, simple, and un-embellished; on one account, indeed, more elaborate and artificial, because they consisted of verse, and were chanted to music'.[3] Lowth starts from the same premise as Johnson, that the more simple the language of a dirge the more it is like the first language of 'the afflicted heart'. However, he admits a complication in this ideal scheme. While, on the one hand, these dirges are modelled on the natural, spontaneous and heartfelt utterances of the mourner, on the other hand, their very artistic nature, the fact that they consist of 'verse' and 'music', makes them 'elaborate and artificial'. Thus he admits that, while the aim of the elegy must be to re-enact that spontaneity and to recapture the natural voice of grief, its very artistic form presents a loss of naturalness and a loss of spontaneous sorrow. To write with art always risks losing the voice of true affliction.

The difference between grief and its poetic representation is one which often turns upon the underlying opposition of speech and writing. The difference between the two is stressed throughout the eighteenth century, and is also one of the central metaphors of *Adonais*. In *A Course of Lectures on the Theory of Language and Universal Grammar* (1762), Joseph Priestley states that in general 'writing...is but a substitute for the art of speaking; and, where both can be used, vastly inferior to it'.[4] The reason for this inferiority is that truth lies, as Jacques Derrida has often pointed out, in proximity to consciousness.[5] The nature of this proximity is described by Hugh Blair, in the *Lectures on Rhetoric and Belles Lettres* (1783), where he writes that 'spoken Language has a great superiority over written Language, in point of energy or force. The voice of the living Speaker, makes an impression on the mind, much stronger than can be made by the perusal of any Writing... For tones, looks, and gestures, are natural interpreters of the sentiments of the mind.'[6] Such superiority of the voice over its representation in writing brings into play a platonic opposition between something living and something dead. It is 'the living Speaker' who most truly expresses 'the sentiments of the mind'. This characteristic of the speaker is then transferred to the language which he speaks.

In his massive and ambitious work *Of the Origin and Progress of Language* (1773–92), which Shelley knew, Monboddo writes: 'Speaking, therefore, may be said to be language *living*; whereas writing is nothing but the *dead* letter, and only a secondary art dependent upon speaking.'[7] This description is linked to other platonic dualisms by which Monboddo divides discourse into soul and body, 'formal' and 'material'.[8] He distinguishes language which is invisible, spiritual and living, from language which is material and dead. The latter must model itself upon the former, but how a dead language can come back to life is never made clear. The opposition is so absolute as to seem irresolvable. Written language is always death to that speech upon which it is nonetheless 'dependent'. According to Derrida, such oppositions contain a denial of the very metaphysics which they seem to affirm. 'We are dispossessed of the longed-for presence in the gesture of language by which we attempt to seize it,'[9] he writes of Rousseau's similar formulations. To proclaim a difference between language living and dead, between speech and writing, is to create a model for poetry which is contradictory, and which dooms it to be always a dead letter. However, such a model also provides the elegist with a formalistic extension of the themes of life and death which are the main content of his poetry. To be living or dead is a quality of language as well as a matter of fact.

In 'A Defence of Poetry' Shelley wrote that all kinds of artistic and political systems of representation 'may be called poetry by that figure of speech which considers the effect as a synonyme of the cause', but adds that 'poetry in a more restricted sense expresses those arrangements of language, and especially metrical language, which are created by that imperial faculty, whose throne is curtained within the invisible nature of man' (VII. 113). In *Adonais* he is still concerned with the relationship between 'metrical language' and 'that imperial faculty' of imagination, but because the poem is an elegy the relationship is also one between a dead writing and a living grief. The question which preoccupies Shelley in *Adonais* is the question of how far the artificial text of a poem can speak like one who truly mourns. It is a question very much concerned with rhetoric, and with the cost, in terms of living grief, of writing at all.

It is interesting to notice how often Shelley's references to the poem in his letters emphasise its artificiality and his own ignorance of the actual events of Keats's death. He writes to the Gisbornes that *Adonais* 'is a highly wrought *piece of art*' (*Letters*, II. 294). Three days later, having completed at least forty stanzas of the poem, he writes to Ollier, 'I could wish that you inquired of some of the friends and relations of Keats respecting the circumstances of his death, and could transmit me any information you may be able to collect' (*Letters*, II. 297). Having received such information a few days later, Shelley writes to John Gisborne, 'I do not think that if I had seen it before that I could have composed my poem – the enthusiasm of the imagination would have been over-powered by sentiment' (*Letters*, II. 299–300). Far from expressing the poet's overpowering 'sentiment', *Adonais* is one of his most consciously rhetorical and stylised poems. It is emphatically a '*piece of art*', and although written, in the true spirit of the sublime, from 'the enthusiasm of the imagination', this motivation is different from the emotion Shelley felt at knowing some of the actual facts about Keats's death. These, far from inspiring a poem, would have incapacitated him from writing altogether. Furthermore, what these letters make clear, is that the actual composition of the poem took place in psychological detachment from the event of which it tells. Shelley asks for information almost as an afterthought, having already written much of the poem. It takes shape, therefore, not from a close involvement in the tragedy of Keats's death, but from a kind of ' "leisure" ' for grief.

It is the self-conscious and stylised rhetorical patterning of *Adonais* which brings into relief the central dilemma of the elegist: the dilemma of how to write truthfully about death and grief in ' "fiction" '. The feelings which attend the writing of this work for a fellow poet are mediated through the ornate and 'highly wrought' conventions of pastoral elegy; through a genre which brings into play certain established topoi of mourning drawn from classical mythology, as well as a host of classical personifications. *Adonais* is based on a tradition of elegiac writing which has already been shaped by many poets and most importantly for Shelley by Bion and Moschus, Milton, Pope and the seventeenth-century Italian poet Giambattista Marino, whose *Adone* was certainly known to him.[10]

From the start, *Adonais* echoes the formulaic phrases of the pastoral elegy:

> I WEEP for Adonais – he is dead!
> O, weep for Adonais! though our tears
> Thaw not the frost which binds so dear a head!   (1–3)

The verb which characterises the poet's special activity is rhetorically decorous and mannered. To 'weep' is an elegiac formula which is distanced from its literal meaning. It refers back to the living language of the heart, but in fact describes the task of writing on which the poet has embarked. Like Milton's 'Who would not sing for Lycidas?' (10),[11] the formula 'I WEEP' is metonymic for the poet's real activity, which is not to give voice to his grief either in weeping or in song, but to write that grief in silent words on the page. It is precisely because this poet no longer weeps, or, as revealed by Shelley's late request for information in the letters, has not yet begun to weep, that he can write such careful stanzas. These formulaic first lines of the poem express a ' "leisure for fiction" ' which is in antithesis to their claim to represent weeping. Yet, the purpose of this elegiac formula is also to refer back to the passion which is spent in writing. Shelley seeks to recapture in this 'highly wrought' figure the sound of a lament that might have flown, in Lowth's words, 'naturally and spontaneously from the afflicted heart'. Thus the phrases 'I WEEP' 'O, weep' suggest at the start the ambiguous claims of elegiac poetry, which are to contrive a verbal fiction, but also to undermine it; to give expression to grief, but also to disturb expression by reference to grief that is inexpressible. The verb 'I WEEP' introduces the poet's task of writing, even while it implies an inability to write coherently or effectively.

The figure is taken up again in stanza III:

> Oh, weep for Adonais – he is dead!
> Wake, melancholy Mother, wake and weep!
> Yet wherefore? Quench within their burning bed
> Thy fiery tears, and let thy loud heart keep
> Like his, a mute and uncomplaining sleep;
> For he is gone, where all things wise and fair
> Descend; – oh, dream not that the amorous Deep
> Will yet restore him to the vital air;
>   Death feeds on his mute voice, and laughs at our despair. (19–27)

The stanza contains first a command to weep and then a command to keep silence. It presents the dilemma of the poet who would express his grief and yet knows that the silence of the 'loud heart' is more in keeping with the event of death: 'let thy loud heart keep / Like his, a mute and uncomplaining sleep'. The repeated injunction to 'weep' is revoked, in order that the mourning song might be more attuned to the state of the dead poet: both 'mute'. The word brilliantly suggests a kind of silence which is not peace, but a stifling of the human voice. The passage subtly associates the mourner and the mourned, Shelley and Keats, in a muteness which is more honestly sorrowful in the case of the one, although deathly in the case of the other. Its objective is thus the objective of the whole poem, which is to make known, behind the persistent speech of the work, the presence of two voices which are without speech. The voice of Keats is 'mute' in death, and thus divorced from the poems of which it was the source, while the voice of his mourner should be 'mute' also, in order to preserve the authentic language of the 'loud heart'. Thus the voices of the two poets are linked, not sentimentally and self-indulgently on Shelley's part, but as one of the main thematic and rhetorical concerns of the poem. This linking lies at the heart of *Adonais*. The poem is concerned with the twin problems of how to recapture the voice of the dead as a living and eternal force, and how to recapture the 'language *living*' of the heart in 'the *dead* letter' of the poem.

This association is made more pronounced by the presence of Urania in place of the traditional Venus, the mother instead of the lover of Adonais. As Wasserman points out, in an earlier draft of stanza IV Shelley invokes 'not Urania, but Poesy',[12] so that, as well as representing 'the earth-mother',[13] she also represents the poetic muse. As such she stands in the same relation to Shelley as to Keats. In a letter to Peacock of some few months before, Shelley describes his intention of replying to 'The Four Ages of Poetry' in terms of 'vindicating the insulted Muses'. He adds that 'I had the greatest possible desire to break a lance with you, within the lists of a magazine, in honour of my mistress Urania' (*Letters*, II. 261). Thus the 'melancholy Mother' who must wake to weep for the death of Keats is both the life-giving force of the man and the inspiratory force of the poet. Shelley's call to her to 'wake and weep' is not only part of the mythological narrative, but also a formula of invocation to his own muse. There is a confusion between the narrative events of life and death and the aesthetic implications of those events for the composition of Shelley's own poem. The question whether Urania should weep or restrain her weeping is one which bears directly on the writing of his elegy.

Thus stanza III expresses as a mythological event the dilemma which besets the elegist. It is significant that after the revocation of weeping in the third line, the language becomes highly figurative and ceremonial. The paradoxical action of 'Quench', as if tears were like fire or thirst, the courtly juxtapositions of 'burning bed' and 'fiery tears', the metonymy 'loud heart' for sorrow which is both expressive and yet inexpressible; all these are in fact a command to keep a more honest silence. Thus, although the first injunctions to weep are revoked, the alternative silence is described in this rich and exaggerated rhetoric. Far from acceding to Johnson's definition of elegy as a 'short poem without points or turns',[14] Shelley's poem, even in its call for silence, remains highly elaborate and figurative. It is as if by the very obtrusiveness of the rhetoric at this point Shelley seeks to distance from language the inexpressible facts of real death and real sorrow: those two kinds of muteness which the stanza desires but necessarily denies.

The identification of mother and muse, of the force which gives life and the force which inspires poetry, recurs in various figurative patterns throughout the poem. One of the most important of these, which is foreshadowed in the 'Ode to the West Wind', is the play upon the word 'breath'. In stanza VII Shelley writes:

> To that high Capital, where kingly Death
> Keeps his pale court in beauty and decay,
> He came; and bought, with price of purest breath,
> A grave among the eternal. (55–8)

The luridly personified description of Death is followed by two lines of strangely beautiful figurativeness. By contrast to the too physical and literal confusion of 'beauty and decay' in the court of Death, the death of Keats is described quite differently: he 'bought, with price of purest breath, / A grave among the eternal'. The effect of the active verb 'bought' is to imply a mere exchange of 'breath' for a 'grave', a willed transaction which buys death for life, but leaves the subject intact.

However, while breath traditionally represents life itself, by way of an almost completely submerged metaphor, 'purest breath' here also means inspiration, that breath from without which the word etymologically contains. This is the breath that bears the voice of song. Breath gives life both to the body and to the body of the poet's verse. Shelley is saying two things at once, by a characteristic conflation of the two themes of death and writing. Keats spent his last 'breath' to buy a 'grave', but Keats also spent the breath of poetic inspiration to buy a 'grave among the eternal'. To lose the life-breath is to die, but to lose the breath of poetic inspiration is to create poetry which entitles Keats to a kind of immortality. The 'funeral elegist', Milton Wilson points out, 'will concern himself with possible consolations or compensations as well as with the loss itself'.[15] The traditional compensation for the poet, which Shelley invokes here, is that of immortal fame. However, what this elegy cannot ignore is that such fame is bought at the cost of life, as well as at the cost of writing any more. If Shelley identifies the breath of life and the breath of inspiration, the problem which he must still face is that both have been spent. In *Adonais* the problem of literal and imaginative loss is greater than its 'possible consolations or compensations'.

It is particularly in the poem's use of personification that this paradox of gain and loss is played out. This characteristic rhetorical strategy of the sublime, which the young Shelley condemned as one of the main supports of a superstitious orthodoxy when he wrote that 'were it not for this embodying quality of eccentric fancy we should be to this day without a God' (*Letters*, I. 101), but which the maturer poet continued to employ, tentatively and distrustfully, in his invocations of the mysterious Power of the universe; this strategy of personification becomes, in *Adonais*, at times grotesquely overworked. The poem is full of lurid presences, which often have little mythological and narrative importance, but which seem to be purely for rhetorical effect, as if advertising their own artificiality. This feature of *Adonais* may be in part attributed to the tradition of pastoral elegy within which Shelley is working, and perhaps in particular to Marino's ingenious and conceited treatment of the same mythological subject in *Adone*.

However, I suggest that the sheer profusion of what are verbal and not metaphysical or narrative personifications in *Adonais* is very much part of Shelley's purpose in this poem. It is as if he needs to polarise as far as possible the literal event and the rhetorical elaborations of death. In stanza VIII, for instance, he writes:

> Within the twilight chamber spreads apace
> The shadow of white Death, and at the door
> Invisible Corruption waits to trace
> His extreme way to her dim dwelling-place;
> The eternal Hunger sits, but pity and awe
> Soothe her pale rage... (65–70)

Such piling up of personified abstractions expresses little more than the poet's own somewhat distracting ingenuity. It is precisely this kind of personification which Wordsworth rejected in the Preface to *Lyrical Ballads* as being merely 'a mechanical device of style'.[16] Yet, if the effect of these contrived presences is to divert attention from the death of Keats and the grief of his elegist to the mere playfulness of poetic language, this might be interpreted as part of Shelley's purpose.

The more subdued and more successful personifications of the following stanza seem to point to this deliberate break between the rhetorical effect of words and the object they would express. Shelley writes:

> Oh, weep for Adonais! – The quick Dreams,
> The passion-wingèd Ministers of thought,
> Who were his flocks, whom near the living streams
> Of his young spirit he fed, and whom he taught
> The love which was its music, wander not, –
> Wander no more, from kindling brain to brain,
> But droop there, whence they sprung; and mourn their lot
> Round the cold heart, where, after their sweet pain,
> They ne'er will gather strength, or find a home again. (73–81)

This is the characteristic language of pastoral elegy. But these 'quick Dreams' and 'Ministers of thought' which Shelley personifies are no more substantial than a strategy of what he once condemned as 'eccentric fancy'. Their nature is a fiction, and lasts only as long as willing belief can sustain it. They belong entirely to the elegist's imagination, and have no grounding in any literal or metaphysical presence. Like the Phantasm of Jupiter in *Prometheus Unbound*, they are externalisations of Keats's mind which have become totally separated from it, and are therefore empty speakers. Theirs is a dead language because cut off from 'the living streams / Of his young spirit'. It is a language broken from its origin as from its life-force. It is this very break which Shelley's own language enacts, by presenting these personified dreams and thoughts as merely verbal substances. Their quality of being mechanical devices of style is precisely the point. Even while these personifications seem actively to 'droop' and 'mourn', their reality is being negated by the fact that the 'heart' which expressed them is 'cold'. The delay between heartfelt inspiration and its external expression is a sign, in *Adonais*, of death. That 'Dreams' or 'thought' may linger to mourn the 'young spirit' who dreamed or thought them is a fantastic artifice; a mere virtuosity of language which, for a short while, resists the void.

The rhetorical fictionalising continues in stanza x, where a 'Dream' appears to speak:

> And one with trembling hands clasps his cold head,
> And fans him with her moonlight wings, and cries;
> 'Our love, our hope, our sorrow, is not dead;
> See, on the silken fringe of his faint eyes,
> Like dew upon a sleeping flower, there lies
> A tear some Dream has loosened from his brain.'
> Lost Angel of a ruined Paradise!
> She knew not 'twas her own; as with no stain
> She faded, like a cloud which had outwept its rain.　　(82–90)

The personification and the imagined direct speech create a sense of animation which is soon, however, shown to be a deception. The Dream does not weep, but is herself the tear. In contrast to the no-time of death, the passage creates an artificial delay, which is a brief moment's grace for the Dream to speak even after the brain is dreamless. But this delay is the product of an impossible desire that ' "Our love, our hope, our sorrow, is not dead." ' It is only this desire which creates the fiction of a still living Dream, and Shelley stresses that it *is* a fiction, thus creating the condition for its dissolution: 'She faded, like a cloud which had outwept its rain.' The Dream was an imaginary personification, a poetic artifice, which cannot survive beyond the death of the poet except as a form of empty rhetoric. Such rhetoric confesses its own elaborations and distortions of the event. Yet, it is a tribute to the peculiar texture of *Adonais* that its rhetoric moves precisely because it admits such emptiness.

It is this effect of deliberate contrivance which characterises the many brief personifications of the poem. These often derive from the traditional topoi of mourning in pastoral elegy: from those Loves and Graces in Bion and Moschus who cut their locks or break their arrows. Elsewhere, they are mere voices of the landscape which seem to echo the poet's lament. 'The choir of nature, divided into many voices, fills space around the poet with the volume of its sound,'[17] writes E. R. Curtius of the later Greek elegy. The many personifications of Shelley's poem: 'Sorrow' (113), 'Pleasure' (114), 'Morning' (120), 'thunder' (124), 'Ocean' (125),

'Winds' (126), 'Echo' (127), 'Spring' (136), seem to provide a responsive chorus to the elegist's song.

> All he had loved, and moulded into thought,
> From shape, and hue, and odour, and sweet sound,
> Lamented Adonais.... (118–20)

However, while these seem to present a universal elegy for the dead poet, nature in this poem is treacherous and inconstant. Unlike the ending of the 'Ode to the West Wind', where the return of spring guarantees change and in a sense relieves the poet of his particular responsibility to effect that change, in *Adonais* the changefulness of the natural world is out of step with the emotional direction of the poem. Generally, in pastoral elegy, the return of spring is a sign that the dead find new life, and that Adonis is resurrected in some form. But in *Adonais* the 'joyous tone' (156) and 'quickening life' (164) of the natural world leave the poet all the more acutely feeling the burden of his grief and the lonely responsibility of putting it into words:

> Alas! that all we loved of him should be,
> But for our grief, as if it had not been,
> And grief itself be mortal! (181–3)

Here the return of spring is a betrayal of human grief, which alone can protect the beloved from total extinction. The personification of the natural world as a reciprocating elegist is a fiction which the poet creates from his own desire, but which is then revealed as a fiction when spring brings different songs.

The spring-time of the natural world then makes itself felt to the poet in stanza xx as another discrepancy between fiction and fact. Shelley writes:

> The leprous corpse, touched by this spirit tender,
> Exhales itself in flowers of gentle breath;
> Like incarnations of the stars, when splendour
> Is changed to fragrance, they illumine death
> And mock the merry worm that wakes beneath;
> Nought we know, dies. Shall that alone which knows
> Be as a sword consumed before the sheath
> By sightless lightning? – the intense atom glows
> A moment, then is quenched in a most cold repose. (172–80)

This recurrent flower imagery in *Adonais*, an imagery associated with the natural return of spring, is frequently an imagery of deception, and specifically of deception wrought by words. Here the flowers of spring 'mock' the worm and 'illumine' the grave. But they are a surface decoration and are incapable of effecting any kind of transformation in the consciousness of the onlooker, who sees in them, not a sign of natural rebirth but merely an ornamentation of the heavy fact of death. The passage characteristically plays upon the meanings of the word 'breath', and brings out a double sense latent in the whole stanza: 'The leprous corpse, touched by this spirit tender, / Exhales itself in flowers of gentle breath.' The verb 'Exhales' is a pun, and opens up two possible perspectives, by describing two very different kinds of breath. The first is the scent of the newly opened flowers, a 'gentle breath', but the second refers to the final harsh exhalation of the dying. The lines look forward in time to the hopeful appearance of the covered grave in spring, but they also look back in time to remind of the man's last breath of life which cannot be recovered in flowers. Such flowers are a pleasing deception, which still cannot conceal the fact which 'they illumine'.

The passage recalls an earlier use of the same imagery near the start of the poem, where Shelley describes Urania's continued ignorance of Adonais' death. In stanza II the association of flowers with speech is made clear:

> With veilèd eyes,
> 'Mid listening Echoes, in her Paradise
> She sate, while one, with soft enamoured breath,
> Rekindled all the fading melodies,
> With which, like flowers that mock the corse beneath,
> He had adorned and hid the coming bulk of Death. (13–18)

These flowers are also a mockery of the facts. In a beautiful reworking of the image of the 'fading coal' which might be rekindled by 'an inconstant wind' (VII. 135) in the 'Defence', Shelley compares the protective language of the Echo to 'flowers that mock the corse beneath'. But such flowers cannot keep back knowledge of the unadorned, heaped grave of the poet. The purpose of the comparison of 'melodies' to 'flowers' is to show the relation between the song and the fact of death, which is a relation of adornment and concealment. These rekindled melodies are a mere brief flowering that, momentarily and deceptively, adorns the 'bulk of Death'. Shelley's own song is hopeful and decorative, like passing flowers.

This association of flowers with poetic speech is an image which seems to belong especially to Shelley's later work. It is the underlying motif of *The Sensitive Plant* (1820), for instance, and also runs through *Epipsychidion* (1821) which was composed a few months before *Adonais*, and which directly compares the poem to offered flowers:

> Lady mine,
> Scorn not these flowers of thought, the fading birth
> Which from its heart of hearts that plant puts forth
> Whose fruit, made perfect by thy sunny eyes,
> Will be as of the trees of Paradise. (383–7)

But where Shelley there looks forward to the transformation of his flowers to fruit which will be, daringly, the fruit of Eden, in *Adonais* the image fails to link speech with transformation, and merely emphasises the dissociation of the song and the facts. Here, the flowers of 'soft enamoured breath' as well as the 'flowers of gentle breath' in the later passage present a tender concealment of death. By comparison to the object, these flowers of poetry are deceptive fancies, and as such they express the underlying message of *Adonais*: that poetic language is a brief ornamentation, a fine and fragile fiction, which only conceals from sight the unimaginable emptiness of the dead.

This preoccupation with the nature of language before the fact of death, a preoccupation with what it means to mourn in leisured syllables and 'highly wrought' images, is evident throughout *Adonais*. Because the language of poetry is always a loss of the object which inspires it, a loss made doubly harsh by being linked to the theme of literal bereavement as well, this language is always aware of its own deceptions and ornamentations. In seeking to record the event of Keats's death and the strength of the later poet's grief, the poem rears a monumental fiction to mark the loss of both. The theme of loss is one which hollows out the language of the poem. It is linked to an aesthetic which proclaims the poet's writing as always a kind of epitaph to the inspiration which has fled. 'We are dispossessed', writes Derrida, 'of the longed-for presence in the gesture of language by which we attempt to seize it.'[18] The overt rhetorical play of *Adonais* becomes a comment on the nature of such dispossession.

In stanza xxv, having lamented the treachery of the natural world and the mortality even of human grief, Shelley returns to the mythological narrative of the poem. He describes the meeting of Urania with the dead poet, in terms of a dramatic meeting with the personified abstraction of death:

> In the death-chamber for a moment Death,
> Shamed by the presence of that living Might,
> Blushed to annihilation, and the breath
> Revisited those lips, and Life's pale light
> Flashed through those limbs, so late her dear delight.
> 'Leave me not wild and drear and comfortless,
> As silent lightning leaves the starless night!
> Leave me not!' cried Urania: her distress
> Roused Death: Death rose and smiled, and met her vain caress.
>
> (217–25)

But this ingenious and Baroque personification of Death serves to distance and undermine any dramatic immediacy or spontaneity of feeling which the event might contain. The drama of the scene is almost entirely a drama of language, and particularly of personification. It is *language* which creates the illusion of life or death in this stanza. Thus Shelley at first personifies Death as an active subject of the verbs 'Shamed' and 'Blushed'. But by creating an animated personification of the dead, he is staging a fiction which only shows us its own duplicity. By being made rhetorically animate, Death becomes the opposite of itself, so that its very blushing into life is a form of 'annihilation'. The rhetorical presence of Death is in contradiction to the literal fact of death. The one presents the illusion of life, if momentarily, while the other presents the unmitigable fact of the dead body.

However, it is with the first that Shelley is mainly concerned. The stanza enacts a rhetorical death of Death, as it 'Blushed to annihilation', and then pursues the idea of a sinister resurrection. As Urania recognises the literal fact before her, she meets a presence which is more like an iconographic, grinning death's-head than a living force: 'her distress / Roused Death: Death rose and smiled, and met her vain caress'. As if to emphasise the discrepancy between the once living object of Urania's 'dear delight' and this new reality, the personification of Death becomes ever more luridly and grotesquely artificial. The effect is to hide the reality, the fact of the dead body, behind a theatrical rhetoric of presence which is confessedly fictional. The personification of a Death which seems to rise and to smile thus serves to disguise the presence which lies behind the fiction: the presence of Keats. If this is not Shelley at his best in *Adonais*, it does nonetheless show him using a language which is so 'highly wrought' that it works by disguise and concealment of its object rather than by a transparent and more honest reference. Personification in *Adonais* is a fiction which obtrudes itself as an unreal and rhetorical presence upon the elegist's consciousness of death.

To read into the language of *Adonais* a commentary on its own intentional artifice in this way is only to extend and elaborate on that theme of loss which is central to Shelley's aesthetic, and which is also the motivating theme of his elegy. Theory and practice are not separate. It could be said that Shelley is engaged in formulating a theory of poetry throughout his life, and that he does so in a language which is already in some sense poetry. Thus the inspirational theory of the 'Defence' is formulated through a series of metaphors which have the effect of a prose poem. For Shelley a description of poetry is to be found in poetry at work, and the vitally metaphorical nature of the 'Defence' is a theoretical extension of all the working metaphors in his actual poems. Conversely, the poems can be interpreted as testing and extending the theory. The very dense and fictitious quality of the language of *Adonais* becomes a comment on its own status, and rings with a certain splendid hollowness before the fact of death. The theme of loss is linked to the distances between an elaborate mythological and rhetorical language and the literal and personal event which inspires its writing. These are the distances once again of Shelley's aesthetic of the sublime.

There is a clear indication of the thematic centrality of such an aesthetic in those controversial stanzas where Shelley himself enters the drama of his poem. In stanza XXXI he writes:

> Midst others of less note, came one frail Form,
> A phantom among men; companionless
> As the last cloud of an expiring storm
> Whose thunder is its knell... (271–4)

and in the following stanza he describes this 'Form' as

> A pardlike Spirit beautiful and swift –
> A Love in desolation masked; – a Power
> Girt round with weakness; – it can scarce uplift
> The weight of the superincumbent hour;
> It is a dying lamp, a falling shower,
> A breaking billow; – even whilst we speak
> Is it not broken? (280–6)

The presence of the poet in his poem has often been a source of condemnation, amusement or embarrassment. But to accuse Shelley of sentimentality, or even blasphemy as his contemporary critics did,[19] is to confuse the man and the poet, and to judge the latter in moral and biographical terms which have no place in a poem of so many rhetorical contrivances. Shelley himself was concerned to discriminate between the two in a letter to the Gisbornes written soon after the completion of *Adonais*. Here he writes, with reference to the poem, that the 'poet & the man are two different natures: though they exist together they may be unconscious of each other' (*Letters*, II. 310). The presence of the poet in his poem should be read, not as a form of sentimental egotism, but, according to Newell F. Ford, as a 'dramatic' objectification of a literary paradox,[20] or, as Judith Chernaik argues, as proof that 'the poet is assuming a literary role as elegist or bard, prophet or dreamer'.[21] The role which is played by the figure of the poet in these stanzas is not a self-portrait, but a dramatisation of an aesthetic process.

It is significant, therefore, that the poet enters his poem in disguise. He is described in a series of images which fail to identify him definitively, and which mark a progressive retreat from his human nature. He appears as a 'frail Form', a 'phantom', a 'last cloud', a 'Spirit', a 'Love', 'a Power', and lastly those failing images of 'lamp', 'shower' and 'billow'. Such images hardly constitute a sentimental self-portrait. Instead, they seem to present that process of cumulative insufficiency and failure which characterises the language of the sublime. Shelley is describing the very condition of poetry, which is the failing image of inspiration. These lines contain a clear echo of that aesthetic of lost signatures and failing light or fire which is elaborated in the 'Defence'. Poetry is a mere trace of the divine passing, and its language is inspiration always on the wane. Thus the poet in his poem is like the absolute force of 'Love' or 'Power' when it is already threatened by 'desolation' or 'weakness'. That these abstractions do not describe the man himself becomes evident at the end, where Shelley asks of the 'breaking billow', 'even whilst we speak / Is it not broken?' Here the 'we' of the speaker is distinguished from the 'it' which claims a grammatical descent from the 'pardlike Spirit'. What breaks like the billow, therefore, is not the life of the poet, but something impersonal and unpersonified: the life-force of poetry. The non-human pronoun 'it' refers to the abstract 'Love' or 'Power' of creativity which for Shelley may only be apprehended as it passes or fails, in its 'desolation' or 'weakness' and in its 'dying', 'falling', 'breaking'. These stanzas are not a histrionic aside, in which Shelley bewails his own plight and portrays himself as yet another dying poet. Instead, they are a characteristic metaphorical statement about the very nature of poetry; about the continual, inevitable pastness of its language and about the failure to sustain the original energy of its inspiration: 'even whilst we speak / Is it not broken?'

These stanzas are not an interpolated commentary on the process of creativity, the meaning of which remains external to the poem, but they are an expression of that imaginative loss which is central to it. It is because the life-force and the inspiratory force have been frequently identified with each other in the metaphorical language of *Adonais* that Shelley can refer to himself as poet without sentimentality. 'The poet & the man are two different natures,' and the poet who enters in these stanzas to lament the death of Keats is an idealised embodiment of the task which he must undertake. Thus Shelley describes him in stanza xxxiv with detached and wry amusement:

> All stood aloof, and at his partial moan
> Smiled through their tears; well knew that gentle band
> Who in another's fate now wept his own,
> As in the accents of an unknown land
> He sung new sorrow ...   (298–302)

The close association of poetry and the poet in Romantic theory is at work here. It was Coleridge who wrote in the *Biographia Literaria* that the question: 'What is poetry? is so nearly the same question with, what is a poet? that the answer to the one is involved in the solution of the other.'[22] The singer of Keats's death in this stanza is the poet as representative of poetry, 'Who in another's fate now wept his own'. The 'fate' of the living poet is to have realised in language not only the death of Keats, but the death of his own inspiration, and to have found the 'lamp' dead, the 'shower' fallen and the 'billow' broken. Thus Shelley turns his characteristic theory of poetry into a vital metaphor for the lost genius of a poet he scarcely knew. As Coleridge proclaimed, poetry is so nearly the same as the poet in their ideal states, that the loss of the one is inextricably tied to the loss of the other. Shelley laments that loss in *Adonais* by raising a fiction to the dead which continually acknowledges the scandal of its own fictitiousness.

However, in the tradition of the elegy, and like its great predecessor *Lycidas*, *Adonais* is structured upon a crucial turning point. There is a change from despair to a kind of hope, and this change takes the form of a new command to silence. In stanza xxxix the mourner who has so recently 'sung new sorrow' is ordered to cease his lamentations:

> Peace, peace! he is not dead, he doth not sleep –
> He hath awakened from the dream of life –

144

> 'Tis we, who lost in stormy visions, keep
> With phantoms an unprofitable strife,
> And in mad trance, strike with our spirit's knife
> Invulnerable nothings. (343–8)

The turning point of the poem proclaims an inversion of roles, an inversion of life and death, waking and sleeping, but above all it proclaims an inversion of the mourner's lament and the dead man's silence. The elegist is recommended to be mute, not now because muteness is the only honest kind of grief, but because only by his muteness will another voice become audible. The traditional paradox of the dead being alive, of their having awakened 'from the dream of life', heralds an important change of voices in the poem. The voice of the mourner must be silenced, and the injunction is repeated like a refrain in the verses that follow: 'Mourn not for Adonais' (362), 'Ye caverns and ye forests, cease to moan! / Cease, ye faint flowers and fountains' (365–6), 'Who mourns for Adonais?' (415). Only when the voice of the elegist is silent may the awakened voice of the dead become audible.

This injunction to silence in the poem clears the way for a different voice, which is a voice to be *heard* differently. In stanza XLII Shelley writes:

> He is made one with Nature: there is heard
> His voice in all her music, from the moan
> Of thunder, to the song of night's sweet bird;
> He is a presence to be felt and known
> In darkness and in light, from herb and stone,
> Spreading itself where'er that Power may move
> Which has withdrawn his being to its own;
> Which wields the world with never-wearied love,
> Sustains it from beneath, and kindles it above. (370–8)

The voice of Keats is heard not as any human language, not as poetry, but as the music of nature: 'He is made one with Nature: there is heard / His voice in all her music.' Once again Shelley is affirming, although in a different context, that 'Nature' is 'the poet' (*Letters*, I. 497). Keats's is no longer a 'mute voice', but a voice that sounds audibly in the voice of creation. In the tradition of the sublime, Shelley is referring creativity back to the model of the creation, and finding in that reunion of the two a means of celebrating Keats's immortality. This is not, like Milton's, the voice of Christian hope, revived through 'the dear might of him that walked the waves' (*Lycidas*, 173), but a typically Shelleyan voice, derived from an aesthetic which gives priority to that voice which sounds beyond the language of any text. The dead Keats is now united to the original creative 'Power' and 'love', to those very forces which in stanza XXXII defined the 'pardlike Spirit' of the living poet. However, those forces are no longer undermined by 'weakness' and 'desolation', but spread unfailingly throughout the creation.

This is not a Christian triumph but an aesthetic one, and its roots are to be found in the principles of the eighteenth-century sublime. 'He is a presence to be felt and known / In darkness and in light, from herb and stone.' Just as the voice of Mont Blanc is not to be heard externally but interpreted and deeply felt, so here the 'voice' and 'presence' of Keats in the natural world are 'to be felt and known'. Keats has achieved that identification of poet and Power which Shelley, the living writer, must still forgo. In celebrating this triumph of the poetic spirit, the poem moves away from a preoccupation with the rhetorical fictions of the literary text to an apprehension of the voice of unfailing inspiration, which speaks through the silence of the living. This triumphant acclamation of creative Power in the universe, like all the previous manifestations of Power in Mont Blanc, Demogorgon, west wind and skylark, celebrates poetic inspiration and, now, immortality.

However, if Keats has been reunited with the Power of original inspiration in death, that Power remains beyond the reach of the poet who still lives and writes. It is this knowledge which permeates the last stanzas of *Adonais*. Having celebrated Keats's natural apotheosis, Shelley addresses a living poet, a 'Fond wretch!' (416) who may be still mourning, and advises him to

> Clasp with thy panting soul the pendulous Earth;
> As from a centre, dart thy spirit's light
> Beyond all worlds, until its spacious might
> Satiate the void circumference: then shrink
> Even to a point within our day and night;

And keep thy heart light lest it make thee sink
When hope has kindled hope, and lured thee to the brink.

(417–23)

These lines express all the daring and the optimism of the Shelleyan sublime as well as all its desperation and knowledge of failure. The poet's spirit is capable of filling space to its furthest horizon 'Beyond all worlds', but it cannot do so without the contrary movement of shrinking 'Even to a point', which is the point of its own small time and place of life. After such expansive hope, there is a sinking. The lines which seem to hold in balance all the possibilities for hope and despair contained in the Shelleyan sublime are those which tell how the spirit's 'spacious might' is able to 'Satiate the void circumference'. The 'human mind's imaginings' can fill empty space with their own spaciousness, but cannot therefore deny that the 'circumference' is 'void'. To reach the very limits of what the poetic spirit can imagine is to reach a boundary which is also nothing. Shelley's brilliant phrase 'the void circumference' comes just short of presenting nothing but also comes just short of presenting a boundary. It is to this perilous edge that the poet must aspire.

In the last stanzas of *Adonais* Shelley acknowledges the despair which lies on the other side of sublime hope. He writes in stanzas LII and LIII:

The One remains, the many change and pass;
Heaven's light forever shines, Earth's shadows fly;
Life, like a dome of many-coloured glass,
Stains the white radiance of Eternity,
Until Death tramples it to fragments. – Die,
If thou wouldst be with that which thou dost seek!
Follow where all is fled! – Rome's azure sky,
Flowers, ruins, statues, music, words, are weak
The glory they transfuse with fitting truth to speak.

Why linger, why turn back, why shrink, my Heart?
Thy hopes are gone before: from all things here
They have departed; thou shouldst now depart! (460–71)

'We mistake this triumph of rhetoric,' writes Harold Bloom, 'if we read it as other than a triumph of human despair.'[23] If the triumph of the poem is to have discovered the dead to be immortal and theirs to be the pure voice of creative Power beyond the deceptive fictions of language, why then does the poet show this reluctance to go towards them? Why should this poet be fearful of leaving behind 'the world's bitter wind' (457) and 'Earth's shadows' in order to gain 'the white radiance of Eternity'? Why is he inclined to 'linger', 'turn back' and 'shrink' from the object of his desire, and from the 'glory', by comparison to which all 'Flowers, ruins, statues, music, words' are merely 'weak'? There seems to be some flaw and some regret in the concept of creativity as a voice calling from beyond the confines of the world's shores. Nor can the fine metaphor of 'Eternity' disguise this regret and uncertainty. For its radiance is gained only by the loss of the coloured dome, which 'Death tramples...to fragments'. If there is a prefiguring here of that ' "Shape all light" ' (352), in *The Triumph of Life*, which treads upon the mind of Rousseau and ' "thought by thought, / Trampled its sparks into the dust of death" ' (387–8), it is one which does not augur well for the nature of such an 'Eternity'. As in 'Mont Blanc' and *Prometheus Unbound*, 'Eternity' is a name which has dire connotations of endlessness and loss. The last verses of *Adonais* seem to contain a haunting suspicion that the poem's triumphant statement of immortality might also be a statement of imaginative despair.

The last stanza does not resolve this doubt. Shelley writes:

> The breath whose might I have invoked in song
> Descends on me; my spirit's bark is driven,
> Far from the shore, far from the trembling throng
> Whose sails were never to the tempest given;
> The massy earth and spherèd skies are riven!
> I am borne darkly, fearfully, afar;
> Whilst, burning through the inmost veil of Heaven,
> The soul of Adonais, like a star,
> Beacons from the abode where the Eternal are. (487–95)

Shelley places the inspiratory formula at the end of the poem, as if it were only a prelude to some greater poetic enterprise. But the seas which must be crossed by the prevailing 'breath' of this last inspiration are not those of poetry or of something to be written.

148

Instead, these seas lead away from the poem to the beckoning voice of the dead and the realm of the 'One'. To reach this place the poet must leave behind the boundary of the 'shore'. Such a shore represents both his life and his poem, both of which must be ended if he is to reach 'Eternity'. This common metaphor of poetic inspiration, the 'breath' which directs the 'spirit's bark', has been transformed into a source of creative despair. The poet is driven by it to end writing altogether. For if to go in search of the immortal dead is to go in search of that Power which originates all things, and particularly the writing of poetry, this is necessarily to go into death and into silence. What lies 'Far from the shore, far from the trembling throng' may be a beacon of unfailing light and it may be the Power of unwaning inspiration, but it is also, almost certainly, beyond imaginative apprehension and beyond its communication in words. To reach inspiration must be to relinquish composition. So, at the end of his poem, Shelley sets out on the stormy sea and leaves behind all the 'Flowers, ruins, statues, music, words' that only weakened and transfused the truth's 'glory'. Particularly, he leaves behind these words of his elegy, which only disguised in artfulness and fiction the 'truth' of grief and death. But to leave all these is to go 'darkly, fearfully'.

The ending of *Adonais* thus offers a merely equivocal celebration of that aesthetic of inspiration which informs the poem. As long as the immortal voice of the dead, the voice of unfailing inspiration, remains lost to the written text, the poem can still play out the drama of its dispossession in words, and its language still promise that inspiration which it defers. But to reach the desired realm of 'the Eternal' is a triumph only gained at the price of silence and despair. Shelley's sceptical aesthetic thus deprives us of Eternity's platonic and religious consolations, and challenges the ideal of pure inspiraton which motivates the poem. But precisely because it challenges these, such scepticism protects and makes precious the poet's ' "leisure for fiction" '.

7

SLEEPERS IN THE OBLIVIOUS VALLEY:
THE TRIUMPH OF LIFE

In *Adonais* the poet's hope of reconciling the work of art to the natural language of the heart is a hope wrecked on the absolute division of the dead and the living. To reach the realm of the immortals is to reach a perfection which denies both life and art. The 'white radiance of Eternity' lies beyond the various and modifying colours of life like an ideal which is unimaginable and which remains in antithesis to the verbal fictions of the poem. As a result, the platonic oppositions of the work are strangely unconfident and distrustful. In stanza xxxix, for instance, Shelley writes of Keats:

> he is not dead, he doth not sleep –
> He hath awakened from the dream of life –
> 'Tis we, who lost in stormy visions, keep
> With phantoms an unprofitable strife,
> And in mad trance, strike with our spirit's knife
> Invulnerable nothings. (343–8)

This reversal of the states of life and death is one which the poet often proclaims, but is reluctant to follow to its conclusion. Although he seeks to leave behind 'the dream of life' in order to wake among the dead, such an aim cannot be achieved in poetry.

It seems fitting, therefore, that Shelley's last great poem is one which presents, as an alternative to the suicidal direction of *Adonais*, an ironic and phantasmagoric celebration of 'life'. It is as if this poem celebrates what *Adonais* only covertly admits: that to write is to relinquish the ideal of Eternity and to return to life's wild 'dream' and 'stormy visions'. *The Triumph of Life* marks a retreat from the desperate ambition which informs the last stanzas of *Adonais*, and signals, in spite of all its pessimism, a renewed confidence in the act of writing as the only means of saving inspiration from that perfection which is the poet's loss.

The poem was composed in the spring and summer of 1822, and was left impressively unfinished at the time of Shelley's death in July of that year. It is hard to dissociate Shelley's great poem about Life from the facts of his death which prematurely ended it, and which give it the significance of a last word. But the meaning of the title and the uncharacteristically allegorical framework of the poem are not so much indications of Shelley's sense of an ending as indications of the influence of Italian literature on his work. As Timothy Webb has shown, it is Dante and Petrarch who give 'the whole flavour and atmosphere'[1] of Shelley's poem. Desmond King-Hele draws on this influence, and particularly the influence of Petrarch, when he claims that the poem would probably have had an optimistic conclusion, on the model of Petrarch's *Trionfi*. He argues that therefore the title is without irony and 'strikes a buoyant note', and speculates that 'Shelley intended to show Man triumphing over his present travails.'[2] Generally, however, critics have been shy of interpreting the poem according to a prognosticated happy ending. Instead, M. H. Abrams contrasts the work to its Dantean sources, claiming that, although *The Triumph of Life* is 'a Dantean dream-vision', Shelley's own aim is to present a 'vision of history as the almost unrelieved tragedy of the defeat of human potentiality'.[3] Harold Bloom interprets the poem as a parodic revision of Dante as well as of Ezekiel and Milton,[4] and, in *Shelley's Mythmaking*, writes that 'the title of the poem needs to be read as the triumph of life over human integrity, and the "life" of the title is Death-in-Life'.[5] Richard Cronin also contrasts the work to its sources, and shows how, while Dante and Petrarch 'represent experience as a series of veils which may be removed one by one...to reveal an absolute and perfect reality', Shelley works in the opposite direction and progressively 'obscures'[6] the ideal.

Most interpretations of *The Triumph of Life* revolve round the meaning of the title in answer to the question which the poem itself raises. At the end of Rousseau's admonitory tale of his own defeat by Life, the poet asks in bewilderment: 'Then, what is Life?' (544).[7] To this question the few lines which follow contain no answer, and the poem as it stands returns the weight of its meaning to that question. Like the final lines of 'Mont Blanc', the poet's sceptical or defiant failure to understand 'what is Life' makes the whole poem still open to interpretation. Rousseau's account of his own inevitable awakening to the nightmarish procession does not answer the poet's search for knowledge, but only prompts the same question to be repeated by him.

However, it is possible to find in this unanswered question some indication of what *The Triumph of Life* is about. In a passage from the earlier essay 'On Life' Shelley gives a partial answer to the question which is so central to his last poem. He writes:

What is life? Thoughts and feelings arise, with or without our will, and we employ words to express them. We are born, and our birth is un-remembered, and our infancy remembered but in fragments; we live on, and in living we lose the apprehension of life. How vain is it to think that words can penetrate the mystery of our being! Rightly used they may make evident our ignorance to ourselves, and this is much. For what are we? Whence do we come? and whither do we go? Is birth the commencement, is death the conclusion of our being? What is birth and death?

(VI. 193–4)

The question 'What is life?' is one which leads to an important distinction between Life as a process and Life as an origin. It is the origin which Shelley desires to recover: that original intense 'apprehension of life' which we forget in 'living'. While it is certainly Wordsworth who influences this description of Life as a process of forgetting birth and infancy, the note of scepticism as to whether these origins can be recalled is peculiarly Shelleyan. 'How vain is it to think that words can penetrate the mystery of our being!' Just as the adult consciousness fails to retain any memory of birth, so words fail to express anything except 'our ignorance' of Life's meaning. It is this failure which characterises Shelley's answer to the question, when he affirms only that 'we live on, and in living we lose the apprehension of life'. Life is something which is lost even while it is lived. Punningly, origin

152

and process converge in the same word. Thus, although the answer to the question 'What is life?' presents itself as a choice between merely 'living' and retaining an imaginative 'apprehension of life', such a choice is not available, because the one is always a loss of the other. Unlike Wordsworth, who is still able to intimate some original glory and freshness beyond the limits of what can be remembered, Shelley claims that the early 'apprehension of life' is inevitably, if poignantly, forgotten.

It is this tension between Life as an imaginative origin and Life as a process of forgetting that origin, which underlies Shelley's last poem. *The Triumph of Life* refers to the triumph of that 'living' which jades the imagination and makes the poet forgetful of his first vision. The title thus expresses the poet's inevitable defeat by Life. Nonetheless, even while the poem describes this process of defeat, it yearns for the alternative meaning, as that original unfamiliarity of the world and that imaginative engagement with it which distinguishes the poet. The poem contains both meanings but linked as they are in the earlier essay. The triumph of 'living' is one which progressively erases from memory the poet's 'apprehension of life', but the rhetorical texture of the poem still saves the second as a source of imaginative regret and loss.

The Triumph of Life is thus Shelley's last poem concerned with the origins of creativity and with the distance between those origins and their recovery in composition. However, this distance is no longer one which is mirrored in the landscapes of the sublime and in the mysterious presences which those landscapes conceal. Instead, it is presented as the distance between the waking adult mind and its forgotten dreams. In this, Shelley's most sceptical and despairing account of the poet's search for Power, he presents the object as perpetually forgotten. Instead of seeking to address the hidden Power and to express it as the imagination's alternative to vacancy, this poem presents a series of wakings which suppress and supplant what went before. The distances of the sublime landscape are now internalised as the distances of memory, where the original object is always forgotten. In *The Triumph of Life*, Shelley confronts the bleakest implications of that aesthetic of lost inspiration which underlies and orders so much of his poetry. He confronts the 'calm' of forgetfulness which is the inevitable fate of the 'living'. 'It is as it were the interpenetration of a diviner nature through our own; but its footsteps are like those of a wind over a sea, which the coming calm erases, and whose traces remain only, as on the wrinkled sand which paves it' (VII. 136), he wrote in 'A Defence of Poetry'. This is the mental landscape of *The Triumph of Life*, with the difference only that 'the coming calm' is now the ever-present condition of the adult mind.

In his last poem Shelley internalises the infinite distances of the sublime as the distances of consciousness, and specifically the distances of the memory. As a result, the poetic activity which orders this brilliantly fragmented and phantasmagoric poem is not the activity of seeing the unseeable or imagining the unimaginable, but of forgetting. What Wordsworth intimates as a heaven, Shelley presents as lost beyond recall. Furthermore, what is forgotten may be, for Shelley, precisely nothing. As Paul de Man writes in his essay 'Shelley Disfigured': 'What one forgets here is not some previous condition, for the line of demarcation between the two conditions is so unclear, the distinction between the forgotten and the remembered so unlike the distinction between two well-defined areas, that we have no assurance whatever that the forgotten ever existed.'[8] It is a characteristic of Shelley's version of the sublime to find origins shading into nothing. However, although *The Triumph of Life* presents the original 'apprehension of life' as a state that is lost in the act of 'living', such an apprehension is not therefore unregretted or undesired. Although this poem, above all others, acknowledges the 'calm' of forgetfulness which erases the wind's 'footsteps' from the mind, it fails to be content with that 'calm'. It is this discontent which makes *The Triumph of Life*, in spite of its pessimism, so defiant and turbulent a poem. Although its main protagonists are always ' "sleepers in the oblivious valley" ' (539), theirs is an oblivion that is charged with desire and regret.

The poem opens with a glad celebration of dawn and day:

> Swift as a spirit hastening to his task
>   Of glory & of good, the Sun sprang forth
> Rejoicing in his splendour, & the mask
>
> Of darkness fell from the awakened Earth.   (1–4)

The swiftness of the rising Sun suggests an equivalent energy of inspiration in the poet's own song. Light rushes upon the scene with the seemingly unequivocal purpose of alleviating the darkness of night and showing the earth in its true colours. The language suggests an equivalent visionary renewal and revelation, as the earth is cleared of night's masks and disguises. Dawn seems to present a triumph of light and clarity over the dubious attributes of night. But although the explicitly glorious and good task of the Sun is in opposition to the masking of night, this is an opposition which the poem will reverse. Whether Shelley's intentions altered in the first few stanzas or whether he intended a deliberate ambiguity is hard to say, but there is in the sixth stanza, as critics have pointed out, a flagging in the tone of celebration and a marked change in the character of the Sun. Here Shelley writes:

> Isle, Ocean, & all things that in them wear
> The form & character of mortal mould
>   Rise as the Sun their father rose, to bear
>
> Their portion of the toil which he of old
>   Took as his own & then imposed on them...   (16–20)

The task of the Sun begins to seem less beneficent than punishing. Significantly, the Sun is no longer portrayed as a swift 'spirit' like the west wind, but as an anthropomorphic father-god, who burdens the earth with toil. The origin of light and Life in these stanzas changes from a spirit beautiful and swift to an old patriarch who imposes Life like a wearisome burden.

This change of perception suggests a collapsed mythological time-scheme. The first stanza describes a prelapsarian world of collaborative energy, but the sixth stanza introduces a fallen world, marked, as it is in Genesis, by 'toil'. From this postlapsarian perspective the origin of Life becomes a god, a 'father'. In these stanzas Shelley is perhaps still acknowledging the difficulty of writing about origins without writing about gods. The language of religious ritual: 'smokeless altars' (5), 'orison' (7), 'matin lay' (8), 'censers' (11), 'incense' (12), however natural the context, leads by a subtle, poetic logic to a presentation of the Sun as Jehovah. The persistent religious imagery of these stanzas acts like a warning. To celebrate the Sun as the origin and giver of Life is to risk falling into a conventional religious anthropomorphism which Shelley elsewhere studiously avoids. The language of religious ritual in these opening verses is heavy with self-distrust.

It is at this point that the poet refuses to be part of the general awakening of the earth, and challenges the universal assumption of dawn by returning to a kind of sleep. The lines which follow the description of the Sun as a father-god have the effect of being an interruption of that first train of thought:

> But I, whom thoughts which must remain untold
>
> Had kept as wakeful as the stars that gem
> The cone of night, now they were laid asleep,
> Stretched my faint limbs beneath the hoary stem
>
> Which an old chestnut flung athwart the steep
> Of a green Apennine: before me fled
> The night; behind me rose the day; the Deep
>
> Was at my feet, & Heaven above my head
> When a strange trance over my fancy grew
> Which was not slumber, for the shade it spread
>
> Was so transparent that the scene came through
> As clear as when a veil of light is drawn
> O'er evening hills they glimmer; and I knew
>
> That I had felt the freshness of that dawn,
> Bathed in the same cold dew my brow & hair
> And sate as thus upon that slope of lawn
>
> Under the self same bough, & heard as there
> The birds, the fountains & the Ocean hold
> Sweet talk in music through the enamoured air.
> And then a Vision on my brain was rolled... (21–40)

The landscape of Shelley's dream-vision is interesting, not so much for the precise geography of the hill in relation to the Sun, but for the way it impresses a characteristic sense of limits. The poet lies where the trunk of 'an old chestnut' is 'flung athwart the steep / Of a green Appenine'. The image of a tree perilously poised over a chasm is one which returns with the force of a self-definition in Shelley's works. In *Alastor*, for instance, the protagonist reaches a place where

> A pine,
> Rock-rooted, stretched athwart the vacancy
> Its swinging boughs, to each inconstant blast
> Yielding one only response...
>
> (*P.W.*, pp. 14–30, lines 561–4)

Similarly in 'Mont Blanc' the pines are described as 'clinging' (20) above the Ravine of Arve in such a way as to give forth a kind of music, 'an old and solemn harmony' (24), as they catch the passing winds. In both examples, Shelley's favourite image of inspired creativity: that of trees which are as a lyre fingered by passing winds, is an image located in a landscape of sublime heights and depths. The interaction of wind and trees creates music on the brink where earth meets space, and thus on the brink of what may be pure 'vacancy'. The trees seem to represent the imagination's last foothold before the abyss, and their music that poetry which would still express something in the face of emptiness.

The image recurs in 'The Two Spirits: An Allegory', where the symbolic opposition of day and night points to the similar opposition in *The Triumph of Life*. The Second Spirit, which is the poet's, ventures beyond the boundaries of day, to where

> Some say there is a precipice
> Where one vast pine is frozen to ruin
> O'er piles of snow and chasms of ice
> Mid Alpine mountains...
>
> (*P.W.*, pp. 615–16, lines 33–6)

This Ariel-like paralysis of the Second Spirit in the form of a solitary pine nonetheless creates those 'Sweet whispers' (44) which comfort passing travellers. The pine over the precipice, even though 'frozen to ruin', holds the Spirit who dares to cross from day to night and who, before the prospect of such desolate and lifeless space, sings. This is the place from which the poet faces either

157

Power or vacancy, and makes them the subject of his song. In *The Triumph of Life* the poet lies on a less desolate edge, but nonetheless the figure of the 'old chestnut flung athwart the steep' suggests something ultimate and perilous in its pose which subtly defines the poet's own trance. If, according to Abrams, the image of the eagle soaring above the abyss represents the revolutionary hopefulness of the Romantic poet, Shelley's image of the tree grasping the last edge of earth implies a more precarious and desperate vision of the world.

Thus the poet lies on the edge of a hill, as well as on an edge between day and night. However, the purpose of the poem is not then to envision a presence in what lies beyond this edge, but rather to exploit the ambiguities of this placing. The poet falls into a kind of sleep which is not sleep, and has a vision which is not a vision. His is a 'strange trance'; a state of waking dream which 'was not slumber, for the shade it spread / Was so transparent that the scene came through'. This is neither sleep nor waking, but a state which allows the poet to witness the visible scene as transparently as if he were awake, and yet with a slight difference: 'as when a veil of light is drawn / O'er evening hills they glimmer'. These stanzas first assert the poet's unique and privileged position in being able to choose not to wake with the dawn, but they then question whether this is a difference at all. The dream-vision is an alternative to the daylight because it is affiliated to 'the stars', those lights which, according to Bloom, represent 'the visionary light of imagination and poetry',[9] and because it retains, even at dawn, a consciousness of 'evening hills'. However, the trance is also described as a clear and transparent rendering of the scene; as an alternative which is no alternative but the same. The traditional licence of the poet to dream is denied here. Unlike the Second Spirit, he cannot cross from day to night, but is forced to see in trance merely what is there in daylight. He witnesses the dawn as if without any 'shade' before its literalness, except that it seems to have the strangely inappropriate and contradictory light of 'evening hills'. Their glimmering subtly suggests the poet's desire to see something that has gone.

This element of haunting from the past is emphasised by the fact that what the poet sees in trance is *déjà vu*. The landscape of dawn, although as nearly transparent as the literal reality, has been seen before. It bears the stamp of something repeated. The 'dawn', the 'cold dew', even this 'slope of lawn' and 'self same bough' seem to have had some prior existence in the poet's consciousness. The present is strangely superimposed upon some identical past, and as a result the experience of the trance for the poet is also the experience of remembering the past: 'And I knew. . . ' The effect of this doubling is to evoke a feeling of the uncanny in a quite specific sense. Freud writes of that 'factor of involuntary repetition which surrounds what would otherwise be innocent enough with an uncanny atmosphere, and forces upon us the idea of something fateful and inescapable when otherwise we should have spoken only of "chance" '.[10] Instead of projecting the imagination's fictions into the scene, Shelley finds in the landscape merely a faint reminder of having seen it before. The creative activity of the mind is not so much one of imagining as of remembering, and the many uncanny repetitions of *The Triumph of Life* work like hauntings of some earlier event.

The dream-vision is thus, in Shelley's hands, peculiarly modern. It offers, not a new way of seeing the world or an alternative scene, but the same again. Yet, at the same time, this 'involuntary repetition' gives to the otherwise literal trance a slight glimmering as of 'evening hills', and an uncanny familiarity. The trance provides an opportunity for remembering

> That I had felt the freshness of that dawn,
> Bathed in the same cold dew my brow & hair
> And sate as thus upon that slope of lawn. . .

It is from this state of uncanny recollection, which is a recollection not in Wordsworth's sense of intimating past glory but merely in the sense of repeating the same thing, that the poem's dream-vision proper springs: 'And then a Vision on my brain was rolled. . .' This leads to the main body of the poem. But its wording is premonitory. If the mind in creation is like sand upon which each wave rolls a new vision, then each vision also erases what has gone before. In *The Triumph of Life* the transitions from one visionary state to another are movements of loss as well as of promise.

The nature of the 'Vision' which the poet sees is like a medieval allegory of death. As Hazlitt wrote in his troubled but acute description of the work in his review of the *Posthumous Poems* (1824): 'The poem entitled the *Triumph of Life,* is in fact a new and terrific *Dance of Death;* but it is thus Mr. Shelley transposes the appellations of the commonest things, and subsists only in the violence of contrast.'[11] The procession which passes before the eyes of the poet and constitutes his 'waking dream' (42) is like a *memento mori*. He sees a throng of people all terrorised or fascinated by their own mortality:

> Some flying from the thing they feared & some
> Seeking the object of another's fear,
>
> And others as with steps towards the tomb
> Pored on the trodden worms that crawled beneath,
> And others mournfully within the gloom
>
> Of their own shadow walked, and called it death... (54-9)

The macabre quality of such passages supports the view that the Triumph of the title is quite simply the victory of that 'living' which destroys the imagination. Such Life is indeed, as Hazlitt saw it, a dull progress of mortality. But although much of the poem is a grotesque allegory of Life as a living death, the other sense of Life as an intense imaginative 'apprehension' is not completely excluded from the work.

This alternative meaning becomes evident in Shelley's description of the chariot of Life which slowly becomes visible to the onlooking poet:

> And as I gazed methought that in the way
> The throng grew wilder, as the woods of June
> When the South wind shakes the extinguished day. –
>
> And a cold glare, intenser than the noon
> But icy cold, obscured with   light
> The Sun as he the stars.... (74-9)

These lines not only recall a more familiarly Shelleyan style of writing, but also introduce a complication in the poet's attitude to the passing procession. The encounter with the chariot is reminiscent of the sublime encounters of the earlier poems, particularly Asia's encounter with Demogorgon. The poet meets an object which defies visual definition and also defies evaluation, being contradictorily both vicious yet beautiful. The whole presentation of the chariot is ambiguous. Its light is preternaturally 'cold' but 'intenser than the noon'; it retains the connotation of an eye, being 'a cold glare', but one which is blank, like a denied 'aura'; its light is most bright, but obscuring. In the manuscript, Reiman notes a cancellation which describes the chariot's light as 'fascinating'.[12] It is not accidental that this description of the chariot is reminiscent of Demogorgon. It is presented, not as an object to be understood, but as a light to be interpreted and shaped by the onlooker. The chariot is not Shelley's allegorical answer to the question 'what is Life?' but is in fact the question. It offers the onlooker a choice of interpretations, in being cold but like the noon, repellent yet fascinating, glaring yet blind. The description of the chariot presents the possibility both of inevitable destruction and of strange beauty.

It is tempting to seek a definitive interpretation of the chariot, as Bloom does when he claims that the 'chariot's glare is the light of life; the sun's, of nature; the stars', the visionary light of imagination and poetry'. He then argues, persuasively, that in the poem 'Nature's light obliterates that of the poet, only to be destroyed in turn by the light of life, the moonlike cold car of Life.'[13] Kenneth Cameron argues that the figure of the chariot driven by the blinded 'charioteer' (99) represents Life driven by 'necessity'.[14] But to interpret the chariot so pessimistically is to ignore the seductively beautiful language by which it is described. The destructive inevitability of Life's passage does not quite destroy the poet's freedom to imagine it differently:

> Like the young moon
>
> When on the sunlit limits of the night
> Her white shell trembles amid crimson air... (79–81)

This distractingly lovely simile is in curious contradiction to the previous description of the chariot as 'intenser than the noon'. This is not just an untidy method of composition, attributable to a rush of inspiration, as Leavis might complain, but rather expresses a conflict which is central to *The Triumph of Life*. Shelley cannot write a poem about that process of 'living' which forgoes the 'apprehension of life' without being haunted by the knowledge of that loss. The epic simile of 'the young moon' is like a reminder of another, earlier time and different light. Just as the poet's first vision of dawn found it strangely like glimmering 'evening hills', so here he finds the dazzling noon light of the chariot to be like the uncertain appearance of the moon at sunset. If this is a logical confusion, it is one which serves the aesthetic interests of the work. Such a confusion asserts the freedom of the imagination to see Life differently, although this is to see it as something that has been lost. For in this poem, the light of evening is always the light of time past.

The alternative beauty of the chariot is again revealed when Shelley writes:

> upon the chariot's beam
> A Janus-visaged Shadow did assume
>
> The guidance of that wonder-wingèd team.
> The Shapes which drew it in thick lightnings
> Were lost: I heard alone on the air's soft stream
>
> The music of their ever moving wings. (93–8)

This passage draws on images which seductively play upon the idea of creativity. The team is either wondrously winged or else driven by the strength of wonder which belongs to the poet. Its movement is like 'lightnings' and the effect of this movement is to create 'music'. The lyricism of the passage supports the new aspect of the chariot as a source of wonder and melody. Like the movement of Asia's progress towards Demogorgon, in which step and sound are simultaneous, the chariot's motion is no longer one which destroys those in its path but one which produces natural and undelaying 'music'. The chariot is briefly a source of sublime creativity. However, Shelley then implies that this alternative aspect is merely the poet's licence. He writes: 'I heard alone on the air's soft stream / The music.' Only this privileged listener can hear, on the other side of storm, destruction and inevitable defeat, the sound of soft music. But for this listener, therefore, the chariot might be, in Ross Woodman's words, 'an emblem of the creative imagination'.[15] As such, it is an emblem of the poet's need to apprehend Life, against all the odds, as wondrous and inspiring.

Thus the chariot of Life is not just a figure of destruction and of the defeat of the imagination in the process of 'living'. It is also a figure of creative hope, specifically the hope that Life itself be still a source of music for the poet. The chariot thus stands in very much the same relation to the poet as did the hidden Power of 'Mont Blanc', for instance, or the unseen Demogorgon. Like those, it represents to some extent the Power of Necessity, 'a blind, insensate force without consciousness or purpose'.[16] But like those, too, such a Power is one which might be converted into the Power of creativity. Shelley's version of the sublime requires the sceptical poet to shape the mysterious, sight-defeating object to his own imaginings, and it is this aim which informs the beautiful, lyrical descriptions of the chariot in these stanzas. Just as the poet wrests from the remote and serene emptiness of Mont Blanc the voice of revolutionary promise, and just as Asia wrests from the 'mighty darkness' of Demogorgon the answers of her own hopeful heart, so here the poet wrests from the 'cold glare' of Life an apprehension of almost impossibly gentle music.

After this brief glimpse of the alternative aspect of the chariot, the poet turns back to the hapless multitudes who are yoked to it. The 'Conqueror' (129) Life subdues all except those few idealistic spirits who die young. Once again it seems that the sheer fact of 'living' is a form of defeat, and Shelley's list of all those who are driven before the chariot attests to the dreary inevitability of that defeat. At one point, however, the poet notices among the crowd 'Maidens & youths' (149) whose passion is no surety against the indifferent progress of the chariot. Their fall is described, poignantly, as a passing of waves over the sand:

163

> One falls and then another in the path
> Senseless, nor is the desolation single,
>
> Yet ere I can say *where* the chariot hath
> Past over them; nor other trace I find
> But as of foam after the Ocean's wrath
>
> Is spent upon the desert shore. (159–64)

The haphazard destruction of lovers by the chariot is expressed by an image of waves and sand which suggests that the passing of Life is like an erasure from memory of all 'trace' of them. The lines imply a landscape of consciousness which would retain some lingering and vestigial sign of what has been lost. It is as if once again the poet's language seeks to save his creative apprehension of the world against the knowledge that Life destroys and obliterates everything in its path. The relentless passage of the chariot leaves nothing except this 'trace' 'as of foam', but the image points to where, in the future, Shelley will find a means of imaginatively retaining for poetry what the process of 'living' erases.

It is soon after this that the poet turns in desperation from the scene, and asks those questions which initiate his dialogue with Rousseau:

> Struck to the heart by this sad pageantry,
> Half to myself I said, 'And what is this?
> Whose shape is that within the car? & why' –
>
> I would have added – 'is all here amiss?' (176–9)

These questions, like the teleological questions of 'Mont Blanc' and *Prometheus Unbound*, for instance, reveal the poet's wish to find an answering voice in the landscape. However, while in the earlier poems this voice takes the form of some imagined Power which answers to the language of the heart, in *The Triumph of Life* the sublime presence is reduced to a form of the absurd. Shelley writes:

> But a voice answered...'Life'...I turned & knew
> (O Heaven have mercy on such wretchedness!)
>
> That what I thought was an old root which grew
> To strange distortion out of the hill side
> Was indeed one of that deluded crew,

164

And that the grass which methought hung so wide
And white, was but his thin discoloured hair,
And that the holes it vainly sought to hide

Were or had been eyes. — (180–8)

Shelley's presentation of Rousseau is an extraordinary surrealist reduction of the sublime presence. Instead of presenting a spirit or Power within the scene, he de-humanises Rousseau till he is materially a part of the scene. Rousseau is a shape at once dead and living, at once natural and human, at once seeing and blind. The poet's desire for an answer to explain the chaos around him is met by this mockery of Power which is, with the contradiction of nightmare, both 'an old root' and a fellow writer.

The figure of Rousseau might be seen as Shelley's last comment on the poet's need for original voices. Rousseau is like a travesty of the god-term of the sublime. Far from being an origin of the hectic scene, Rousseau is merely another of its victims: 'one of that deluded crew', and far from being an invisible Power, he is visible to the point of being almost literally part of the earth. Rousseau's role of explaining to the younger poet the meaning of Life is undermined from the start. He is one of those who have been defeated by the process of 'living', and who have thus lost their first idealistic 'apprehension' of things. The answer which Rousseau gives merely repeats the inevitability of that loss. His role is to repeat, uncannily, that 'in living we lose the apprehension of life', and the remainder of the poem brilliantly turns that repetition into a series of wakings which are like the poet's own waking at the start of the poem.

At first Rousseau promises to answer the poet's questions by recounting the history of his own life: his loss of the original 'spark' (201) and his resultant fall into the common 'dance' (189). However, what is interesting about his narrative is that it fails to explain *why* he falls. The event is merely reiterated by him. Rousseau's long catalogue of all the other spirits who have been defeated by Life fails to give the cause or origin of that defeat. His answer proves to be no answer at all because it merely recounts the inevitable. The general unsatisfactoriness of his reply, which has been the source of some critical debate, is also perceived by the poet himself who insistently renews his questions at the end: ' "Whence camest thou & whither goest thou? / How did thy course begin," I said, "& why?" ' (296–7). As in the essay 'On Life', the poet's quest for knowledge is mainly a quest to know the origin of things. The poem looks backwards in time, and it is this retrospective movement which then characterises Rousseau's attempt to answer the younger poet's ' "thirst of knowledge" ' (194).

Rousseau's story begins in ' "the April prime" ' (308), and the lush valley which he describes is like a neoplatonic landscape of entry into birth. Both time and place suggest a point of origin. However, the beginning of consciousness or Life is curiously arbitrary. Rousseau remembers that

> 'I found myself asleep
> Under a mountain which from unknown time
>
> 'Had yawned into a cavern high & deep...'   (311–13)

His story starts in the middle of a sleep which stretches back infinitely, it seems, into ' "unknown time" '. Rousseau's description of this first sleep then emphasises how unoriginal a point of departure it is. He tells of the sound of ' "a gentle rivulet" ' (314)

> 'which all who hear must needs forget
>
> 'All pleasure & all pain, all hate & love,
>   Which they had known before that hour of rest:
> A sleeping mother then would dream not of
>
> 'The only child who died upon her breast
> At eventide, a king would mourn no more
>   The crown of which his brow was dispossest
>
> 'When the sun lingered o'er the Ocean floor
>   To gild his rival's new prosperity. –
> Thou wouldst forget thus vainly to deplore
>
> 'Ills, which if ills, can find no cure from thee,
> The thought of which no other sleep will quell
>   Nor other music blot from memory –
>
> 'So sweet & deep is the oblivious spell. –'   (318–31)

The music of this Lethean stream seems at first to be a remedy for all social ills. It might cure the childless mother of her grief

166

and the dispossessed king of his humiliation. But in fact, what the passage makes clear is that these ills are immedicable. The child still dies, as Shelley knew too well, and the king is still deposed. The state of forgetfulness induced by the stream's music is not utopian but is merely anaesthetising, because it dulls pleasure as well as pain, love as well as hate, and more disturbingly, it dulls the impulse ' "to deplore" '.

But the most sinister sense of the passage emerges in the last lines. The stream's music is able to ' "blot from memory" ' all thought of past states and to engulf the mind in its ' "oblivious spell" '. The word ' "blot" ' contains a hidden violence which seems out of keeping with the lulling sweetness of the music, but which will be stressed in a similar erasing later in the poem. The ' "oblivious spell" ' also recalls earlier senses of the word 'spell', to mean an iconic message or a superstitious formula of words which have become dissociated from purpose and action. The effect of this music is to induce oblivion by being a language broken from human will and utterance. This is the first and earliest of Rousseau's memories. But what he remembers at the beginning of life is a vague and seemingly endless sleep, and a state of general oblivion. 'Our birth is but a sleep and a forgetting' (58), Wordsworth wrote in 'Intimations of Immortality'. Shelley's comment on that 'forgetting' is characteristically sceptical. Before that sleep Rousseau does not know if life was the ' "Heaven which I imagine, or a Hell" ' (333). The origin of Life has already receded from memory and, in his attempt to answer the poet's questions, he remembers only that, almost from the beginning, he began to forget. The origin of Life is both unspecific and deferred. It lies beyond what Rousseau can remember, because Life makes him already one of the ' "sleepers in the oblivious valley" '.

He then describes his waking from this first sleep:

> 'I arose & for a space
> The scene of woods & waters seemed to keep,
>
> 'Though it was now broad day, a gentle trace
> Of light diviner than the common Sun
> Sheds on the common Earth, but all the place

'Was filled with many sounds woven into one
Oblivious melody, confusing sense
Amid the gliding waves & shadows dun...' (335–42)

As critics have noted, this waking parallels the poet's own waking
in the first section of the poem. Rousseau rises to find that it is
' "broad day" ' and that the light of the Sun fills the place. However, this waking quickly becomes another kind of oblivion. As
so often in this poem, the daylight erases the dreams of the night,
and ' "the common Sun" ' supplants the rarer lights of the stars.
Life is a waking into oblivion of what went before. However, this
oblivion is not absolute, but keeps ' "a gentle trace / Of light diviner
than the common Sun" '. Shelley's language of paradoxical remembering and forgetting recalls the description of inspiration in
the 'Defence', as the 'footsteps...whose traces remain only, as on
the wrinkled sand' (VII. 136). The new harsh light of the Sun
cannot quite obliterate, as yet, ' "a gentle trace" ' of some earlier
and ' "diviner" ' light which lingers on like a faint memory. This
different light is as if traced upon the sunlight like an alternative
way of seeing the world which the waker has not quite forgotten.
Rousseau's description of his first awakening to Life thus echoes
the poet's own trance at dawn and his vision of the chariot. Just
as that dawn retained the alternative glimmer as of evening, and
the chariot retained a likeness to tremulous moonlight, so here
Rousseau's dawn waking is haunted by a 'trace' of the earlier
time. Oblivion, in this poem, is threaded with memory.

It is in this, his second stage of forgetting, that Rousseau sees
the ' "shape all light" ' (352) upon the stream:

'there stood

'Amid the sun, as he amid the blaze
Of his own glory, on the vibrating
Floor of the fountain, paved with flashing rays,

'A shape all light...' (348–52)

Whether this shape represents 'Wordsworthian nature' which puts
out the starlight of the imagination,[17] as Bloom's very Blakean interpretation has it, or whether she is 'Rousseau's epipsyche',[18] as Ross

Woodman writes, the shape is akin to the earlier configurations of light and sound in the poem:

> 'As one enamoured is upborne in dream
>   O'er lily-paven lakes mid silver mist
> To wondrous music, so this shape might seem
>
>   'Partly to tread the waves with feet which kist
> The dancing foam, partly to glide along...'   (367–71)

The shape is strangely like the chariot of Life in being both a crystallising of light and a source of ' "wondrous music" '. The measures of her step and of her sound are simultaneous, as if she represented Shelley's ideal of inspired and effective creativity. But although a source of music and wonder, the shape is, like the chariot, destructive. Light, in this poem, is consistently linked with waking and forgetting, and the action of the shape is one which forces another wave of oblivion upon Rousseau. She holds ' "a crystal glass / Mantling with bright Nepenthe" ' (358–9) and a cancelled version of her ' "ceaseless song" ' (375) reads 'opiate song'.[19] This must challenge any interpretation of the shape as purely beneficent. She is another manifestation of that Life which usurps the poet's memory of origins, and as such she represents Life's potential to be visionary and entrancing, but also vicious and deathly.

This destructive aspect is made clear in the verses which follow:

> 'And still her feet, no less than the sweet tune
> To which they moved, seemed as they moved, to blot
>   The thoughts of him who gazed on them, & soon
>
> 'All that was seemed as if it had been not,
>   As if the gazer's mind was strewn beneath
> Her feet like embers, & she, thought by thought,
>
>   'Trampled its fires into the dust of death,
> As Day upon the threshold of the east
>   Treads out the lamps of night, until the breath
>
> 'Of darkness reillumines even the least
>   Of heaven's living eyes – like day she came,
> Making the night a dream...'   (382–93)

These lines are a pessimistic reworking of Shelley's theory of inspiration in the 'Defence'. Unlike the footsteps of the wind, the footsteps of the shape are not traced on the bed of consciousness, like an after-patterning in words of the visionary event. Instead, they ' "blot / The thoughts of him who gazed on them" '. The verb punningly makes ' "thoughts" ' like writing. The shape destroys her own representation in the mind as something lingeringly seen or written, and the oblivion which she induces is like death to the mind in creation. Her influence is destructive because the ' "embers" ' of thought are not fanned by an 'invisible influence' to fire again. Shelley's two main images of inspired creativity are denied in this passage. The shape's footsteps erase all thought without trace, and the fading embers die. The shape enforces a loss of inspiration which is like an absolute forgetfulness of the past: ' "All that was seemed as if it had been not." '

It is significant that in *The Triumph of Life* this denial of creativity stems from images of too much light. These different configurations of the Sun and of dawn all have the same effect as of 'the coming calm'. Each successive image of the day and of the day's light is one which makes the poetic mind oblivious, and wakes the poet to a reality which powerfully out-shines his imagination: ' "like day she came, / Making the night a dream" '. But although Rousseau's narrative seems to repeat this event of forgetting, he still retains a regret or desire for earlier knowledge. It is for this reason that he asks the shape: ' "Shew when I came, and where I am, and why —" ' (398). These questions mockingly echo those which the poet first addressed to Rousseau and their repetition opens up a prospect of infinite regress within the poem. The impulse of the sublime to find an original and authorising voice within the landscape is thwarted here. Instead, the same unanswered questions echo retrospectively down the strange mental vistas of the poem.

Rousseau's pleas to know the cause and origin of his present state, like that of the younger poet, meet no answer except a repetition of his ignorance:

> ' "Arise and quench thy thirst," was her reply.
> And as a shut lily, stricken by the wand
> Of dewy morning's vital alchemy,

'I rose; and, bending at her sweet command,
    Touched with faint lips the cup she raised,
And suddenly my brain became as sand

    'Where the first wave had more than half erased
The track of deer on desert Labrador,
    Whilst the fierce wolf from which they fled amazed

'Leaves his stamp visibly upon the shore
    Until the second bursts – so on my sight
Burst a new Vision never seen before. –'   (400–11)

Rousseau's thirst for knowledge is answered by this dull opiate drink which, so familiarly now, erases thought from the mind. The repetitiveness of all these oblivious spells has the uncanny effect of halting the narrative around an event which is terrifyingly *déjà vu*. Oblivion is a kind of blocking mechanism, which halts the search for origins, and makes the poem circle round a single event of waking and forgetting, which is like Freud's uncanny dream of always returning to the same place.[20] Rousseau's search for the beginnings of Life is one which always returns to the same ' "oblivious valley" '. Thus Rousseau is answered by the cup which makes the mind as sand over which the first wave has already ' "half erased" ' the imprint of deer. This very Shelleyan landscape, which is a landscape of the sublime from which the god has disappeared, is internalised as the desert of consciousness. While the desert is Shelley's most appropriate image for that oblivion which afflicts Rousseau in this latest wakening into Life, it is also the landscape of possible creativity, because it is a landscape which might retain a 'trace' of what has gone. Such a trace is the imprint of deer, described in an earlier draft as 'legible'.[21] The markings on the sand are specifically those natural writings which, like the poet's verse, attest to a presence which has fled.

These haunting lines describe Rousseau's forgetfulness as an erasure of signs. But this time, the writing on the sand is only ' "half erased" '. The process of forgetting is held in suspension for a moment so that the mind can remember what it must forget. Whatever the precise meaning of the deer, their movement is that of the wind of inspiration over the sea. They leave a natural writing in the sand of the mind which is like a brief memory

171

before the 'calm' of oblivion. Their tracks are like the inscriptions of poetry after inspiration has passed. The desert landscape, for Shelley, is nearly always one which tells of the absence of the gods and of the loss of inspiration. Thus in 'Ozymandias', the death of gods and kings is inscribed in writing in the infinitely empty desert: 'boundless and bare / The lone and level sands stretch far away' (*P.W.*, p. 550, lines 13–14). Rousseau's failure to remember the origins of Life is a failure which lies at the very heart of Shelley's aesthetic of poetry. Thus *The Triumph of Life* presents the act of forgetting as the equivalent of that decline of inspiration which characterises composition. The mind in creation is as sand on which the wind's footsteps are hardly retained. Thus, the living consciousness hardly retains its memory of origins because Life has always passed like a wave of oblivion across it. Yet, paradoxically, it is the very calm of Life's forgetfulness which allows the mind to be haunted by its loss. In *The Triumph of Life* oblivion is creative because it is, like composition, a forfeiting of something else.

Then a second wave of oblivion erases even the sign of the wolf, and ' "bursts" ' like ' "a new Vision" ' upon Rousseau's consciousness:

> 'But the new Vision, and its cold bright car,
> With savage music, stunning music, crost
>
> 'The forest, and as if from some dread war
> Triumphantly returning, the loud million
> Fiercely extolled the fortune of her star. –'   (434–8)

Thus Rousseau forgets and wakes once more, and finds himself in the procession of Life. His perception of the chariot differs, however, from the poet's, and marks his fallen condition. For him, the ' "music" ' is not mild and wondrous but ' "savage" ' and ' "stunning" '. He has lost any creative 'apprehension of life' and has become merely another of those caught in the dreary procession of 'living'. From this perspective, Life is a savage and defeating spectacle, and its music leaves the mind still oblivious and stunned.

The effect of progress and development in Rousseau's narrative is a deception. There is no beginning to his story and he fails to communicate any knowledge to the younger poet. He only remembers, as if over and over again, the event of waking into the oblivious light of Life, which is where he has always been, except for some forgotten time of the imagination which still haunts him. Life is the savage daylight which has dominated the poem from its opening, and the alternative evening light is merely a brief and quickly fading memory. However, although this is the poem which most pessimistically denies the poet's wish to recover some original state of imaginativeness, it is a poem which also seeks to make the act of forgetting inspirational. The paradox of *The Triumph of Life* is that, although the origin is always forgotten, that movement of oblivion is also, subtly, a way of saving what is lost. The past may still be traced on the blank daylight or on the empty sand. The poem is too full of regret to be the exponent of its own message of defeat, and Shelley does not, in the end, confirm absolutely that 'in living we lose the apprehension of life'.

This element of imaginative regret is evident in that passage where Rousseau describes his final waking to the savage procession of Life:

> 'So knew I in that light's severe excess
> The presence of that shape which on the stream
> Moved, as I moved along the wilderness,
>
> 'More dimly than a day appearing dream,
> The ghost of a forgotten form of sleep,
> A light from Heaven whose half extinguished beam
>
> 'Through the sick day in which we wake to weep
> Glimmers, forever sought, forever lost. –' (424–31)

To wake into Life is still to be haunted by what went before. The new ' "light's severe excess" ' makes the shape into a ' "dream" ', a ' "sleep" ', a ' "half extinguished beam" '. The different light of her presence ' "Glimmers" ', like those 'evening hills' which complicate the poem's opening dawn. In a sense this is the same landscape and the same event. Rousseau's final waking uncannily repeats the poet's own trance at dawn, upon which also lingered a memory of gentler light. Rousseau's long narrative tells as much as the younger poet has already experienced, and the whole poem thus repudiates his search for answers.

This last passage also comments revealingly on the nature of the glimmering ' "presence" '. The shape upon the stream is now like a lost, alternative light; a light that is allied to dream and sleep. However, it is an alternative that only the waking mind can know. It is only because Rousseau has waked again that he remembers the shape more dimly and glimmeringly than she ever was in fact. Her ' "presence" ' is like nothing more than a trick of the new light. Shelley's scepticism in this poem makes the original and elusive Power one which is a mere figment of the waking mind. It is the harsh glare of Life which makes the past seem ghostly, and makes it therefore ' "forever sought, forever lost" '. The two activities of seeking and losing go together. The poet desires what is absent and regrets what is forgotten. It is the strength of his desire and his regret which then creates these ghosts of memory. *The Triumph of Life* sceptically and relentlessly asserts that the original presence which the poet desires to recover is shaped by his loss of it, and that the alternative haunting lights of the poem are shaped by its perpetual daylight.

This is Shelley's last venture into that region which divides inspiration from writing, origins from their recovery in consciousness. It is a venture, not so much into the emptiness of the landscape but into the 'calm' of oblivion, which is an internalised, psychological equivalent of that landscape. The image for both is that of the desert. The sand of the mind may retain the tracks of the deer like a natural writing, but those tracks are always quickly erased by the sea, and it is this process of erasure or forgetting which is the main concern of the poem. It is for this reason that *The Triumph of Life* is a poem which seems to exist in a perpetual present, in spite of its historical and biographical scope. Although Rousseau describes a series of wakings, these only emphasise that he is what he was at the beginning: one of the ' "sleepers in the oblivious valley" ' of Life. He is always one of those who have forgotten any other condition except this of Life's too clear and literal dawn.

Yet, like its ambiguous title, *The Triumph of Life* presents loss and defeat as still a means of imaginative regret and gain. For while the triumph of Life is to reduce all to a state of mere 'living', which is like the glare of unrelieved daylight, nonetheless it is this very prevalence of daylight which gives to the forgotten night the quality of an ideal and visionary time: a time worth imagining. To wake and forget is to retain a brief memory of different light against the glare of day, or to retain a trace of writing upon the mind's desert sand. Just as Rousseau, in his waking state, remembers the shape upon the stream as ' "a forgotten form of sleep" ' and as a lingering ' "dream" ', so the whole poem imagines with regret a ghostly origin of Life, whose loss and absence it commemorates in writing.

The Triumph of Life is Shelley's most severe expression of that divided aesthetic of inspiration and composition which constitutes his version of the sublime. It is a poem which forbids any recovery of the Power which has been lost, because the wave of oblivion has always passed, from the very beginning of Life. However, the poem still brilliantly and fiercely commemorates in its writing the idea of what is lost or absent. Although this is no more than a figment of the poet's desire, it is strong enough to pull against the self-sufficiency of his composition. While inspiration is a trick of memory in this poem, or a trick of the waking consciousness, it is nonetheless an idea which still draws the poet's imagination. There is, in *The Triumph of Life*, for all its declared pessimism, an insufficiency and a 'hidden want' which makes its writing, like so much of Shelley's work, brave in its expression of what is lost. In the end, it is the ' "sleepers in the oblivious valley" ' who are Shelley's representatives of the sublime poet. To sleep and forget inspiration is paradoxically to be able to commemorate it.

This act of commemoration is the real triumph, not only of Shelley's last poem, but of all those compositions which seek to bear witness, like traces 'on the wrinkled sand', to the imagined origin of creativity which directs their writing but has always passed from consciousness. To lose that origin is still, for Shelley, to feel in composition the keen pressure of its loss.

NOTES

1 The sublime in the eighteenth century

1. John Locke, *An Essay Concerning Human Understanding*, ed. Peter H. Nidditch (Oxford, Clarendon Press, 1975), Book II, chapter viii, paragraph 8, p. 134.
2. C. R. Morris, *Locke Berkeley Hume* (Oxford, Clarendon Press, 1931), pp. 30–1.
3. Locke, II, i, 24, p. 118.
4. *Ibid.*, II, ix, 2, p. 143.
5. David Hume, *An Enquiry Concerning Human Understanding*, in *Enquiries Concerning Human Understanding and Concerning the Principles of Morals*, ed. L. A. Selby-Bigge, rev. P. H. Nidditch (Oxford, Clarendon Press, 1975), Section II, paragraph 12, p. 18.
6. Locke, II, xxix, 2, p. 363.
7. Hume, *An Enquiry Concerning Human Understanding*, I, 6, p. 11.
8. *Ibid.*, II, 13, p. 18.
9. *Ibid.*, II, 14, p. 19.
10. Michael Foucault, *The Order of Things: An Archaeology of the Human Sciences*, trans. from the French (London, Tavistock Publications, 1970), p. 56.
11. Locke, III, ii, 1, p. 405.
12. Locke, III, x, 34, p. 508.
13. George Berkeley, *A Treatise Concerning the Principles of Human Knowledge*, in *The Works of George Berkeley Bishop of Cloyne*, ed. A. A. Luce and T. E. Jessop (9 vols., London, Nelson, 1948–57), Introd. paragraph 20; II, 37.
14. *Ibid.*, Introd. par. 21; II, 38.
15. Hume, *An Enquiry Concerning the Principles of Morals*, in *Enquiries*, Appendix IV, par. 262, p. 314.
16. *Ibid.*, App. IV, 261, p. 312.
17. Locke III, ix, 21, p. 488.
18. Joseph Addison, *The Spectator*, ed. Donald F. Bond (5 vols., Oxford, Clarendon Press, 1965), 21 June 1712, III, 535, 536.
19. P. N. Furbank, *Reflections on the Word 'Image'* (London, Secker & Warburg, 1970), p. 29.
20. Addison, 27 June 1712, III, 560.
21. Hugh Blair, *Lectures on Rhetoric and Belles Lettres* (2 vols., London, 1783), II, 378.
22. Lord Monboddo (James Burnet), *Of the Origin and Progress of Language* (6 vols., Edinburgh, 1773–92), VI, 101.

23. Blair, 1, 297.
24. Lord Kames (Henry Home), *Elements of Criticism*, 7th edn corr. (2 vols., Edinburgh, 1788), 11, 329.
25. William Drummond, *Academical Questions* (1 vol. only, London, 1805), p. 309.
26. *Dionysius Longinus On the Sublime*, trans. William Smith (London, 1739), p. 3.
27. *Ibid.*, p. 18.
28. Nicolas Boileau-Déspreaux, 'Préface: Traité du sublime', in *Oeuvres de Boileau*, ed. M. Amar (Paris, 1856), p. 363.
29. Ernest Tuveson, 'Space, Deity, and the "Natural Sublime"', *Modern Language Quarterly*, 12 (1951), 21.
30. Thomas Burnet, *The Sacred Theory of the Earth*, ed. Basil Willey (1690; rpt. London, Centaur Press, 1965), pp. 109–10.
31. Marjorie Hope Nicolson, *Mountain Gloom and Mountain Glory: The Development of the Aesthetics of the Infinite* (Ithaca, N.Y., Cornell University Press, 1959), p. 194.
32. Angus Fletcher, *Allegory: The Theory of a Symbolic Mode* (Ithaca, N.Y., Cornell University Press, 1964), p. 249.
33. Addison, 24 June 1712, 111, 545.
34. Longinus, p. 86.
35. Thomas Reid, *Essays on the Intellectual Powers of Man* (Edinburgh, 1785), p. 725.
36. Thomas Weiskel, *The Romantic Sublime: Studies in the Structure and Psychology of Transcendence* (Baltimore and London, John Hopkins University Press, 1976), p. 249.
37. Samuel H. Monk, *The Sublime: A Study of Critical Theories in XVIII-Century England* (New York, Modern Language Association of America, 1935), p. 74.
38. Addison, 23 June 1712, 111, 540.
39. Edmund Burke, *A Philosophical Enquiry into the Origin of our Ideas of the Sublime and Beautiful*, ed. James T. Boulton (London, Routledge & Kegan Paul, 1958), p. 82.
40. Dugald Stewart, *Philosophical Essays* (Edinburgh, 1810), p. 368.
41. *Journals of Dorothy Wordsworth*, ed. William Knight (London, Macmillan, 1930), p. 195.
42. William Wordsworth, 'The Sublime and the Beautiful', in *The Prose Works of William Wordsworth*, ed. W. J. B. Owen and Jane Worthington Smyser (3 vols., Oxford, Clarendon Press, 1974), 11, 350.
43. Addison, 25 June 1712, 111, 549.
44. William Duff, *An Essay on Original Genius* (London, 1767), pp. 150–2.
45. John Dennis, *The Grounds of Criticism in Poetry* (London, 1704), p. 16.
46. *Ibid.*, p. 17.
47. William Blake, *Vision of the Last Judgment*, in *William Blake's Writings*, ed. G. E. Bentley, Jr. (2 vols., Oxford, Clarendon Press, 1978), 11, 1027.

48. Duff, p. 171.
49. *Ibid.*, p. 156.
50. Robert Lowth, *Lectures on the Sacred Poetry of the Hebrews*, trans. G. Gregory (2 vols., London, 1787), I, 79.
51. Addison, 27 June 1712, III, 561.
52. *Ibid.*, 23 June 1712, III, 541.
53. Burke, p. 63.
54. *Kant's Critique of Judgement*, trans. J. H. Bernard, 2nd edn rev. (London, Macmillan, 1931), p. 102.
55. Thomas Gray, 'The Progress of Poesy', in *Thomas Gray and William Collins: Poetical Works*, ed. Roger Lonsdale (Oxford University Press, 1977), p. 50.
56. Lowth, I, 354.
57. *Ibid.*, I, 353.
58. Longinus, p. 40.
59. P. W. K. Stone, *The Art of Poetry: 1750–1820* (London, Routledge & Kegan Paul, 1967), p. 75.
60. Weiskel, p. 23.
61. Kant, p. 134.
62. Burke, p. 39.
63. *Ibid.*, p. 71.
64. Sigmund Freud, 'The "Uncanny"', in *The Standard Edition of the Complete Psychological Works of Sigmund Freud*, ed. James Strachey (24 vols., London, Hogarth Press, 1953–74), XVII, 240–1.
65. Walter Benjamin, 'On Some Motifs in Baudelaire', in *Illuminations*, ed. Hannah Arendt, trans. Harry Zohn (London, Jonathan Cape, 1970), p. 190.
66. Geoffrey H. Hartman, 'The Sacred Jungle 2: Walter Benjamin', in *Criticism in the Wilderness* (New Haven, Conn., and London, Yale University Press, 1980), p. 77.

2 *Shelley: from empiricism to the sublime*

1. Roy Park, *Hazlitt and the Spirit of the Age: Abstraction and Critical Theory* (Oxford, Clarendon Press, 1971), p. 12.
2. Kenneth Neill Cameron, *The Young Shelley: Genesis of a Radical* (New York, Collier Books, 1962), p. 37.
3. *Ibid.*, p. 78.
4. Longinus, p. 14.
5. Albert Gérard, 'On the Logic of Romanticism', *Essays in Criticism*, 7 (1957), 267.
6. Marilyn Butler, *Peacock Displayed: A Satirist in his Context* (London, Routledge & Kegan Paul, 1979), p. 291.
7. Thomas Love Peacock, 'The Four Ages of Poetry', in *The Works of Thomas Love Peacock*, ed. H. F. B. Brett-Smith (10 vols., London, Constable, New York, Gabriel Wells, 1924–34), VIII, ii.
8. *Ibid.*, VIII, 20.

9. *Ibid.*, VIII, 5.
10. *Ibid.*, VIII, 18.
11. *Ibid.*, VIII, 11.
12. M. H. Abrams, *The Mirror and the Lamp: Romantic Theory and the Critical Tradition* (New York, Oxford University Press, 1953), p. 126.
13. Weiskel, p. 36.

3 Scepticism and sublime Power: 'Hymn to Intellectual Beauty' and 'Mont Blanc'

1. Wordsworth, 'The Sublime and the Beautiful', in *Prose Works*, II, 353–4.
2. Clarence DeWitt Thorpe, 'Coleridge on the Sublime', in *Wordsworth and Coleridge: Studies in Honor of George Mclean Harper*, ed. Earl Leslie Griggs (Princeton University Press, 1939), p. 198.
3. Wordsworth, 'The Sublime and the Beautiful', in *Prose Works*, II, 354.
4. *Ibid.*, II, 354.
5. *Ibid.*, II, 349.
6. Geoffrey Hartman, *Wordsworth's Poetry 1787–1814* (New Haven, Conn., and London, Yale University Press, 1964, 1971), p. 26.
7. Wordsworth, 'Tintern Abbey', in *Wordsworth: Poetical Works*, ed. Thomas Hutchinson, rev. Ernest de Selincourt (London, Oxford University Press, 1936), pp. 163–5.
8. *Ibid.*, pp. 460–2.
9. Cameron, *Shelley: The Golden Years* (Cambridge, Mass., Harvard University Press, 1974), p. 238.
10. Harold Bloom, *The Visionary Company: A Reading of English Romantic Poetry*, rev. and enlarged edn (Ithaca, N.Y., and London, Cornell University Press, 1971), p. 291.
11. Judith Chernaik, *The Lyrics of Shelley* (Cleveland, Ohio, and London, Case Western Reserve University Press, 1972), p. 33.
12. Cameron, *Shelley: The Golden Years*, p. 242.
13. Chernaik, *The Lyrics of Shelley*, p. 186.
14. Timothy Webb, *Shelley: A Voice Not Understood* (Manchester University Press, 1977), p. 39.
15. *Byron's Letters and Journals*, ed. Leslie A. Marchand (11 vols., London, John Murray, 1973–81), v, 165.
16. Charles E. Robinson, *Shelley and Byron: The Snake and Eagle Wreathed in Fight* (Baltimore and London, Johns Hopkins University Press, 1976), p. 36.
17. *Collected Letters of Samuel Taylor Coleridge*, ed. Earl Leslie Griggs (6 vols., Oxford, Clarendon Press, 1956–71), I, 349.
18. Norman Fruman, *Coleridge, The Damaged Archangel* (London, Allen & Unwin, 1972), pp. 26–30.
19. *Collected Letters of Samuel Taylor Coleridge*, IV, 974.
20. Coleridge, 'Hymn Before Sun-Rise, in the Vale of Chamouni', in *The*

Complete Poetical Works of Samuel Taylor Coleridge, ed. Ernest Hartley Coleridge (2 vols., Oxford, Clarendon Press, 1912), I, 376–7.

21. Richard Holmes, *Shelley: The Pursuit* (London, Weidenfeld & Nicolson, 1974), p. 342.
22. Peacock, 'Memoirs of Percy Bysshe Shelley', in *Works*, VIII, 71.
23. Patricia Meyer Spacks, 'Horror-Personification in Late Eighteenth-Century Poetry', *Studies in Philology*, 59 (1962), 560.
24. Wordsworth, Preface to *Lyrical Ballads*, in *Poetical Works*, p. 735.
25. Donald Davie, *Purity of Diction in English Verse*, enlarged edn (London, Routledge & Kegan Paul, 1967), p. 38.
26. I. J. Kapstein, 'The Meaning of Shelley's "Mont Blanc"', *PMLA*, 62 (1947), 1046.
27. C. E. Pulos, *The Deep Truth: A Study of Shelley's Scepticism* (1954; Lincoln, University of Nebraska Press, 1962), p. 62.
28. Earl R. Wasserman, *The Subtler Language: Critical Readings of Neo-classic and Romantic Poems* (Baltimore, Johns Hopkins Press, 1959), p. 73.
29. Weiskel, p. 36.
30. Chernaik, *The Lyrics of Shelley*, p. 289.
31. Kapstein, p. 1052.
32. Cameron, *Shelley: The Golden Years*, p. 248.
33. I use the alternative version, 'In such a faith', here, as printed in 'The Byron and Shelley Notebooks in the Scrope Davies Find', by Judith Chernaik and Timothy Burnet, *The Review of English Studies*, NS 29 (1978), 47.
34. Webb, *Shelley: A Voice Not Understood*, p. 138.
35. *Ibid.*, pp. 138–9.

4 *The politics of creativity:* Prometheus Unbound

1. Abrams, *Natural Supernaturalism: Tradition and Revolution in Romantic Literature* (London, Oxford University Press, 1971), p. 344.
2. P. M. S. Dawson, *The Unacknowledged Legislator: Shelley and Politics* (Oxford, Clarendon Press, 1980), p. 283.
3. *Mary Shelley's Journal*, ed. Frederick L. Jones (Norman, University of Oklahoma Press, 1947), p. 93. '*Monday*, MAR. 16 [-21]. – Shelley reads Schlegel aloud to us.'
4. Augustus William Schlegel, *A Course of Lectures on Dramatic Art and Literature*, trans. John Black (2 vols., London, 1815), I, 30.
5. *Ibid.*, I, 31.
6. *Ibid.*, I, 92.
7. Abrams, *Natural Supernaturalism*, pp. 448–62.
8. Milton Wilson, *Shelley's Later Poetry: A Study of his Prophetic Imagination* (New York, Columbia University Press, 1959), p. 61.
9. Wasserman, *Shelley: A Critical Reading* (Baltimore and London, Johns Hopkins University Press, 1971), p. 266.

10. Susan Hawk Brisman, '"Unsaying His High Language": The Problem of Voice in *Prometheus Unbound*', *Studies in Romanticism*, 16 (1977), 68.
11. Dawson, p. 111.
12. Wasserman, *Shelley: A Critical Reading*, p. 260.
13. Schlegel, 1, 105.
14. Cameron, *Shelley: The Golden Years*, p. 488.
15. Schlegel, 1, 73–4.
16. Paul Foot, *Red Shelley* (London, Sidgwick & Jackson, 1980), p. 194.
17. *Ibid.*, p. 197.
18. Schlegel, 1, 74.
19. Abrams, *Natural Supernaturalism*, p. 344.
20. *Shelley's 'Prometheus Unbound': The Text and the Drafts*, ed. Lawrence John Zillman (New Haven, Conn., and London, Yale University Press, 1968), p. 134.
21. Wasserman, *Shelley: A Critical Reading*, p. 318.
22. Wilson, p. 140.
23. W. B. Yeats, '*Prometheus Unbound*', in *Essays and Introductions* (London, Macmillan, 1961), p. 420.

5 Inspiration and the poet's skill: 'Ode to the West Wind'
and 'To a Skylark'

1. Duff, p. 156.
2. George N. Shuster, *The English Ode from Milton to Keats* (1940; Gloucester, Mass., Peter Smith, 1964), p. 12.
3. *Ibid.*, p. 262.
4. *Ibid.*, p. 255.
5. *Ibid.*, p. 12.
6. Dennis, p. 112.
7. Lowth, 1, 37.
8. *Coleridge's Miscellaneous Criticism*, ed. Thomas Middleton Raysor (London, Constable, 1936), p. 412.
9. Samuel Johnson, *A Dictionary of the English Language* (2 vols., London, 1755), 11, see under 'Ode'.
10. Lowth, 11, 196.
11. Norman Maclean, 'From Action to Image: Theories of the Lyric in the Eighteenth Century', in *Critics and Criticism: Ancient and Modern*, ed. R. S. Crane (University of Chicago Press, 1952), p. 419.
12. Lowth, 11, 198.
13. *Ibid*, 11, 250.
14. Martin Price, 'The Sublime Poem: Pictures and Powers', *The Yale Review*, 58 (1968), 194–5.
15. Davie, p. 133.
16. F. R. Leavis, *Revaluation: Tradition & Development in English Poetry* (London, Chatto & Windus, 1936), p. 206.
17. *Ibid.*, p. 216.

18. *Ibid.*, p. 231.
19. *Ibid.*, p. 227.
20. Webb, *Shelley: A Voice Not Understood*, p. 75.
21. *Ibid.*, p. 177.
22. Bloom, *Shelley's Mythmaking* (New Haven, Conn., Yale University Press, 1959), p. 1.
23. Irene H. Chayes, 'Rhetoric as Drama: An Approach to the Romantic Ode', *PMLA*, 79, no. i (1964), 68.
24. John Keats, 'To Autumn', in *The Poetical Works of John Keats*, ed. H. W. Garrod, 2nd edn (Oxford, Clarendon Press, 1958), p. 273.
25. Webb, *Shelley: A Voice Not Understood*, p. 178.
26. Wasserman, *Shelley: A Critical Reading*, p. 240.
27. Bloom, *Shelley's Mythmaking*, p. 79.
28. Wasserman, *Shelley: A Critical Reading*, p. 240.
29. *Ibid.*, p. 247.
30. Webb, *Shelley: A Voice Not Understood*, p. 38.
31. *Ibid.*, p. 178.
32. Leavis, p. 214.
33. *Ibid.*, p. 215.
34. Chernaik, *The Lyrics of Shelley*, p. 127.
35. Shuster, p. 260.
36. Peacock, 'Memoirs of Percy Bysshe Shelley', in *Works*, VIII, 41–2.
37. Price, p. 210.
38. Wordsworth, 'To the Cuckoo', in *Poetical Works*, pp. 145–6.
39. Duff, p. 156.
40. Coleridge, 'Dejection: An Ode', in *The Complete Poetical Works*, I, 364. 'I see, not feel, how beautiful they are!' (38).
41. Bloom, *The Visionary Company*, p. 303.
42. Holmes, p. 599.
43. Chernaik, *The Lyrics of Shelley*, p. 125.

6 Shelley's leisure for fiction: Adonais

1. A. E. Powell, *The Romantic Theory of Poetry: An Examination in the Light of Croce's Aesthetic* (1926; New York, Russell & Russell, 1962), p. 218.
2. Johnson, 'Milton', in *Lives of the English Poets*, ed. George Birkbeck Hill (3 vols., Oxford, Clarendon Press, 1905), I, 163.
3. Lowth, II, 127.
4. Joseph Priestley, *A Course of Lectures on the Theory of Language and Universal Grammar* (Warrington, 1762), p. 22.
5. Jacques Derrida, *Of Grammatology*, trans. Gayatri Chakravorty Spivak (Baltimore and London, Johns Hopkins University Press, 1974), p. 12.
6. Blair, I, 136.
7. Monboddo, III, 4.
8. *Ibid.*, I, 8.

9. Derrida, p. 141.
10. Shelley ordered Marino's *Adone* from Lackington on 9 November 1815, and an ambiguous reference to him in a letter of 18 June 1822 indicates that he had at least perused this lengthy and ornate moral epic. Evidently Marino was himself influenced by the Greek Bucolic poets, and there are few echoes of the *Adone* in Shelley's poem which do not ultimately stem from Bion or Moschus, whose elegies Shelley knew and translated. Although there are some tempting similarities between *Adonais* and *Adone*, such as the stylised personifications of Morning and Death, the references to Urania and the play on flower imagery, the influence of Marino shows mainly, I think, in the unusually tight rhetorical figures of Shelley's poem and in his sometimes lurid and Baroque language, which is reminiscent of seventeenth-century wit: of 'ingegno'.
11. John Milton, *Lycidas*, in *The Poems of John Milton*, ed. John Carey and Alastair Fowler (London, Longman, 1968), pp. 232–54.
12. Wasserman, *Shelley: A Critical Reading*, p. 496.
13. *Ibid.*, p. 497.
14. Johnson, *A Dictionary of the English Language*, I, see under 'Elegy'.
15. Wilson, p. 242.
16. Wordsworth, Preface to *Lyrical Ballads*, in *Poetical Works*, p. 736.
17. Ernst Robert Curtius, *European Literature and the Latin Middle Ages*, trans. Willard R. Trask (London, Routledge & Kegan Paul, 1953), p. 92.
18. Derrida, p. 141.
19. Contemporary reviews in *The Literary Gazette* and *Blackwood's Edinburgh Magazine* both objected to the description of the poet's 'brow' as 'like Cain's or Christ's' (305–6) on the score of blasphemy. See *Shelley: The Critical Heritage*, ed. James E. Barcus (London and Boston, Routledge & Kegan Paul, 1975), pp. 299, 306.
20. Newell F. Ford, 'Paradox and Irony in Shelley's Poetry', *Studies in Philology*, 57 (1960), 655–6.
21. Chernaik, 'The Figure of the Poet in Shelley', *Journal of English Literary History*, 35 (1968), 578.
22. Coleridge, *Biographia Literaria*, ed. J. Shawcross (2 vols., London Oxford University Press, 1907), II, 12.
23. Bloom, *The Visionary Company*, p. 349.

7 *Sleepers in the oblivious valley:* The Triumph of Life

1. Webb, *The Violet in the Crucible: Shelley and Translation* (Oxford, Clarendon Press, 1976), p. 327.
2. Desmond King-Hele, *Shelley: His Thought and Work* (London, Macmillan, 1960), p. 350.
3. Abrams, *Natural Supernaturalism*, pp. 441, 442.
4. Bloom, *The Visionary Company*, p. 354.
5. Bloom, *Shelley's Mythmaking*, p. 223.

6. Richard Cronin, *Shelley's Poetic Thoughts* (London, Macmillan, 1981), pp. 203, 205.
7. I quote throughout from Donald Reiman's transcription of the poem in *Shelley's 'The Triumph of Life': A Critical Study* (Urbana, University of Illinois Press, 1965), pp. 136–210.
8. Paul de Man, 'Shelley Disfigured', in *Deconstruction and Criticism* (London, Routledge & Kegan Paul, 1979), p. 50.
9. Bloom, *The Visionary Company*, p. 354.
10. Freud, 'The "Uncanny"', in *Works*, XVII, 237.
11. William Hazlitt, 'Shelley's Posthumous Poems', in *The Complete Works of William Hazlitt*, ed. P. P. Howe (21 vols., London and Toronto, Dent, 1930–4), XVI, 273.
12. Reiman, p. 143.
13. Bloom, *The Visionary Company*, p. 354.
14. Cameron, *Shelley: The Golden Years*, p. 454.
15. Ross Greig Woodman, *The Apocalyptic Vision in the Poetry of Shelley* (University of Toronto Press, 1964), p. 186.
16. Cameron, *Shelley: The Golden Years*, p. 454.
17. Bloom, *The Visionary Company*, p. 359.
18. Woodman, p. 186.
19. Reiman, p. 187.
20. Freud, 'The "Uncanny"', *Works*, XVII, 237.
21. Reiman, p. 193.

BIBLIOGRAPHY

Primary texts

Addison, Joseph. *The Spectator*, 5 vols., ed. Donald F. Bond, Oxford, Clarendon Press, 1965.

Aristotle. *The Works of Aristotle*, 12 vols., ed. W. D. Ross and partly J. A. Smith, Oxford, Clarendon Press, 1908–52.

Berkeley, George. *The Works of George Berkeley Bishop of Cloyne*, 9 vols., ed. A. A. Luce and T. E. Jessop, London, Nelson, 1948–57.

Blair, Hugh. *Lectures on Rhetoric and Belles Lettres*, 2 vols., London, 1783.

Blake, William. *William Blake's Writings*, 2 vols., ed. G. E. Bentley Jr., Oxford, Clarendon Press, 1978.

Boileau-Déspreaux, Nicolas. *Oeuvres de Boileau*, ed. M. Amar, Paris, 1856.

Burke, Edmund. *A Philosophical Enquiry into the Origin of our Ideas of the Sublime and Beautiful*, ed. James T. Boulton, London, Routledge & Kegan Paul, 1958.

Burnet, Thomas. *The Sacred Theory of the Earth*, 1690; rpt. London, Centaur Press, 1965.

Byron, Lord. *Byron's Letters and Journals*, 11 vols., ed. Leslie A. Marchand, London, John Murray, 1973–81.

Byron: Poetical Works, ed. Frederick Page, corr. John Jump, London, Oxford University Press, 1970.

Campbell, George. *The Philosophy of Rhetoric*, 2 vols., London, 1776.

Coleridge, Samuel Taylor. *Biographia Literaria*, 2 vols., ed. J. Shawcross, London, Oxford University Press, 1907.

Coleridge's Miscellaneous Criticism, ed. Thomas Middleton Raysor, London, Constable, 1936.

Collected Letters of Samuel Taylor Coleridge, 6 vols., ed. Earl Leslie Griggs, Oxford, Clarendon Press, 1956–71.

The Complete Poetical Works of Samuel Taylor Coleridge, 2 vols., ed. Ernest Hartley Coleridge, Oxford, Clarendon Press, 1912.

Dennis, John. *The Grounds of Criticism in Poetry*, London, 1704.

Drummond, William. *Academical Questions*, 1 vol. only, London, 1805.

Duff, William. *An Essay on Original Genius: And its Various Modes of Exertion in Philosophy and the Fine Arts, Particularly in Poetry*, London, 1767.

Freud, Sigmund. *The Standard Edition of the Complete Psychological Works of Sigmund Freud*, 24 vols., ed. James Strachey, London, Hogarth Press, 1953–74.

Godwin, William. *Enquiry Concerning Political Justice and Its Influence on Morals and Happiness*, 3rd edn, 2 vols., London, 1798.

Bibliography

Gray, Thomas. *Thomas Gray and William Collins: Poetical Works*, ed. Roger Lonsdale, Oxford University Press, 1977.

Hazlitt, William. *The Complete Works of William Hazlitt*, 21 vols., ed. P. P. Howe, London and Toronto, Dent, 1930–4.

Hume, David. *Enquiries Concerning Human Understanding and Concerning the Principles of Morals*, ed. L. A. Selby-Bigge, rev. P. H. Nidditch, Oxford, Clarendon Press, 1975.

Johnson, Samuel. *A Dictionary of the English Language*, 2 vols., London, 1755.

   Lives of the English Poets, 3 vols., ed. George Birkbeck Hill, Oxford, Clarendon Press, 1905.

Kames, Lord (Henry Home). *Elements of Criticism*, 2 vols., 7th edn corr., Edinburgh, 1788.

Kant, Immanuel. *Kant's Critique of Judgement*, trans. J. H. Bernard, 2nd edn, rev., London, Macmillan, 1931.

Keats, John. *The Poetical Works of John Keats*, ed. H. W. Garrod, 2nd edn, Oxford, Clarendon Press, 1958.

Locke, John. *An Essay Concerning Human Understanding*, ed. Peter H. Nidditch, Oxford, Clarendon Press, 1975.

Longinus, Dionysius. *Dionysius Longinus On the Sublime*, trans. William Smith, London, 1739.

Lowth, Robert. *Lectures on the Sacred Poetry of the Hebrews*, 2 vols., trans. G. Gregory, London, 1787.

Marino, Giambattista. *L'Adone, Poema del Cavalier Marino*, 3 vols., London, 1789.

   Adonis: Selections from 'L'Adone' of Giambattista Marino, trans. Harold Martin Priest, Ithaca, N.Y., Cornell University Press, 1967.

Milton, John. *The Poems of John Milton*, ed. John Carey and Alastair Fowler, London, Longman, 1968.

Monboddo, Lord (James Burnet). *Of the Origin and Progress of Language*, 6 vols., Edinburgh, 1773–92.

Peacock, Thomas Love. *The Works of Thomas Love Peacock*, 10 vols., ed. H. F. B. Brett-Smith, London, Constable, New York, Gabriel Wells, 1924–34.

Priestley, Joseph. *A Course of Lectures on the Theory of Language and Universal Grammar*, Warrington, 1762.

Reid, Thomas. *Essays on the Intellectual Powers of Man*, Edinburgh, 1785.

   An Inquiry into the Human Mind on the Principles of Common Sense, 3rd edn corr., London, 1769.

Schlegel, Augustus William. *A Course of Lectures on Dramatic Art and Literature*, 2 vols., trans. John Black, London, 1815.

Shelley, Mary. *Frankenstein: Or The Modern Prometheus*, London, Oxford University Press, 1969.

   Mary Shelley's Journal, ed. Frederick L. Jones, Norman, University of Oklahoma Press, 1947.

Shelley, Percy Bysshe. *The Complete Works of Percy Bysshe Shelley*, 10

Bibliography

vols., ed. Roger Ingpen and Walter E. Peck, London, Ernest Benn, New York, Charles Scribner's Sons, 1926–30.

The Letters of Percy Bysshe Shelley, 2 vols., ed. Frederick L. Jones, Oxford, Clarendon Press, 1964.

Shelley: Poetical Works, ed. Thomas Hutchinson, corr. G. M. Matthews, London, Oxford University Press, 1970.

Shelley's 'Prometheus Unbound': The Text and the Drafts, ed. Lawrence John Zillman, New Haven, Conn., and London, Yale University Press, 1968.

Shelley's Prose: Or The Trumpet of a Prophecy, ed. David Lee Clark, corr. edn, Albuquerque, University of New Mexico Press, 1966.

Shelley's 'The Triumph of Life': A Critical Study, ed. Donald H. Reiman, Urbana, University of Illinois Press, 1965.

Stewart, Dugald. *Account of the Life and Writings of Thomas Reid*, Edinburgh, 1802.

Philosophical Essays, Edinburgh, 1810.

Wordsworth, Dorothy. *Journals of Dorothy Wordsworth*, ed. William Knight, London, Macmillan, 1930.

Wordsworth, William. *Wordsworth: Poetical Works*, ed. Thomas Hutchinson, rev. Ernest de Selincourt, London, Oxford University Press, 1936.

The Prose Works of William Wordsworth, 3 vols., ed. W. J. B. Owen and Jane Worthington Smyser, Oxford, Clarendon Press, 1974.

Yeats, W. B. *Essays and Introductions*, London, Macmillan, 1961.

Secondary texts

Abrams, M. H. *The Mirror and the Lamp: Romantic Theory and the Critical Tradition*, New York, Oxford University Press, 1953.

Natural Supernaturalism: Tradition and Revolution in Romantic Literature, London, Oxford University Press, 1971.

Alston, William P. *Philosophy of Language*, Englewood Cliffs, N. J., Prentice-Hall, 1964.

Baker, Carlos. *Shelley's Major Poetry: The Fabric of a Vision*, Princeton University Press, 1948.

Barrell, Joseph. *Shelley and the Thought of His Time: A Study in the History of Ideas*, New Haven, Conn., Yale University Press, 1947.

Benjamin, Walter. *Illuminations*, ed. Hannah Arendt, trans. Harry Zohn, London, Jonathan Cape, 1970.

Bennett, Jonathan. *Locke Berkeley Hume: Central Themes*, Oxford, Clarendon Press, 1971.

Bloom, Harold. *Shelley's Mythmaking*, New Haven, Conn., Yale University Press, 1959.

The Visionary Company: A Reading of English Romantic Poetry, rev. and enlarged edn, Ithaca and London, Cornell University Press, 1971.

Brisman, Susan Hawk. '"Unsaying His High Language": The Problem of Voice in *Prometheus Unbound*', *Studies in Romanticism*, 16 (1977), 51–86.

187

Bibliography

Butler, Marilyn. *Peacock Displayed: A Satirist in his Context*, London, Routledge & Kegan Paul, 1979.

Cameron, Kenneth Neill. *Shelley: The Golden Years*, Cambridge, Mass., Harvard University Press, 1974.

The Young Shelley: Genesis of a Radical, New York, Collier Books, 1962.

Chayes, Irene H. 'Rhetoric as Drama: An Approach to the Romantic Ode', *PMLA*, 79, no. i (1964), 67–79.

Chernaik, Judith S. 'The Figure of the Poet in Shelley', *Journal of English Literary History*, 35 (1968), 566–90.

The Lyrics of Shelley, Cleveland, Ohio, and London, Case Western Reserve University Press, 1972.

and Burnet, Timothy. 'The Byron and Shelley Notebooks in the Scrope Davies Find', *The Review of English Studies*, NS 29 (1978), 36–49.

Cohn, Jan, and Miles, Thomas H. 'The Sublime: In Alchemy, Aesthetics and Psychoanalysis', *Modern Philology*, 74 (1977), 289–304.

Cronin, Richard. 'Shelley's Language of Dissent', *Essays in Criticism*, 27 (1977), 203–15.

Shelley's Poetic Thoughts, London, Macmillan, 1981.

Curran, Stuart. *Shelley's Annus Mirabilis: The Maturing of an Epic Vision*, San Marino, Calif., Huntington Library, 1975.

Curtius, Ernst Robert. *European Literature and the Latin Middle Ages*, trans. Willard R. Trask, London, Routledge & Kegan Paul, 1953.

Davie, Donald. *Purity of Diction in English Verse*, enlarged edn, London, Routledge & Kegan Paul, 1967.

Dawson, P. M. S. *The Unacknowledged Legislator: Shelley and Politics*, Oxford, Clarendon Press, 1980.

de Man, Paul. 'Shelley Disfigured', in Harold Bloom (ed.), *Deconstruction and Criticism*, London and Henley, Routledge & Kegan Paul, 1979, pp. 39–73.

Derrida, Jacques. *Of Grammatology*, trans. Gayatri Chakravorty Spivak, Baltimore and London, Johns Hopkins University Press, 1974.

Fletcher, Angus. *Allegory: The Theory of a Symbolic Mode*, Ithaca, N.Y., Cornell University Press, 1964.

Foot, Paul. *Red Shelley*, London, Sidgwick & Jackson, 1980.

Ford, Newell F. 'Paradox and Irony in Shelley's Poetry', *Studies in Philology*, 57 (1960), 648–62.

Foucault, Michel. *The Order of Things: An Archaeology of the Human Sciences*, trans. from the French, London, Tavistock Publications, 1970.

Fruman, Norman. *Coleridge, The Damaged Archangel*, London, Allen & Unwin, 1972.

Furbank, P. N. *Reflections on the Word 'Image'*, London, Secker & Warburg, 1970.

Fussell, Paul. *The Rhetorical World of Augustan Humanism: Ethics and Imagery from Swift to Burke*, Oxford, Clarendon Press, 1965.

Gérard, Albert S. *English Romantic Poetry: Ethos, Structure, and Symbol in Coleridge, Wordsworth, Shelley, and Keats*, Berkeley and Los Angeles, University of California Press, 1968.

Bibliography

'On the Logic of Romanticism', *Essays in Criticism*, 7 (1957), 262–73.

Grabo, Carl. *The Magic Plant: The Growth of Shelley's Thought*, Chapel Hill, University of North Carolina Press, 1936.

Grave, S. A. *The Scottish Philosophy of Common Sense*, Oxford, Clarendon Press, 1960.

Hacking, Ian. *Why Does Language Matter to Philosophy?* Cambridge University Press, 1975.

Hartman, Geoffrey H. *Criticism in the Wilderness*, New Haven, Conn., and London, Yale University Press, 1980.

The Fate of Reading and Other Essays, Chicago and London, University of Chicago Press, 1975.

Wordsworth's Poetry 1787–1814, New Haven, Conn., and London, Yale University Press, 1964, 1971.

Holmes, Richard. *Shelley: The Pursuit*, London, Weidenfeld & Nicolson, 1974.

Hughes, Daniel. 'Prometheus Made Capable Poet in Act One of *Prometheus Unbound*', *Studies in Romanticism*, 17 (1978), 3–11.

Kapstein, I. J. 'The Meaning of Shelley's "Mont Blanc"', *PMLA*, 62 (1947), 1046–60.

King-Hele, Desmond. *Shelley: His Thought and Work*, London, Macmillan, 1960.

Kuhns, Richard. 'The Beautiful and the Sublime', *New Literary History*, 13 (1982), 287–307.

Leavis, F. R. *Revaluation: Tradition & Development in English Poetry*, London, Chatto & Windus, 1936.

Maclean, Norman. 'From Action to Image: Theories of the Lyric in the Eighteenth Century', in R. S. Crane (ed.), *Critics and Criticism: Ancient and Modern*, University of Chicago Press, 1952.

Manuel, Frank E. *The Eighteenth Century Confronts the Gods*, Cambridge, Mass., Harvard University Press, 1959.

Medwin, Thomas. *The Life of Percy Bysshe Shelley*, ed. H. Buxton Forman, Oxford University Press, 1913.

Monk, Samuel H. *The Sublime: A Study of Critical Theories in XVIII-Century England*, New York, Modern Language Association of America, 1935.

Morris, C. R. *Locke Berkeley Hume*, Oxford, Clarendon Press, 1931.

Morris, David B. *The Religious Sublime: Christian Poetry and Critical Tradition in 18th-Century England*, University Press of Kentucky, 1972.

Nicolson, Marjorie Hope. *Mountain Gloom and Mountain Glory: The Development of the Aesthetics of the Infinite*, Ithaca, N.Y., Cornell University Press, 1959.

Notopoulos, James A. *The Platonism of Shelley: A Study of Platonism and the Poetic Mind*, Durham, N. Carolina, Duke University Press, 1949.

Park, Roy. *Hazlitt and the Spirit of the Age: Abstraction and Critical Theory*, Oxford, Clarendon Press, 1971.

Bibliography

Powell, A. E. *The Romantic Theory of Poetry: An Examination in the Light of Croce's Aesthetic*, 1926; New York, Russell & Russell, 1962.

Price, Martin. 'The Sublime Poem: Pictures and Powers', *The Yale Review*, 58 (1968), 194–213.

Pulos, C. E. *The Deep Truth: A Study of Shelley's Scepticism*, 1954; Lincoln, University of Nebraska Press, 1962.

Robinson, Charles E. *Shelley and Byron: The Snake and Eagle Wreathed in Fight*, Baltimore and London, Johns Hopkins University Press, 1976.

Schulze, Earl J. *Shelley's Theory of Poetry: A Reappraisal*, The Hague, Paris, Mouton, 1966.

Shelley, Percy Bysshe. *Shelley: The Critical Heritage*, ed. James E. Barcus, London and Boston, Routledge & Kegan Paul, 1975.

Shuster, George N. *The English Ode from Milton to Keats*, 1940; Gloucester, Mass., Peter Smith, 1964.

Solve, Melvin T. *Shelley: His Theory of Poetry*, 1927; New York, Russell & Russell, 1964.

Spacks, Patricia Meyer. 'Horror-Personification in Late Eighteenth-Century Poetry', *Studies in Philology*, 59 (1962), 560–78.

Stone, P. W. K. *The Art of Poetry: 1750–1820*, London, Routledge & Kegan Paul, 1967.

Thorpe, Clarence DeWitt. 'Coleridge on the Sublime', in Earl Leslie Griggs (ed.), *Wordsworth and Coleridge: Studies in Honor of George Mclean Harper*, Princeton University Press, 1939, pp. 192–219.

Tuveson, Ernest Lee. *The Imagination as a Means of Grace: Locke and the Aesthetics of Romanticism*, Berkeley, University of California Press, 1960.

'Space, Deity, and the "Natural Sublime"', *Modern Language Quarterly*, 12 (1951), 20–38.

Wasserman, Earl R. 'The Inherent Values of Eighteenth-Century Personification', *PMLA*, 65 (1950), 435–63.

Shelley: A Critical Reading, Baltimore and London, Johns Hopkins University Press, 1971.

The Subtler Language: Critical Readings of Neoclassic and Romantic Poems, Baltimore, Johns Hopkins Press, 1959.

Webb, Timothy. *Shelley: A Voice Not Understood*, Manchester University Press, 1977.

The Violet in the Crucible: Shelley and Translation, Oxford, Clarendon Press, 1976.

Weiskel, Thomas. *The Romantic Sublime: Studies in the Structure and Psychology of Transcendence*, Baltimore and London, Johns Hopkins University Press, 1976.

Willey, Basil. *The Eighteenth Century Background: Studies on the Idea of Nature in the Thought of the Period*, London, Chatto & Windus, 1940.

The Seventeenth Century Background: Studies in the Thought of the Age in Relation to Poetry and Religion, 1934; London, Chatto & Windus, 1967.

Bibliography

Wilson, Milton. *Shelley's Later Poetry: A Study of his Prophetic Imagination*, New York, Columbia University Press, 1959.

Woodman, Ross Greig. *The Apocalyptic Vision in the Poetry of Shelley*, Toronto, University of Toronto Press, 1964.

INDEX

Index